THE WHALE WATCHER'S GUIDE

WHALE–WATCHING TRIPS IN NORTH AMERICA

To the world's whales,
and to those who dare to watch them

NorthWord Press
5900 Green Oak Drive
Minnetonka, Minnesota 55343
1-800-328-3895

Cover Photograph © Jeff Foott
Designed by Wayne C. Parmley
Icons by Amy Monday
Whale illustrations by David Peters
Printed and bound in U.S.A.

Library of Congress Cataloging-in-Publcation Data

Corrigan, Patricia.

    The whale watcher's guide : whale-watching trips in North America /
by Patricia Corrigan : foreword by Roger Payne. — [Rev. ed.]

      p.   cm.

Includes index.
ISBN 1-55971-683-5 (sc)
1. Whale watching—North America—Guidebooks. 2. Whales—North America—Identification. I. Title.
QL737.C4C66   1999
599.5′097—dc21   98-44878
                                                     CIP

THE WHALE WATCHER'S GUIDE

WHALE–WATCHING TRIPS IN NORTH AMERICA

PATRICIA CORRIGAN

FOREWORD BY ROGER PAYNE

NORTHWORD PRESS
Minnetonka, Minnesota

ILLUSTRATIONS

TABLE OF CONTENTS

FOREWORD

If after reading this book you cannot meet the whale of your dreams when and where you wish, it may be time to reprioritize your life.

Every time I approach the guidebooks in a bookstore and scan the new offerings, I wonder the same thing: Did the person who undertook this daunting task do a thorough job, or did he or she get part way into it and run out of gas?

Pat Corrigan has done her job. She did not run out of anything. The clarity with which she writes and the fresh, concise way she sets forth her information means that you and I can find what we're looking for at once. But better: Not only does she think out what you and I want to know more clearly than we do, she presents it straight, succinctly, and without ever saying too much, or being patronizing. What a treat for us, when a fine writer and journalist decides to do a book like this.

She tells us the basics about whales and the areas they frequent and then offers good advice on everything surrounding whale watching: how to choose among the competing tours, what to wear, what to bring with you, what to eat, how to avoid seasickness, and so on. She garnishes it with remarks such as "Inhale deeply of the fresh air and taste the salt on your lips. Memorize the moment with your every pore, and it won't matter whether or not the photographs turn out."

Good advice, that.

That it is possible to get so much solid information about a subject as specialized as whale watching is one of life's little delights. It says that in spite of all the disappointments that sprout like weeds in our society, we still grow some straight-grained hardwood. Pass over the weeds and buy this guide and then follow its advice. You won't be disappointed, and you will see whales.

ROGER PAYNE, PRESIDENT
Whale Conservation Institute
Lincoln, Massachusetts
September 1998

ACKNOWLEDGMENTS

Heartfelt gratitude and deep affection are due to the following parties for the reasons noted here.

My son, Joel Krauska, loves learning about and watching whales as much as I do. The wonderful tour operators listed in this book—my new extended family—sent me not only tidily filled-out questionnaires but warm words of encouragement, updates on whale conservation issues, invitations to visit, snapshots of whales, T-shirts, and audio and video tapes of assorted whale songs and behaviors. And some of them called, just to chat, or to tell me that they remember meeting me or that they grew up in St. Louis, too.

Roger Payne and Stephen Leatherwood spared time for me and my questions, both on and off whale-watch boats. Peter C. Beamish at Ocean Contact Ltd., Scott Kraus at the New England Aquarium, and Richard Sears at the Mingan Island Cetacean Study Inc. all reviewed the chapter on whale biology. Thanks, too, to the scientists and researchers who contributed to "What You May See At Sea": Peter Beamish, Steven Katona, Scott Kraus, Stephen Leatherwood, Roy Nickerson, Richard Sears, Ted Walker and Hal Whitehead.

Bob Wilds and the crew of the *Mystery* escorted me on my first whale-watch trip on September 25, 1982. Erich Hoyt directed me to several later whale-watching adventures. Robert Packard wrote the article on whale watching that first captured my imagination.

Thanks, too, to my agent, Jeanne Hanson, to Linda Piel Gwyn, Betty Dameris, Joan Bray, Sanda Rosenblum and other special friends who provided emotional support, cheerfully attended all my whale parties and bought me great whale presents. Some of them even went whale watching!

I would be remiss if I failed to mention the whales, who chose me to write this book so you could go find them.

WELCOME TO WHALE WATCHING

Whales! The greatest show on Earth is in the water, and anyone willing to go where whales are will see it. Whales—swimming, all sea-shiny and slick; diving, flashing enormous fan-shaped tails; spouting, baptizing one and all with a hearty expulsion of air and water as the mighty mammals breathe; whales with vast open mouths feeding on microscopic shrimp; whales hurtling their 50-ton bodies up, up, and completely out of the water, then falling back with a thunderous crash.

Blue whales, fin whales, rare right whales, humpbacks, gray whales, killer whales, minkes, and beluga whales—I've seen them all, in the Atlantic Ocean off Cape Cod, in Hawaiian waters, off Trinity in Newfoundland, in Alaska's Prince William Sound, off the coast of British Columbia, in Canada's St. Lawrence Seaway, near Peninsula Valdes in Argentine waters, in the lagoons off Baja California, off the coast of San Diego, and just yards from the Oregon shore.

I am not a marine biologist, research scientist, conservation specialist, wildlife photographer, or anyone at all with a specialized entree to the world of whales. I do watch whales, as often as I can manage, and so can you. Extraordinary experiences are available to anyone willing to go where the whales are.

Humpbacks sometimes smack their fifteen-foot flippers on the water's surface.

The first whale I ever met was a finback, a creature just slightly smaller than the 80-foot, 76-ton boat on which I was a passenger. The whale came toward us, dived, swam under the boat, and was gone before we could comprehend what we had seen. Finback whales are the second largest creatures ever to live on Earth, surpassed in size only by the mighty blue whales, and they are among the fastest swimmers in the sea, reaching speeds of 20 knots (30 miles per hour).

That trip was in 1982, out of Barnstable Harbor, off Cape Cod. We spent much of the day watching humpback whales feeding, their huge open mouths rising up through the columns of bubbles they blow under water to trap krill and tiny fish. The humpbacks also waved their tails ("threw their flukes") over and over, and two swam and dived together in unison, as though their dance had been choreographed. It was a magic day.

Once I had seen whales, I wanted to see more, to experience again the awe and exhilaration, the sense of deep privilege I felt when I was among them. Seeing whales became a priority, and I began to seek out opportunities to go where whales were whenever possible.

In 1984, during a three-day business trip to Maui, I boldly abandoned my traveling companions and headed for Lahaina, where I signed on for back-to-back whale-watch trips, a day's worth of expeditions. The morning trip reaped only a few far-distant flukes, and the afternoon threatened to be even less satisfying. But just as the captain started the boat's engine to leave, a humpback whale in the distance breached—hurled itself completely out of the water—seven times.

One look at that was simply not enough. Two years later, in May of 1986, I was on a ferryboat trip across Prince William Sound in Alaska when a humpback whale approached the boat and stayed nearby for forty-five minutes. Right in front of us, only yards from the boat, the whale breached over and over, slapped its 15-foot flippers on the water, waved its tail each time it dived, and smacked its tail repeatedly at the water's surface. Just before the graceful behemoth swam away, it appeared to wave "good-bye" with one long flipper.

The captain said that in his seventeen years of crossing the sound, he hadn't ever seen such a breathtaking spectacle. The thirty passengers, most of us strangers when we had boarded, were all hugging one another and laughing and crying. The captain

When a humpback whale breaches—heaves its entire body out of the water—it falls back with a thunderous crash.

joined in the celebration by declaring a round of drinks on the house, and we all offered up toasts to "our" whale.

In 1987, I returned to Cape Cod with my then-twelve-year-old son in tow. We took whale-watch trips on four consecutive days, and we saw whales every day. One afternoon, a humpback that had been lolling around several hundred yards away suddenly surfaced alongside the boat, so we had an unusual up-close look at the whale's impressive 40-foot length. We also saw five fin whales and at least thirty Atlantic white-sided dolphins.

From the back decks of cruise ships, I've seen orcas (killers). Surely, sighting blue whales is one of the rare privileges in life. In June of 1987, I was on the St. Lawrence River, aboard the *S.S. Bermuda Star.* The ship's pilot from Quebec had warned me that it was too early in the season to see any whales, yet four blue whales showed up on my thirty-ninth birthday, and I also saw a dozen or so belugas arching their backs out of the sun-sparkled water at the mouth of the Saguenay River.

Whale watching became up close and personal one day in Trinity Bay, off the north coast of Newfoundland, when a frisky adolescent humpback whale, measuring about 35 feet long and weighing about a ton per foot, draped its 10-foot-wide scalloped tail across the bow of our little rubber boat and gave us a hearty shove.

Late in the summer of 1991, off Bar Harbor, Maine, I saw fish flying above the ocean's surface and then saw the cause of their distress—a 70-foot-long finback whale that lunged halfway out of the water, mouth agape and ventral pleats bulging, enjoying a good meal.

"Hope you got a good look," said the narrator on the boat. "They usually only do that once." Suddenly, the finback hurled itself right out of the water a second time.

In San Ignacio Lagoon, off Baja California, Mexico, I watched a gray whale roll its big blue eye and watch me as I stroked her massive head. The moment was intensely moving, and I started to cry. Another day out in the lagoon that February of 1992, I found myself with a ringside seat at an orgy, watching white water roil up in a flurry of fins and flukes as three gray whales courted.

In 1993, I spent a week on a sailboat in the Bahamas, in the company of spotted dolphins, and another week cruising among feeding humpbacks on Stellwagon Bank, off the Massachusetts coast.

How did a nice Midwestern woman living on the banks of the Mississippi River become entranced with these magnificent marine mammals?

In July of 1982, I read an article in the New York Times travel section about a whale-watch trip off Cape Cod. A photograph of a whale leaping out of the water accompanied the article. After reading just a few paragraphs, I became obsessed with the idea of meeting a whale. The first opportunity was a week-long business trip to Washington, D.C., that autumn. I made arrangements to add a two-day visit to Cape Cod to the end of the trip. Then I headed for the library for books on whales, so that I would know what I was looking at in case I saw one.

I did see a whale, and it changed my life. Now I want to change yours.

HOW TO USE THIS BOOK

This is a book for people who watch whales, people who have been inexplicably moved, often deeply touched, by the sight of these glorious animals in their natural habitat. This is also a book for people who want to watch whales and for people who are about to discover that they too are fascinated with the mighty beasts. What you hold in your hands is a nature guide, a travel planner, an adventure book, and an inspirational text in the broadest sense.

Listed here are more than two hundred commercial whale-watch tour operators who are ready and waiting to escort you on more than two hundred fifty trips to see whales off the coasts of the United States (including Alaska and Hawaii), Canada, and Mexico. (Note: If we missed you, or if you know of a tour operator who is not included in this book, please see the note at the end of the book so we can include you in revised editions.)

You may use this book to plan a single whale-watching expedition, to devise an entire itinerary devoted to watching whales, or to find information on package tours and research expeditions. You pick a trip, pick a place or time, or pick a certain whale species that you want to see, and the book will point the way.

Guidelines for picking and choosing are in this chapter, and what to expect when you go whale watching (including what to wear) is covered in the next. Next, you'll read "What You May See at Sea," exciting tales—contemporary legends, actually—told by whale scientists. The following chapter, "Whale Tales," includes information on sixteen species of whales and dolphins. The book's final chapter is a calendar of sorts, indicating what whales are where, when. This book also includes information on more than thirty museums, aquariums and national marine sanctuaries and parks that have special whale exhibits or programs about marine life, names and addresses to write for tourism information, names and addresses of more than sixty whale conservation and research organizations, information on thirteen adopt-a-whale programs, a bibliography, and list of tour operators who sponsor package whale-watch trips in areas not covered here.

THE DIRECTORY

The chapters cover the following geographic areas: Northeast U.S. Coast, Pacific Northwest, California, Hawaii, Alaska, Canada, and Mexico. Most of the listings are arranged north to south, and maps are included in each chapter. Each listing includes the tour operator's name, address, and telephone number; what sort of whales you can expect to see; what time of year the trips are available; the type of boat (or boats) on which they take place; a daily schedule, if available; the cost; whether or not reservations are recommended or advised; the point of departure (with simple directions to that point); and a note about whether or not a naturalist or narrator is on board. Symbols indicate what you may expect in the way of a sheltered area on board, food, drink, binoculars, and hydrophones to let you hear the whales while you watch them, and whether or not a brochure is available from the tour operator.

Whale watchers using wheelchairs are welcome and are made comfortable on many boats, including kayaks. On some boats that do not have ramps accessible to wheelchairs, tour operators will carry the passenger—and the wheelchair—aboard. In general, tour operators do not recommend day-long trips for people in wheelchairs as bathrooms on boats ("heads," as they are called) are uniformly tiny and not at all accessible for wheelchairs. Also tour

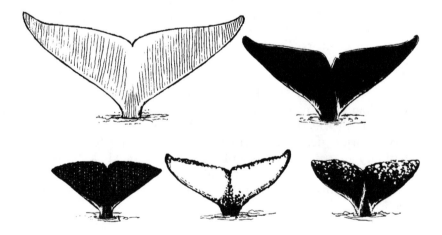

Whale tails, or flukes, come in different sizes and shapes. **Top Row:** Blue whale, right whale. **Bottom row:** sperm whale, Humpback whale, gray whale.

operators suggest that physically disabled whale watchers go out on calm days, as ocean swells may make boarding dangerous on some boats and may make securing a wheelchair tricky. All that said, most tour operators reported that they regularly take out whale watchers in wheelchairs. When you call for reservations, please mention that you will need help boarding and that you are concerned about finding a safe place for your chair.

All prices and departure times are subject to change. Since this book went to press, some tour operators may have added boats to their fleet or replaced less-comfortable vessels with sleek new boats designed for whale watching. Still others may have merged or gone into another line of work. The moral of this paragraph is this: Call or write to tour operators before you arrive at the pier. If you call or write off-season, you may not get an immediate response. Keep at it. Whale watching is worth it!

PICK A TRIP

Whale-watch trips may last one hour, two hours, half a day, a full day, two or three days, or on up to ten or fourteen days. You may spend as little as $7 per person for an hour-long trip or as much as $3,000 for a two-week expedition with several stops. Vessels listed in this book include large excursion boats, small excursion boats, fishing boats, small motor craft, sailboats, motorized rafts, and sea kayaks.

Some trips are strictly for pleasure, some are research oriented, and some successfully combine both elements. Most whale-watch tours listed here are family-run businesses; some are sponsored by scientific institutions and research organizations. Most of the trips are suitable for almost everyone, from the exceptionally sea hardy to those who rely on pills or patches to stave off the possibility of motion sickness. Trips to the Farallon Islands off San Francisco are particularly rigorous; the outings within the confines of Depoe Bay off the coast of Oregon can be remarkably calm. Otherwise, you pay your money and you take your chances—and chances are you'll be just fine.

PICK A PLACE OR TIME

Most of the trips are listed according to the point of departure. The exceptions are trips in Mexico, all of which are sponsored by tour operators in the United States and Canada. These trips are organized by destination. Otherwise, if you already know where you are going, you can look up that city (or one close by) and see what's available in the way of whale watching. If you don't have a destination in mind, you can check the calendar to see where whales are when and make your plans accordingly.

In some communities where whale watching is big business, local hotels and motels offer package deals, usually in the form of discount coupons for some tours. Where available, these packages are noted in the listings. Usually guests are given a choice of departure times but not of tour operators. Call or write to the tour operators, rather than the hotels, for details.

PICK A WHALE

If you've met humpback whales and you want to watch gray whales next time out, you can turn immediately to the listings for tours off the west coast of the United States and Canada and in the lagoons of Baja California, Mexico. If you want a peek at the rarest large whale in the world, the northern right whale, look for trips in the North Atlantic. Blue whales can be found with some certainty in the St. Lawrence Seaway in Canada and occasionally off the coast of California, and orcas patrol the waters off the San Juan Islands and off the west coast of Canada. Humpbacks and

Sometimes humpbacks (and other whales) stick their heads out of the water, a behavior called "spyhopping."

18

minkes? Head for Alaska, Hawaii, or the northeast coast of the United States. These are just general guidelines, as the migration paths of the world's whales meander through all the oceans.

ABOUT PICKING AND CHOOSING

A word is in order about the nature of "naturalists." The term generally refers to the person or persons on board who narrate the whale-watch trips, providing educational information about the whales, their behaviors and habitat, and the other creatures that share the marine environment. Some naturalists are marine biologists or oceanographers. Some are affiliated with, and trained by, research organizations and scientific institutions. On some trips, narration is provided by knowledgeable captains, people who have been going to sea with whales for years and have made a point of educating themselves so they can answer passengers' questions correctly. On some trips where no narration is provided, tour operators show an educational video on whales and hand out written materials provided by whale conservation organizations.

Probably it is unwise to judge a trip's worth based solely on whether or not a naturalist is on board. Once, when I was on a commercial trip off Cape Cod with a "certified" naturalist, said naturalist identified a passing whale as a humpback. My son, then with only one previous whale-watch trip under his belt, took a good look at the animal and insisted it was a finback, based on its color and the shape of its dorsal fin. Off he went to talk to the "expert." Moments later she was back on the public address system, admitting her mistake.

Some tour operators work with scientific research organizations and advertise that affiliation. The tie-in may be full-time and permanent, in that each whale-watch trip is a fact-finding research mission; or it may be that the boat has been chartered from time to time by organizations for its members. Boarding a boat that actively shares in a research effort or donates part of each day's profits to that research doesn't necessarily mean that you'll have a more rewarding trip, unless participating in research is exactly what you have in mind.

Also, booking passage on a whale-watch trip that boasts the presence of a naturalist is no reason not to educate yourself before you get on the boat. Many wonderful books about whales and whale biology are in print, available at libraries and bookstores all over the country. (For more than seventy such titles, see the

Bibliography.) Learning about the animals ahead of time makes the experience that much richer and will allow you to ask more specific questions if there is a naturalist on the trip you take.

OTHER CONSIDERATIONS

In any given area, all the tour boats go to the same places, sometimes staying in radio contact with one another in case someone sights whales that others have overlooked. For the most part, all whale-watch tour operators are infused with enthusiasm for the sport and are proud to be sharing the experience with their passengers. Cooperation among tour operators, rather than cutthroat competition, is most often the case. Therefore, if you're not particularly concerned about the size of the boat or the credentials of the naturalist, you might choose a trip that simply departs at a time convenient for you or that charges a fare that suits your budget. If you're a skeptic, seek out those tour operators who "guarantee" that you'll see a whale or they'll give you a free trip—not an uncommon offer in those areas where whales are practically willing to keep appointments with tour operators, year after year. And if you can afford it and you're so inclined, sign up for more than one trip. Because of the nature of the beast, every trip is unique.

Dolphins in all of the world's oceans enjoy bow riding, frolicking in the wake made by boats and ships.

WHAT TO EXPECT ON A WHALE WATCH

Before you can do any whale watching, you will likely have to do some whale waiting. While you're waiting, watch the water's surface for flying fish, other marine mammals, or even shark fins. Confronted with a vast expanse of ocean, many people initially think that "there's nothing out there." But that's just not true. Everything is out there. A whole world is just beneath the water's surface, and if you watch carefully, you will see evidence of that world. Also, look up and meet assorted seabirds that you're not likely to see flying over land-locked cities.

En route to where whales are supposed to be, you can always scan the horizon, just in case a whale might have meandered into new territory. Whales are blissfully ignorant of our schedules and calendars and maps, and they often pop up when and where we least expect them. An experienced captain once assured me we were well past the area off British Columbia where orcas are sighted, and thirty minutes later, four tall dorsal fins came into view along the shore.

Another orca spent a recent summer off Provincetown, Massachusetts, playing in the surf and delighting tourists and townspeople alike. Government officials actually met several times to determine what to do about the whale, which wasn't where it "should" have been at that time of year. Some gray whales appear to take a liking to the coast of Oregon, Washington and western Canada, and they spend twelve months in residence, rather than joining their species' annual trek between Alaska and Mexico.

Keep your eyes open and watch for that first thrilling sight of a whale spout against the horizon. One naturalist once described it as similar to a car radiator "blowing off steam"; after the steam subsides, look for a glimpse of what appears to be a shiny black stretch limo.

WHAT NOT TO EXPECT

What you can't expect is to see whales where you want them to be exactly when you want them to be there. This is nature, real life; not a multimillion-dollar theme park where every surprise is scheduled. Patience must rule the day. When you do see whales, you will realize they were worth the wait. Also, you will return to

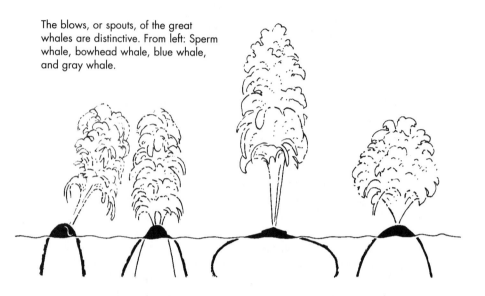

The blows, or spouts, of the great whales are distinctive. From left: Sperm whale, bowhead whale, blue whale, and gray whale.

shore exhilarated, better educated about a fascinating animal, and more aware of what's at stake if we lose even one species to extinction.

WHAT YOU NEED TO KNOW AHEAD OF TIME

Sometimes people are disappointed when they first see a whale spout. "That's it?" they say. "That little puff of steam that the wind blew away?" But when you've had a chance to do some whale watching, you will find out that each of the great whales has a distinctive spout. Literally a large roomful of air and mist is exhaled each time a whale breathes. If you're familiar with the height and shape of the different blows, and if the wind isn't too strong, and if you're facing the whale head on, sometimes you can tell exactly what sort of whale you're seeing even if you don't get a glimpse of the body or the dorsal fin or some other telltale sign. And sometimes, of course, you can't.

If you know what to expect, if you know that the great whales range in size from 45 to 90 or 100 feet and weigh as much as 1.5 tons per foot, you're less likely to be disappointed at the sight of a spout. If you know that a blue whale can weigh as much as thirty-two elephants or that a toddler could crawl through the arteries of any full-grown great whale or that a humpback's flipper is more than twice the height of the tallest person you know, then your sense of excitement about even a distant sighting will increase.

Chances are good—guaranteed at some spots during certain times of year—that you will see much more than a spout. Take binoculars, if you have them, to get a closer look at whales in the distance. If you don't have binoculars, don't despair. Most likely you won't need them.

There are laws that restrict how close whale-watch boats may approach the animals. For the most part, the laws are designed to protect the whales from harassment by overeager whale-watch vessels and small pleasure craft. Whales, unaware of our laws and good intentions, often approach idling boats for what appears to be a closer look at whale watchers. In the words of Dr. Peter Beamish, who operates Ocean Contact Ltd. out of Trinity Bay in Newfoundland, "Whale watching is free in Newfoundland. You can sit on a cliff near Trinity all day and watch whales. We guide people into our spectacular marine environment so that the whales can watch us."

WHAT TO WEAR

Of course, no matter how close whales come to the boat, you can't watch them comfortably if you're not dressed appropriately. No matter how sunny and warm it is in town or even at the dock, once you're out on the water the temperature may be cooler by ten to twenty degrees. If the wind is blowing, it may be even chillier. Also, there is always the possibility that you will get wet, either from occasional spray or from the unanticipated rain cloud.

When you pack a backpack or tote for whale watching, put in the obligatory sunscreen, a hat or visor, a sweatshirt or sweater, and a waterproof windbreaker, poncho, or jacket. Earmuffs, mittens, and scarves may come in handy too. And if you forgo the gloves, remember to smear some sunscreen on your hands, even if they are the only part of you that is exposed. (Don't forget your ears!) Wear sunglasses, long pants or jeans, a comfortable shirt, socks, and rubber-soled shoes. Female whale watchers clad in dresses, pantyhose, and tasteful grown-up-lady shoes and whale watchers of both sexes in cutoffs and tank tops have a hard time staying on a spray-splashed deck long enough to enjoy the trip.

As you sail over the bounding main, you may be aware of how wild the ocean seems, how uncontrollable a force it is to reckon with. For most people, that's part of the thrill. If you're not accustomed to being at sea, or if you've never managed it comfortably, plant your feet firmly on the deck and keep your knees loose and slightly bent. That way, you're not fighting the motion—and it's fun!

WHAT TO BRING

A camera is the obvious answer, and this from a person who has an album fully of fuzzy, out-of-focus pictures of whales and pictures of where whales just were. Unless you are a professional nature photographer accustomed to shooting from boats rocking gently (and not so) on the sea, you probably won't get profession-al-quality nature photos. However, you probably will get perfectly acceptable snapshots of tail flukes, dorsal fins, a flipper or two, and maybe even a whole whale at midbreach. And so you should bring your camera.

That said, it is also true that documenting whale behavior through a camera lens is not nearly as exciting as taking in the experience with all your senses turned up high. At some point, put down the camera and bring your mind's eye into sharp focus. Stare hard at the creature, noting the texture and color of its skin, any scars or scratches, the flash of baleen when it opens its mouth, the way the water streams down the ventral pleats under

Human beings are only as large as some of the smallest cetaceans. Shown here, from top to bottom, are the blue whale, sperm whale, bottlenose dolphin, humpback whale, and orca.

The humpback whale has a pleated throat that expands when the animal feeds. The whale then filters out the water through its baleen plates.

the whale's chin, or the places where barnacles are gathered. Listen to that most amazing sound when the whale breathes, the explosion of air and water that may well rain down upon you. Inhale deeply of the fresh air and taste the salt on your lips. Memorize the moment with your every pore, and it won't matter whether or not the photographs turn out.

WHAT NOT TO BRING

In order for motion sickness pills to be effective, you must take them at least thirty minutes before you board the boat. After you've put out to sea (or worse, started feeling bad), it's too late to take a pill, so be sure to swallow yours in time. Dramamine makes most people sleepy; Bonine makes only some people sleepy. Both are available over the counter. Medicated patches, worn behind the ear, are generally effective if they don't cause a reaction and make the wearer sick. Ginger has a reputation for preventing motion sickness, and is available in capsule form at most health food stores. On a positive note, even the queasiest passengers feel better when the whales show up.

Of course, many people who take no precautions at all never become seasick. Please don't stay home because you are worried that you might get sick—after all, you might not. If you do start to feel uncomfortable, stay outside in the open air, keep your eyes on the horizon, and breathe deeply. Nibble on plain soda crackers; sip ginger ale. Stave off panic by thinking about anything except being sick. If none of that works, comfort yourself with the thought that everyone, even experienced sailors, gets seasick at least once.

Few children under age five enjoy being confined on a boat for an extended period of time. As for older children, please take into consideration the individual child's behavior in public, level of intellectual curiosity, and need for unrestricted space. If you do decide to bring along a young child, tell him or her what to expect on the expedition and what behavior will be expected.

Most whale-watch boat operators allow passengers to smoke cigarettes in a restricted area out on deck, but they discourage pipe or cigar smoking.

WHAT YOU WILL SEE FROM SHORE

Sometimes people who have seen whales from shore, either from an official lookout or just meandering along the beach one day, feel that they've had the whole experience and think that they don't need to book passage on a whale-watch boat. Certainly, seeing a whale from shore is a thrill. I actually spotted a gray whale once through a living room window. But it's not the same. Watching whales from shore instead of going out to sea is something like watching a play on television instead of going to the theater and seeing the live performance. Watching from shore is fun, but it's a passive experience, not nearly as exciting as being smack in the middle of the action.

This book is set up to help you get to where the whales are. Make plans to go soon—and let me know what happens.

WHAT YOU MAY SEE AT SEA

S ay you've been cruising along for longer than you care to recall, with no sea creatures in sight. Suddenly, off the starboard bow, you hear what sounds like an exploding building. You look over just in time to see the wind carrying away the last wafts of a huge column of vapor, and you watch the mottled back of an 86-foot-long blue whale break the water's surface just 30 yards from the boat.

That's exactly what happened one November day off the coast of Big Sur, California, on a trip that was advertised as a good opportunity to sight sea birds and dolphins.

Such are the rewards of putting out to sea for a day of whale watching. Expect the unexpected: Every whale-watch trip, every excursion, is completely different from the last. Scott Kraus, an associate scientist at the New England Aquarium in Boston, puts it this way: "If you watch whales long enough, you're always seeing something new."

Kraus and other "professional" whale watchers, scientists, and naturalists who have spent years observing whales in the wild say they have seen sights and experienced encounters while on the water that they could never have anticipated. Eight of them—Peter Beamish, Steven Katona, Scott Kraus, Stephen Leatherwood, Roy Nickerson, Richard Sears, Ted Walker, and Hal Whitehead—shared some of their stories of amazing moments for this chapter.

This is the stuff of legends.

CURIOUS CALVES AND PROUD MOTHERS

Stephen Leatherwood says he will never forget the first time that a curious humpback calf left the protection of its mother to swim over to have a look at him.

Leatherwood is chairman of the Cetacean Specialist Group for the World Conservation Union. He also is the coauthor of several books, including *The Sierra Club Handbook of Whales and Dolphins*, *The Sierra Club Handbook of Seals and Sirenians*, and scientific texts on gray whales and bottlenose dolphins.

Back in 1973, Leatherwood was studying humpback whales off Maui. One calm day, a mother and calf swam toward Leatherwood's boat, and he slipped into the water with the animals.

"As I swam toward the mother, she swept the calf under her 15-foot flipper. The calf kept twisting its body and rolling its eye to look at me. At one point the calf peeled out from under Mom's wing and came right for me, staring right at me the whole time," Leatherwood recalls. "At the last minute, it veered off, and I reached out. The whale pressed against my hand, still moving, just like a cat."

That was Leatherwood's first close encounter with a humpback whale. More recently, underwater off the Bahamas in June of 1991, Leatherwood found another mother and calf—this time, a dolphin.

"There was an Atlantic spotted dolphin I was familiar with after visits to the area for three years, but I had never known her to have a calf," Leatherwood said. "One day, I was out on deck when a small group of dolphins came up to the boat. I saw there was a calf among them, so when I got in the water, I just hung there, not moving around. First, the dolphin I knew swam by with the calf on her opposite side. They made another pass by me, this time with the calf between us. Then the mother paused a short distance away. The calf came toward me. When it started to move away, she headed it back toward me.

"I couldn't help but get the impression that she was bringing her calf over to introduce it to me."

ATTACKS OF CURIOSITY

For years, tales have been told of attacks by orcas, or killer whales, on gray whales as the grays make their annual migration from the Bering and Chukchi seas to Baja California and back again.

Dr. Theodore J. Walker, an authority on gray whales, is convinced that sometimes the orcas are victims of bad press.

"The most dramatic thing I ever saw was a so-called attack on three gray whales by 44 killer whales," Walker said. "It happened in 1969, and the U.S. Navy logged the observation."

Walker, who spent 21 years at Scripps Institution of Oceanography as a research marine biologist, is the founder of the whale observatory at Cabrillo National Monument in San Diego, the first such observatory on the West Coast. He is the author of *Whale Primer*, and he has lectured widely since 1971.

That day in 1969, Walker went up in a small plane to check out the report of the killer whale attack. Flying at an altitude of 500 feet, he saw the 44 orcas traveling north from Ensenada,

Mexico. They located three gray whales that were in a circle just below the surface, with their heads together, a formation called a rosette.

"The killer whales made several runs at the gray whales, but nothing ever happened. We did not observe any blood in the water or any signs that the gray whales were impaired," Walker said. "We concluded that the killer whales were not attacking. The three gray whales were courting, and it appeared that the killer whales were having a look."

He added, "I'm of the opinion that unless you can produce the body, it didn't happen."

One day, Walker witnessed a dramatic orca attack, but a gray whale was not the victim. Walker was up in a helicopter, scanning the coast of Southern California for migrating gray whales. He saw an adult male orca swimming alone. The pilot made a few passes high above the animal, and then reported he saw a large shark near the surface of the water not far from the whale.

"I saw it, too, and I photographed it," Walker recalled. "We saw the killer whale attack the shark. And then that whale jumped clear out of the water, up toward the helicopter, with the shark in its mouth, broken in half.

"I have a very bad photograph of that," Walker said, laughing.

WHALES WATCHING PEOPLE

Richard Sears, director of the Mingan Island Cetacean Study, based in Sept-Iles, Quebec, spends several months each year studying blue whales—the largest animal ever to live on earth—in the Gulf of St. Lawrence and several months in the Sea of Cortez, off Baja California. In his work, Sears also encounters several other species, including some particularly curious humpbacks.

In the Gulf of St. Lawrence, in the fall of 1990, some 25 humpback whales, all known to the researchers, took turns approaching Sears' boat about six at a time and began to spyhop—stick their heads up out of the water very close to the boat. "Eventually, most of the whales moved off, but two stayed for several hours, continuing to spyhop, looking down into the boat, right at me."

Another day, Sears set out in choppy water and was immediately surrounded by two humpbacks that "followed us all day like dogs."

One of his favorite stories about blue whales is about a calf with a touch of colic.

"In 1989, we were off Baja, observing mother whales with their calves. Flip Nicklin was swimming with one pair, photographing them, when we saw a calf swim up to the water's surface with its mouth open," Sears said. "It was spitting up milk, having a fit of colic."

A year later, Sears was out in the Sea of Cortez, about two miles off Loreto, following a mother and calf. "The whales dived, and the mother's head was within feet of the boat," Sears said. "Then the calf surfaced right off our bow, and suddenly we were framed in blue whales."

Another day in the Sea of Cortez, Sears and company saw what they first thought was a harbor porpoise and then identified as a day-old, nine-foot-long finback calf. A few days later, a pod of 17 orcas, including three calves, swam and played by the research boat for eight full hours.

"That was an amazing sighting," Sears said.

CAREFUL RESEARCH AMONG COURTING WHALES

Scott Kraus, an associate scientist at the New England Aquarium in Boston, has a special fondness for the right whales, which he has studied in the Bay of Fundy since 1980 and off the southeastern U.S. coast since 1984.

Off the Nova Scotia shelf, Kraus and his colleagues are accustomed to seeing right whales in courting groups, which usually consist of one female and as many as 20 males or more.

"The courting groups are oblivious to us," Kraus said. "We like to shut down the engines and observe the whales from a distance, but more than once, a female has tried to use the boat as a barrier, to get away from the males. Once, a large male moved us out of the way to get to a female. That's when you need those engines running because it can be dangerous to be in the way of courting whales."

Kraus said that every year he sees something he never expected to see. "The first time you see a calf nursing, you don't realize what you're looking at. And the behavior of the older calves is always fun to watch," he said. "Once, a right whale calf swam alongside the boat, rubbing its body against a $20,000 piece of scanning equipment that tracks whales underwater. We were afraid we were going to lose the scanning sonar."

Kraus said there are about 300 right whales in the North

Atlantic, and each year, 10 or 12 whales swim south to give birth off the southeastern U.S. coast. "We strongly discourage attempts at whale watching there because it is a nursery area. Besides, very few animals are involved, and you never know if you will see them on any given day."

FOOD FOR THOUGHT

Giant baleen whales troll the oceans in search of the tiny fish and crustaceans that nourish them. Two scientists, Dr. Steven Katona and Dr. Hal Whitehead, have observed how the baleen whales sometimes get a little help from their friends.

Dr. Katona teaches and conducts research in marine biology at the College of the Atlantic in Bar Harbor, Maine. He is the author of *A Field Guide to the Whales, Porpoises, and Seals of the Gulf of Maine and Eastern Canada*. Dr. Whitehead, on the faculty at Dalhousie University in Halifax, Nova Scotia, has studied whales all over the world and is the author of *Voyage to the Whales*, a book about sperm whales in the Indian Ocean.

The two coauthored a paper on the ecological importance of whales, and in that paper they described some communal feeding practices they have observed in Nova Scotian waters. Once, they saw white-sided dolphins herding herring "into balls so dense that we scooped up 30 fish in a single dip of a five-gallon bucket."

"Humpback whales gently maneuvered to eat these schools, after which the dolphins quickly circled the fishes to herd them close together again," Katona and Whitehead reported. "The fish schools appeared to offer a surfeit of food for the dolphins, and we consider it possible that the dolphins were playing and/or herding for the benefit of the whales. We could not identify any immediate mutualistic benefit for the dolphins, although they swam with the whales throughout our observation period."

Katona and Whitehead have also watched communal feasting on the part of whales, herring gulls, and greater black-backed gulls.

While watching a humpback whale in 1987 near Mount Desert Rock, Maine, the scientists saw this feeding pattern repeated for several hours: "The whale exhaled underwater, creating a patch of ascending bubbles. Krill rose to the surface during the next 30 seconds, coloring the surface pink. During the following 30 seconds, herring appeared at the surface jumping so energetically in pursuit of krill that their splashing sounded like a heavy rainstorm.

"Herring gulls and greater black-backed gulls gathered and snatched herring. Apparently, in response to the marauding fishes, the krill pressed together into tight discrete schools up to two meters in diameter. The whale then surfaced, open-mouthed, to engulf krill from these tight schools, which were so thick that our dip net was packed full in one pass."

CLOSE ENCOUNTERS WITH HUMPBACK WHALES

Dr. Peter Beamish, president of Ocean Contact Limited and director of Ceta-Research based in Trinity, Newfoundland, recalls a breathtaking incident from 1982.

"We arrived at Newman's Cove, a tiny outport in eastern Newfoundland, to find three humpback whales feeding near the community wharf. For one hour, we, in our 15-foot Zodiac, came as close to entering their world as you could imagine, theirs being three dimensional and ours only two."

Beamish said the smallest of the whales (about 35 feet in length) suddenly appeared almost stationary at the surface.

"Then, heading in the same direction as our Zodiac, the whale moved its tail sideways and placed it under the midsection of our vessel. The whale gently lifted the Zodiac approximately two feet into the air and then slowly lowered the boat."

Interspecies communication—not serving as toys for whales—is Beamish's special area of interest. One day in June of 1990, the whales cooperated willingly.

"We were transmitting short underwater sounds exactly every two minutes," Beamish said. "Two humpback whales came near our vessel, and then one animal exhaled exactly as we transmitted a sound."

Beamish issued an opening message of tones underwater, and the animal mimicked the rhythm of the message.

"Then we repeated the experiment using three different sounds, and the whale mimicked the message using three different signals: a tailslap, a full breach, and an exhalation. Message had become independent of signal," Beamish said. "We repeated the experiment, and whales have demonstrated that 'rhythm-based' information can be transmitted independently of signal quality."

Beamish continues, "We must change our emphasis in commu-nication from what animals are doing to when they are doing it."

MORE HUMPBACK WHALES AND "THE FRIENDLIES"

Roy Nickerson, an eloquent author (*Brother Whale* and *The Friendly Whales*) and naturalist, moved back to Hawaii in 1991 after an absence of 10 years. The whales had a few surprises in store for him.

"A behavior that was new to me was watching several instances of adult humpback whales breaching in unison, two at a time, only yards apart from each other," Nickerson said. Then, in April of 1992, the humpbacks upped the ante. For the first time, Nickerson observed three humpbacks breaching together in the Auau Channel, the seven miles of water between Maui and Lanai.

"At first, two breached together twice, then they were joined by a third and all three jumped three times in a row together. Then they each jumped three or four more times, but not in unison. It was an astounding display," he said.

"To me, this indicates some intelligent purpose in breaching, and to me, breaching just for the fun of it is an intelligent purpose."

Some of his favorite stories are about the gray whales off Baja California, Mexico, that have come to be called "the Friendlies."

"In San Ignacio Lagoon, I was able to pat baby gray whales on the head, and one mother whale lifted our skiff up out of the water briefly—a very gentle experience that did startle and amaze all six of us in the skiff, as well as those who were watching in nearby boats," Nickerson said.

"Tail lobbing" is what scientists call the humpback's penchant for smacking its tail on the water's surface.

"These experiences only reaffirm that whales are thinking, reasoning, and intelligent animals; that they have been protected for enough generations now so they no longer remember that men came at them with harpoons, and today, they enjoy interacting with us."

Nickerson sees "our love affair with whales" as a wonderful thing.

"Without it, the gray whales would not have come back to their historic population, nor would the humpbacks be making such good progress toward their historic populations, and the same with other whales, both great and small."

WHALE TALES

Say "whale" and what comes to most people's minds is an image of a sperm whale. Moby Dick was a sperm whale, and the distinctive shape of Herman Melville's Great White Whale is so familiar that illustrations of that one species are often used to represent all whales. In fact, the mighty sperm whale, with its rectangle-shaped head and its long, narrow lower jaw, is unique among whales.

What the sperm whale has in common with all other whales is that it is a mammal. Aristotle was the first to record the observation that whales were not giant fish; that they did not breathe through gills. Whales are warm-blooded, air-breathing creatures that spend most of their time under water, rising to the surface to exhale and then take in great gasps of fresh air before submerging again.

More than 345 million years ago, an amphibian relative of the land vertebrates climbed out of the water and began to adapt to life on land. One group of mammals eventually returned to the water, and those were the early ancestors of today's whales. Over time, the noses of these air-breathing mammals moved from the front to the top of the head. A special valve evolved, so the whales can seal off their air passages when they are under water, and their external ears disappeared completely. Some whales hear with dense bones located on each side of their heads, where their external ears once were, picking up the smallest of vibrations.

All whales are cetaceans, a word derived from their biological order, Cetacea, from the Greek *ketos* or the Latin *cetus,* which both mean "whale." The order includes at least seventy-seven species of whales, porpoises, and dolphins. One ancient suborder of whales disappeared more than twenty million years ago, but two suborders survive today. The existing suborders are Odontoceti ("toothed whales") and Mysticeti ("mustached whales").

The "mustache" is actually baleen—hard, keratinous fibers that overlap in the whales' mouths and serve as a sieve. When the whales eat, the hundreds of strips of baleen filter water out and leave behind the krill and small fish. Baleen was once known as "whalebone," and whales were butchered so the baleen could be used in corsets, shirt collar stays, brushes, and buggy whips and as ribs for umbrellas and lamp shades.

Except for sperm whales, all larger whales are baleen whales. All baleen whales—except for gray whales, right whales, bowhead whales, and pygmy right whales—are rorquals, whales with ventral (underside) pleats that allow their throats to expand while feeding. Baleen whales have two external blowholes. Toothed whales—sperm whales, orcas, narwhals, beluga whales, dolphins, and porpoises—have just one.

Whales are generally believed to be intelligent, curious, and not aggressive toward humans. Most whales travel in "pods," social or family groups. Among behaviors common to some species of the larger whales are spyhopping, where a whale lifts its massive head out of the water and appears to look around, and breaching, where the whale leaps completely out of the water and then falls back with a thunderous crash. Several species raise their broad tails completely out of the water when they "sound," or begin a deep dive. Some whales stick their flippers or tails out of the water or slap them against the water's surface.

Scientists can't explain any particular behavior of whales, though they have formulated theories based on years of research. Because whales are difficult to study in their natural habitat, we actually know very little about the live animals.

We know a great deal about dead whales. The United States was once the world's greatest whaling power. By the nineteenth century, Yankee whalers no longer killed whales for meat, to survive, but for oil for lamps and machines and for by-products used in candles, crayons, dog food, fertilizer, cosmetics, and perfume. With hand-held harpoons thrown from wooden whaleboats, Yankee whalers had almost depleted the right and bowhead populations; then the modern age of whaling ushered in the exploding harpoon and the fleets of mechanized factory ships that have contributed to

Baleen varies widely in size among whales. Shown here, to scale, are baleen strips from the bowhead whale (top), the blue whale (left), and the gray whale (right).

the slaughter of
millions of whales
in the twentieth
century.

Krill, a shrimplike crustacean only 2 inches in
length, is the primary diet of the baleen whales.

Today there is a relatively inexpensive substitute for every
product once sought from whales. Yet eight of the twenty species
of "great whales"—the larger whales—are endangered, close to
extinction.

And in spite of a moratorium on commercial whaling
declared in 1986, Japan, Norway, and Iceland continue to kill
whales, claiming "scientific research" is their purpose.

But whales and dolphins also face other threats. Oil spills,
such as the one in 1989 from the Exxon *Valdez* in Prince William
Sound, kill whales, as do nylon fishing nets (also known as ghost
nets) that drift through the open seas, entangling marine mammals and seabirds. Even more insidious are the tens of thousands
of human-produced toxic substances that we dump into the sea—
chemicals that, if we continue dumping, will practically guarantee
the eventual extinction of marine mammals and all other life in
the ocean. As we sit poised at the top of the food chain, we must
ask ourselves, "Will we be next?"

The organizations listed in Appendix 2 believe that it's not
too late to save whales and, by extension, to save ourselves. Write
to those that interest you to learn how you can help.

Some of what scientists do know about sixteen species of
whales and dolphins follows here. This general information relates
to the species you are most likely to see on the whale-watch trips
in this guidebook. The whales are listed according to size: blues,
finbacks, rights, bowheads, sperm whales, humpbacks, gray
whales, minkes, orcas, pilot whales, narwhals, belugas, bottlenose
dolphins, common dolphins, white-sided dolphins (Atlantic and
Pacific), and harbor porpoises. By no means is this information
complete. Several fine books on whale biology are listed in the
Bibliography.

Population estimates, where available, are based on statistics from the International Whaling Commission. Still, many of the figures are speculative, as estimates change frequently. The range in length and weight of the different species is based, unfortunately, primarily on measurements taken from dead whales.

Blue whale *(Balaenoptera musculus).* The blue, or sulphur bottom, whale is the largest creature ever to live on Earth. Blue whales are blue-gray, often with gray mottling. Though they can attain a length of more than 100 feet and weigh between 130 and 150 tons, most of the largest blue whales were killed before the species was granted protected status. Today, most blue whales sighted are between 70 and 90 feet long.

The heart of a blue whale is about the size of a Volkswagen Beetle, and there is room on its tongue for a full-grown elephant. A newborn blue whale measures 20 to 25 feet and weighs about 3 tons. The calf gains as much as 200 pounds a day while nursing, and an adult blue whale can eat as much as 2 tons of krill a day.

Blue whales are an endangered species. Only between 4,000 and 6,000 are left.

The blue whale is the largest creature ever to live on earth and eats as much as two tons of food a day.

Fin whale *(Balaenoptera physalus).* Though the fin, or finback, whale has to settle for being the second largest animal on Earth, it is the fastest of the large whales. The sleek finback can attain a speed of 30 miles an hour, a record only occasionally threatened by the sei whale. Fin whales grow to 80 feet in length and weigh 60 to 70 tons.

Fin whales are dark gray to brownish black, with a characteristic white lower right jaw. A narrow ridge on the animal's back extends from the dorsal fin to the tail and gives the whale its nickname of "razorback."

The United States considers fin whales endangered, though they have not been granted that status internationally. An estimated 120,000 live in the seas of the world, down from a pre-exploitation population of 548,000.

The fin whale is the second largest animal ever to live on earth and is known as "the greyhound of the sea" because it swims so swiftly.

Right whale *(Eubalaena glacialis/australis).* Unfortunately, the right whale got its name from nineteenth-century whalers who considered it the "right" whale to kill because it swims slowly, it has abundant oil, and its carcass floats. The arched upper jaw holds baleen that grows to 7 feet long.

Northern and southern right whales, black in color, attain a length of 50 to 60 feet and weigh as much as 45 tons. They have callosities, patches of thickened skin, that grow in the same places that human males have facial hair—mustaches, eyebrows, beard, and sideburns. The callosities are often covered with cyamid crustaceans, or whale lice. The distinctive number, size, shape, and placement of callosities on each right whale make it possible to recognize individual whales.

The right whale is the rarest of all the large whales. Both southern and northern right whales are endangered.

The North Atlantic right whale is the rarest of all whales because the whaling industry slaughtered so many of the animals.

When the Pilgrims landed in what is now Massachusetts, the North Atlantic Ocean was home to an estimated 20,000 right whales. A journal entry noted that one could almost walk across Cape Cod Bay on the backs of the animals, so plentiful were they. Today, only about 300 right whales live in the North Atlantic, and fewer than 2,000 live in the Southern Hemisphere. Some scientists fear that it is too late to save the species from extinction.

Bowhead whale *(Balaena mysticetus)*. Bowheads take their name from the exaggerated arch of the jaw, which houses baleen that grows up to 14 feet long. These whales are primarily black, with a white band underneath the chin. They grow as large as 65 feet long and weigh as much as sixty-five tons.

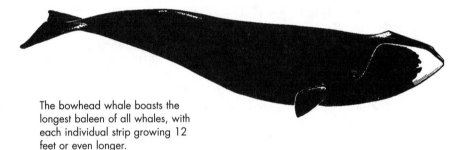

The bowhead whale boasts the longest baleen of all whales, with each individual strip growing 12 feet or even longer.

These mighty giants aren't easy to find, but you may be lucky enough to see one if you travel in the arctic regions. Bowhead whales are endangered, but they are still hunted by Alaskan natives, who are allotted a certain number of "subsistence" kills each year. They particularly enjoy muktuk, a delicacy consisting of the outer skin layers of bowhead whales: a tough outer layer, the true skin, and oily blubber. Muktuk may be eaten fresh, frozen, cooked, or pickled. The baleen is used to make intricately woven baskets. As someone once noted, "Nothing is wasted except the whale."

Fewer than 7,000 bowhead whales are believed to exist today, compared with a pre-exploitation population of 30,000.

Sperm whale *(Physeter macrocephalus)*. The rectangle-shaped head of the 50- to 60-foot sperm whale accounts for about one third of the animal's length and contains a "case" full of rich oil. Some scientists think that during dives below the surface of the ocean, the waxlike oil solidifies, which reduces buoyancy and helps the whale extend the distance of its dives.

Male sperm whales weigh as much as 59 tons and have the largest brain of any creature on Earth. They are dark grayish-brown to brown and have a wrinkled skin behind the head. The animal's lower jaw is long and narrow and contains up to 60 conical teeth, which fit into corresponding sockets in the upper jaw. Sperm whales feed on giant squid; the squid can grow to 55 feet and weigh some 4,500 pounds.

One-third of the sperm whale's body is the head, which holds a huge "case" of waxy oil.

Those teeth were once prized by whalers, who carved miniature scenes on them, an art known as scrimshaw. Another once-valued product from sperm whales is ambergris, a product from the intestinal bile used by the perfume industry to make permanent blends of various fragrances. The United States considers sperm whales an endangered species; fewer than one million live in the world's oceans. The peak of exploitation was reached in the 1960s, when 29,000 sperm whales were killed each year.

Humpback whale *(Megaptera novaeangliae)*. The "big-winged New Englander" is perhaps the most gregarious of all the large whales. If you've seen a whale breach, slap the water with its flipper or tail, poke its head up to watch you watching it, and raise its beautiful scalloped tail high out of the water before a long dive, chances are you've seen a humpback whale. The males also sing long, haunting songs.

Humpback whales, basi-
cally black or gray with some
white on the throat or belly, flippers,
and tail, grow to about 50 feet and
can weigh as much as 45 tons. The
animal boasts the longest flippers of
any whale, sporting 15-foot "wings" that have scalloped edges
and are often white underneath. The "stovebolt" knobs on the
humpback's head usually hold hair follicles, and some scientists
think the single hair that protrudes from each may be a sensor.
The pattern on the underside of each humpback's tail is unique,
and individual whales are easily recognizable.

The humpback whale has distinctively long flippers and a reputation for curiosity about whale-watch boats.

Humpback whales are endangered, down to about 10,000
compared to 65,000 estimated to have lived prior to the rise of
the whaling industry.

Gray whale *(Esrichtius robustus)*. The gray whales are the
conservationists' success story. Though the North Atlantic population was brought to extinction in the 1600s, the North Pacific
populations have recovered twice from near extinction. In the
mid-nineteenth century, so many gray whales were killed that they
became classified as "economically extinct," which meant that
there were so few left, it wasn't worth the time or trouble to hunt
them. The species began to recover, only to be nearly wiped out
again in modern times with the advent of mechanized whaling
techniques. The government stepped in, and today between
17,000 and 24,000 gray whales migrate each year from the
Bering, Chukchi, and western Beaufort seas to breeding grounds
off Baja California, Mexico.

Some scientists believe the gray whales are primitive in many
ways and may be direct descendants of the ancient ancestral
baleen whales. The body, flippers, and flukes (tail) of the stocky
animals are mottled, with gray and white splotches. The whale's
head is bumpy and warty, with bristly facial hairs, and patches of
barnacles, algae, and whale lice cover much of the rest of the

Some scientists believe the gray whale is the most closely related to the archaic whales.

body. Gray whales grow to lengths of 45 to 50 feet and weigh about a ton per foot.

Beauty is only skin deep, of course, and gray whales delight more than two million whale watchers off the west coast of the U.S. and Canada each year. In the quiet lagoons off Baja California, some gray whales known as "the friendlies" have been known to approach small boats full of whale watchers and come in close enough to be petted. And you may recall that the international effort expended off Point Barrow, Alaska, in the fall of 1988 was on behalf of three gray whales trapped in the ice.

In the United States, gray whales are no longer considered an endangered species. Also, the International Whaling Commission has reclassified them from "protected stock" to the status of "sustained management" stock.

Minke whale *(Balaenoptera acutorostrata)*. Legend has it that a Norwegian whaler named Minke mistook this smallest of the baleen whales for a mighty blue, and his amused peers promptly named the whale after him to commemorate forever his error.

Minkes are black to dark gray on the back, white on the belly and across an "armband" on the flipper (in the Northern Hemisphere). There may be as many as three subspecies of minkes, but generally these streamlined animals grow to about 30 feet and weigh up to 7 tons. Some minkes

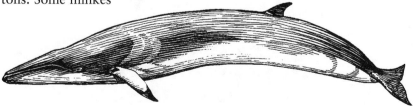

Minke whales are occasionally mistaken for other, larger, baleen whales.

43

have a reputation for being feisty, swimming close to shore in inlets and bays and popping up right in front of moving boats.

These whales are not considered endangered, and many are killed each year by those nations still active in commercial whaling. Also, several minke whales have been held in captivity in Japan, as they are the only member of the genus small enough to be displayed and researched.

Orca whale *(Orcinus orca)*. Some orcas, or killer whales, spend their lives in show business at theme parks and oceanariums, and many people have seen the shiny black and white whales up close. Orcas are members of the dolphin family, and like dolphins they are acrobatically inclined. Still, some scientists say that orcas in captivity rarely achieve their full growth potential.

In the wild, male orcas grow to about 30 feet, weigh up to 8 tons, and sport striking 6-foot dorsal fins. Females are slightly smaller. The animals have ten to thirteen conical teeth on each side of each jaw, and they prey on fish, squid, birds, seals, turtles, porpoises, and, occasionally, whales.

Research has shown that most orcas kill for food, not for sport, and orcas do not go after human beings without extreme provocation. Legend has it that these whales were originally known as "whale killers" and that over time the name was reversed to the more ominous version. No population estimates are available, and orcas are not considered an endangered species.

Orcas, commonly called "killer whales," often swim in family groups within the pod.

The long-finned pilot whale is one of the largest animals ever kept in captivity. You may have met one in a marine life park.

Pilot whale *(Globicephala melaena* and *G. macrorhynchus).* At aquariums and theme parks, you can distinguish between long-finned and short-finned pilot whales because there will be large signs identifying them, but at sea even experts find it nearly impossible to tell the two species apart. A good guess is possible, however, because the long-finned pilot whale is generally found in nontropical waters and the short-finned pilot whale is seen in tropical waters.

Both species have large bulbous foreheads, stocky elongated bodies, and prominent dorsal fins and are slate gray to black in color. The short-finned pilot whales, not surprisingly, have shorter flippers than long-finned pilot whales. Males of both species reach a length of 19 or 20 feet, with females slightly smaller. Both species feed on squid and schooling fish and travel in herds of up to several hundred individuals, often in the company of bottlenose dolphins.

Narwhal *(Monodon monocerus).* Male narwhals go through life armed to the teeth, so to speak. The adult male of this unusual species boasts a tooth that grows through the upper lip into an 8-foot-long tusk, which may have inspired the legend of the unicorn. No one is sure of the tooth's function, though males have been seen battling with their built-in swords. Eskimo and Alaskan Indian tribes prized the narwhal's tusk most

The male narwhal has an 8-foot-long tusk, unique among whales, that may have inspired the legend of the unicorn.

highly, and such a gift to the chief or the tribal elder was considered a great tribute.

Narwhals are stocky animals, slow swimmers, that range in color from dark blue-gray in juveniles to mottled dark brown in adults. Males grow to about 15 feet, excluding the tusk, and weigh about 3,500 pounds. Females are slightly smaller. The whales live in arctic waters, where they feed on squid, fish, shrimp, and crab.

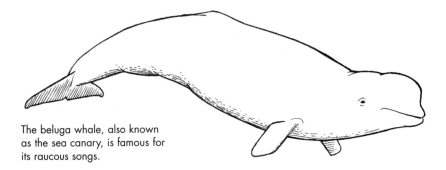

The beluga whale, also known as the sea canary, is famous for its raucous songs.

Beluga whale *(Delphinapterus leucas)*. The only true "white" whales are the belugas. The whales are born gray or brown and turn white as they mature.

Belugas, which are not the source of the famous caviar that comes from sturgeons, are also known as "sea canaries" because of their impressive range of vocalizations. They squeal and chirp and are considered among the most vocal of all whales.

The animals are stocky, with a disproportionately small head. Generally they grow to about 16 feet and weigh as much as 2,400 pounds, though there are size differences among different geographical populations. Scientists estimate there are about 50,000 belugas, all living in arctic or subarctic water: The 500 left in the St. Lawrence Seaway are believed to be at the greatest risk because of the toxic pollutants in the river.

Bottlenose dolphin *(Tursiops truncatus)*. Remember Flipper? That particular bottlenose dolphin may have been the first, last, and only bottlenose dolphin to star in its own television series, but it was largely responsible for the fond associations many people have with the species.

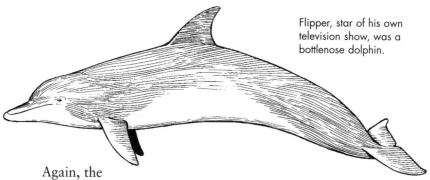

Flipper, star of his own
television show, was a
bottlenose dolphin.

Again, the
animals vary slightly in different
geographical regions of the world, and at least two distinct subspecies may exist. In general, bottlenose dolphins range from dark
to lighter gray in color. They grow to about 13 feet and weigh as
much as 1,400 pounds. They live in shallow water and are often
seen riding the surf.

Common dolphin *(Delphinus delphis)*. These are the aerial
acrobats that Herman Melville probably had in mind when he
wrote, "They always swim in hilarious shoals which upon the sea
keep tossing themselves to heaven like caps in a Fourth of July
crowd." The pods, or herds, may number as many as two thousand individuals. In addition to the acrobatics, common dolphins
are said to change course for the opportunity to ride the bow
wave of a passing ship, or even of a passing larger whale, for that
matter.

Common dolphins are often tricolored: black, gray, and
cream. They reach a length of 7 to 8 feet and weigh 200 to 300
pounds. Unlike the bottlenose dolphin, common dolphins do not
thrive in captivity. They live in temperate and tropical waters of
all oceans.

The common dolphin is found in many areas.

White-sided dolphin *(Lagen-orhynchus acutus* and *L. obliq-uidens).* Atlantic and Pacific white-sided dolphins are not classified as the same species, but they share more than a name.

Both are primarily black on top and white on the underbelly, with a gray stripe running from behind the eye to the beginning of the tail. The Atlantic white-sided dolphin has a characteristic yellow patch that begins just under the dorsal fin and extends back. Both species have dorsal fins that are tall and quite pointed, and both travel in herds of up to one thousand animals.

Atlantic white-sided dolphins are the larger of the two, growing to 10 feet and weighing 400 to 550 pounds. Pacific white-sided dolphins are 7 to 8 feet in length and weigh at least 330 pounds. Both species feed on hake, squid, and sardines.

Top: The Atlantic white-sided dolphin is often sighted in the North Atlantic Ocean.
Bottom: The Pacific white-sided dolphin is a frequent bow-wave rider on whale-watch trips off the California coast.

Harbor porpoise *(Phocena).* The harbor porpoise is the most commonly seen of all porpoises, and though it does not ride the bow waves of ships, it has been known occasionally to approach small boats. The stocky little animal is usually brown or dark gray, with lighter gray coloring at the flanks.

Harbor porpoises grow to about 6 feet in length and weigh up to 200 pounds. They surface to breathe about every fifteen seconds and do not stay submerged longer than 3 or 4 minutes. The animals have been described as generally undemonstrative, with a "businesslike" approach to life.

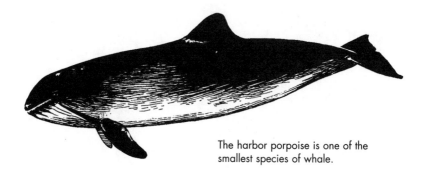

The harbor porpoise is one of the smallest species of whale.

TOURS, MUSEUMS, AQUARIUMS, AND NATIONAL PARKS

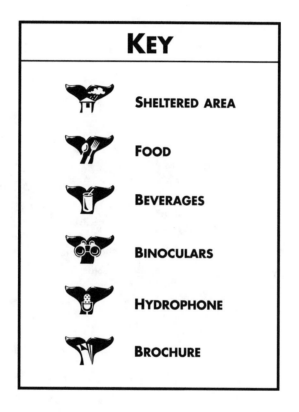

KEY

SHELTERED AREA

FOOD

BEVERAGES

BINOCULARS

HYDROPHONE

BROCHURE

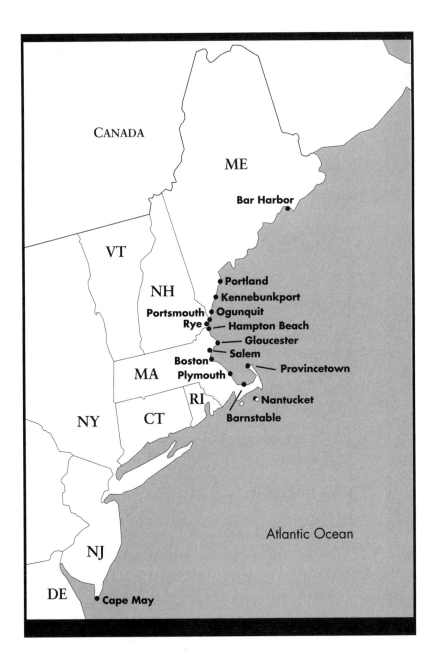

CANADA

ME

Bar Harbor

VT

NH

Portland
Kennebunkport
Portsmouth • Ogunquit
Rye • Hampton Beach
Gloucester
Salem
Boston
Plymouth • Provincetown

MA

RI

NY

CT

Nantucket

Barnstable

Atlantic Ocean

NJ

DE

Cape May

NORTHEAST U.S. COAST

Commercial whale-watch tours are said to have originated on the Northeast Coast, and today three New England states plus New York and New Jersey take advantage of the whales that come to feed in the Gulf of Maine from April through October. Whale-watch trips depart from numerous cities and towns in Maine, Massachusetts, New Hampshire, New York, and New Jersey, setting out to see humpbacks, finbacks, minkes, the occasional rare right whale, and assorted dolphins.

Massachusetts leads the way, with nearly twenty whale-watch tours. Provincetown, on Cape Cod, boasts four! Maine is active in the industry, with trips originating from six cities along the coast. Four tours operate out of New Hampshire and one each from New Jersey and New York. The whale-watch tours on the Northeast Coast range from trips sponsored by small charter companies to research-oriented trips run by institutions and organizations. Here, too, are excursion boats built specifically for whale watching.

TOURISM INFORMATION

MAINE
Maine Office of Tourism
59 Statehouse Station, Augusta, ME 04333
(207) 287-5710

MASSACHUSETTS
Cape Cod Chamber of Commerce
P.O. Box 790, Hyannis, MA 02601
(508) 362-3225

Massachusetts Office of Travel & Tourism
100 Cambridge Street, 13th Floor, Boston, MA 02202
(800) 447-MASS or (617) 632-8038 in Massachusetts

NEW HAMPSHIRE
New Hampshire Office of Vacation Travel
P.O. Box 1856, Concord, NH 03302
(603) 271-2666

NEW JERSEY
New Jersey Division of Tourism
P.O. Box 826, Trenton, NJ 08625
(609) 292-2470

NEW YORK
Department of Economic Development
One Commerce Plaza, Albany, NY 12245
(800) CALL NYS

WHALE-WATCHING TRIPS

BAR HARBOR

Acadian Whale Watcher

Golden Anchor Pier, 55 West Street, Bar Harbor, ME 04609
(800) 421-3307 or (207) 288-9794 or 2025

Whales:	Humpback, fin, minke, right, Atlantic white-sided dolphin
Season:	Mid-May through late October
Boats:	One boat, the 94-ft. *Acadian Whale Watcher*; 150 passengers
Trips:	Three 4-hour trips daily in summer at 8 a.m., 12:30 p.m. and 4:30 p.m. Some trips combine whale watching with bird watching. Call for information. Midweek is busiest.
Fare:	Adults, $28; senior citizens, $25; children: ages 7 to 15, $17; 6 and under, free. Fare includes free admission to the Bar Harbor Whale Museum. Reservations advised.
Departure:	Trips leave from the Golden Anchor Pier on West Street in Bar Harbor, at the foot of Rodick Street about half a mile from Route 3.
Naturalist:	Naturalist aboard.

"The *Acadian* is perfect for the sightseer," says a spokeswoman. "We sail around Acadia National Park on our way to the whales' feeding grounds. Also, we whale watch in an area where there are very few vessels." Tapes of the Acadian trips are for sale, available free to groups who charter the boat.

Bar Harbor Whale Watch Company

39 Cottage Street, Bar Harbor, ME 04609
(800) WHALES-4 or (207) 288-2386; Fax (207) 288-4393;
E-mail humpback@acadia.net; Web site www.whalesrus.com

Whales: Humpback, fin, minke, Atlantic white-sided dolphin

Season: June through mid-October

Boats: One boat, the *Friendship V*, a 112-foot catamaran that holds 350 passengers

Trips: One trip daily at noon June 1 through June 14 and from October 2 through October 20. Two trips daily at 9 a.m. and 1 p.m. June 15 through June 30 and August 30 through October 1. Three trips daily at 8:15 a.m., 12:30 p.m. and 4:15 p.m. June 30 through August 29.

Fare: Adults, $31; senior citizens, $27; children ages 6 to 14, $19; 5 and under, free. Reservations advised.

Departure: Trips leave from marina at the Regency Holiday Inn on Route 3, one mile from Bar Harbor.

Naturalist: Naturalist aboard.

Friendship V, a catamaran built in 1996, has two hulls that assure a smooth, stable ride with less rocking motion, says Barbara Bridges, operations manager. The Bar Harbor Whale Watch Company offers a 100 percent money-back guarantee that you will see whales.

Whale Watcher Inc.

1 West Street, P.O. Box 153, Bar Harbor, ME 04609
(800) 508-1499 or (207) 288-3322; Fax (207) 288-5626;
E-mail info@atlantiswhale.com; Web site www.atlantiswhale.com

Whales: Fin, humpback, right, minke, Atlantic white-sided dolphin

Season: June through mid-October

Boats: The 116-foot *Atlantis*, launched in 1998, which carries 300 passengers

Trips: Three 2-1/2-hour trips daily at 8:30 a.m., 12:30 p.m., and 4:30 p.m. from June through August. Two 2-1/2-hour trips at

9 a.m. and 1:30 p.m. in September. One 2-1/2-hour trip at 12:30 p.m. in October. Midweek is busiest in the summer.

Fare: Adults, $30; senior citizens, $27; children 6 to 15, $20; under 5, free. Reservations advised.

Departure: Trips leave from the Town Pier at the corner of Main and West streets on the waterfront in Bar Harbor.

Naturalist: Naturalist aboard.

Founded in 1978, Whale Watcher Inc. acknowledges that the ocean is a very special environment. "Whales control if and when they will be watched," notes Gary Mohr, "which makes it all the more special when a captain's patience and soft touch on the controls are rewarded by a whale's lack of concern at our presence." Your money back if no whales are sighted.

KENNEBUNKPORT

Cape Arundel Cruises

P.O. Box 2775, Kennebunkport, ME 04046
(207) 967-0707

Whales: Humpback, fin, minke, Atlantic white-sided dolphin

Season: Mid-May through late September

Boats: The *Nautilus*, which carries 100 passengers

Trips: One 5- to 6- hour trip daily at 10 a.m. with sunset whale watches scheduled at 4 p.m. every day in July and August.

Fare: Adults, $25; children 3 through 12, $15. Reservations advised.

Departure: Trips leave from the Kennebunkport Marina, off Route 9.

Naturalist: Captain serves as naturalist.

"We promise an exciting opportunity to observe firsthand some of the largest and rarest wild animals on Earth," says a spokesman.

Indian Whale Watch

P.O. Box 2672, Kennebunkport, ME 04046
(207) 967-5912

Whales:	Humpback, fin, minke, right, Atlantic white-sided dolphin
Season:	June through October
Boats:	One boat, the *Indian*; 72 passengers
Trips:	One 5- to 6-hour trip daily at 10 a.m
Fare:	Adults, $30; senior citizens (60 and older), $25; children: 13 to 18, $25; 6 to 12, $15; under 5, free. Group rates and private charters available. Reservations advised.
Departure:	Trips leave from Arundel Wharf Restaurant on Ocean Avenue in Kennebunkport.
Naturalist:	Yes

"We try to make every trip a good time as well as an educational experience," says Captain Dick Brindle. "Each member of my crew is an enthusiastic whale lover and they have been with us for years. Our naturalist gives a commentary as well as answers questions, and every day we offer a free ticket to anyone who can stump the crew."

Brindle adds, "Our feeling is that everyone should experience these wondrous creatures and if we didn't have to make a living, I would take everyone out for free." Whale sightings are guaranteed.

Ugly Anne

P.O. Box 863, 9 King's Lane, Ogunquit, ME 03907
(207) 646-7202; Web site www.uglyanne.com

Whales:	Humpback, fin, minke
Season:	Mid-June to Labor Day
Boats:	One, the *Ugly Anne*; 35 passengers
Trips:	Two 4-hour trips daily at 8 a.m. and 1:15 p.m.
Fare:	$30 per person. Reservations required.

Departure: Trips leave from Perkins Cove in Ogunquit. Take Shore Road to Oarweed to the dock.

Naturalist: No

Owners Jeanne and Ken Young, Sr., note, "The *Ugly Anne* is primarily a charter fishing boat, but we do see a lot of whales in August and September." Charters are available. And you can buy *Ugly Anne* T-shirts and sweatshirts.

PORTLAND

Olde Port Mariner Fleet

634 Cape Road, Standish, ME 04084
(800) 437-3270 or (207) 775-0727

Whales: Finback, humpback, minke, right, Atlantic white-sided dolphin

Season: Mid-May through mid-October

Boats: One, the *Odyssey*; 95 passengers

Trips: One 6-hour trip daily at 10 a.m. Weekend day trips are the busiest.

Fare: Adults, $35; senior citizens, $30; children: 13 to 17, $25; 12 and under, $20 on the day trips. Reservations advised.

Departure: Trips leave from Long Wharf on Commercial Street in Portland. From the Maine Turnpike, take Exit 7, then take the exit ramp for Route 295 North. Take Exit 4 off 295 and follow signs for Route 1A, Commercial Street, or the waterfront. Ticket booth is next to Key Bank, just before DiMillo's Restaurant.

Naturalist: Naturalist aboard.

"Humpbacks! Finbacks! Minkes! And the anticipation of sighting a rare right whale, sei or blue whale," says a spokesman. "White-sided dolphin, basking sharks, ocean sunfish, sea turtles, and countless seabirds accompany us as we course our way to the whales."

MASSACHUSETTS

BARNSTABLE

Hyannis Whale Watcher Cruises

P.O. Box 254, Barnstable Harbor, Barnstable, MA 02630
(888) WHALEWATCH or (508) 362-6088; Fax (508) 362-9739

Whales:	Humpback, finback, minke, right
Season:	April through October
Boats:	One boat; 300 passengers
Trips:	Three 4-hour trips daily in summer. Departure times change daily, but you can count on one trip in the morning, one at mid-day and one late afternoon or early evening. One or two trips daily in the fall.
Fare:	Rates vary with season and time of day; range is from $10 to $22 per person, with discounts for AAA members, children, senior citizens, and groups. Reservations advised. Discount coupons for trips are available at all lodging facilities on Cape Cod.
Departure:	Trips leave from Barnstable Harbor, just 3 miles from Hyannis. Take Exit 6 off the mid-Cape highway (Route 6) and make a right turn onto Route 132. At the first traffic light, turn left and follow for 3 miles, straight to the harbor.
Naturalist:	Yes

"We are the only whale watch located in the mid-Cape area," says a spokeswoman. "Our crew is always friendly and in uniform, and our galley staff offers complete food and beverage service."

BOSTON

A. C. Cruise Line

290 Northern Avenue, Boston, MA 02210
(800) 422-8419 or (617) 261-6633; Fax (617) 261-4747;
E-mail a.c.cruise@worldnet.attnet; Web site www.accruise.com

Whales: Humpback, finback, Atlantic white-sided dolphin

Season: Mid-April through mid-October

Boats: Two boats; 146 and 400 passengers

Trips: One 6-hour trip at 10:30 a.m. Wednesdays through Sundays. Weekends are busiest.

Fare: Adults, $18; children, $12. Reservations advised.

Departure: Trips leave from Pier 290 Northern Avenue in the South Station area of Boston. Take the John F. Fitzgerald Expressway to either Northern Avenue or Congress Street.

Naturalist: Naturalist aboard.

Captain Alan Circeo cruises among the harbor islands and out to Stellwagen Bank to view the humpbacks and fin whales feeding.

"It's possible to see dolphins, various seabirds, ships, yachts—there's always a surprise every trip," he says. Whale sightings are guaranteed, and the *Cape Ann* and *Virginia C II* are both available for private charters.

Boston Harbor Cruises

Number One Long Wharf, White Ticket Center, Boston, MA 02110
(617) 227-4321

Whales: Humpback, fin, minke, right, pilot, dolphin

Season: Mid-May through mid-September

Boats: The *Milennium*, a catamaran new in 1998 that carries 350 passengers, and the *Hurricane*, which holds 300.

Trips: One 3-hour trip on weekdays at 10:30 a.m., three 3-hour trips on weekends at 8:30 a.m., 12:30 p.m., and 5:30 p.m. and one 5-hour trip on weekends at 2:30 p.m.

Fare: For 3-hour trips: Adults, $26; senior citizens, $22; children under 12, $20. For 5-hour trips: Adults, $23; senior citizens, $20; children, $17. Reservations required.

Departure: Three-hour trips leave from Number One Long Wharf in Boston off I-93 Blue Line Aquarium T Station. Five-hour trips leave from nearby Rowes Wharf.

Naturalist: Naturalist aboard.

Boston Harbor Cruises is family owned and operated and has been in business since 1926, says a spokeswoman. "Whale watching is a favorite among us all, and because of that personal feeling that we have for whales and other marine life, we feel that our whale watch is the best in Boston."

Boston Harbor Whale Watch

60 Rowes Wharf, Boston, MA 02110
(617) 345-9866

Whales: Finback, humpback, minke

Season: June through early September

Boats: One boat; 325 passengers

Trips: One 4-1/2-hour trip daily at 10 a.m. on weekdays; two trips on weekends, at 9 a.m. and 2 p.m.

Fare: Adults, $21; senior citizens and children under 12, $18. Reservations advised.

Departure: Trips leave from Rowes Wharf in Boston, directly behind the arch at the Boston Harbor Hotel.

Naturalist: Naturalist aboard.

Owner Jerry Van Dalinda says the Boston Harbor Whale Watch is "the home of fast whales—we'll get you there, fast."

New England Aquarium

Central Wharf, Boston, MA 02110
(617) 973-5277 for information or (617) 973-5281 for reservations;
Web site www.neaq.org

Whales: Humpback, finback, minke, right, Atlantic white-sided dolphin

Season: April through late October

Boats: One boat, the *Voyager II*; 299 passengers

Trips: Trips last 4-1/2 to 5 hours. April weekends at 10 a.m.; May and June, weekdays at 10 a.m. and weekends at 9:30 a.m. and 3 p.m. July and August, daily at 11 a.m. and 5 p.m.; September 7 through October 10, weekdays at 2 p.m., weekends at 9:30 a.m. and 3 p.m.; October, weekends at 10 a.m.

Fare: Adults, $24; senior citizens and college students, $19; youths 12 to 18, $17.50; children 3 to 11, $15.50. Group rates available. Reservations advised.

Departure: Trips leave from the New England Aquarium's dock. Boarding begins 30 minutes before departure.

Naturalist: Naturalist from the Aquarium staff on board.

"During the trip, our experienced staff will teach you how to identify the different species of whales and the other marine life that inhabit the area," notes Captain Ken Wright. "On the rare occasion that whales are not seen during your voyage, we will be happy to reschedule you for another trip."

The New England Aquarium is a private, nonprofit organization dedicated to education, conservation, and research that has sponsored whale-watch trips since 1978. The Aquarium is building a new, faster boat that will debut in 1999.

GLOUCESTER

Cape Ann Whale Watch

P.O. Box 345, Rose's Wharf, Gloucester, MA 01931

(800) 877-5110 or (508) 283-5110; Web site www.caww.com

Whales:	Humpback, finback, minke, right, Atlantic white-sided dolphin
Season:	Early May through mid-October
Boats:	Two boats; 149 passengers each
Trips:	Two 4-hour trips daily in the summer at 8:30 a.m. and 1:30 p.m. Usually one midmorning trip in early spring and late fall. Weekend afternoon trips are the busiest.
Fare:	Adults, $24; senior citizens over 60, $19; children under 16, $15. Reservations required.
Departure:	Trips leave from Rose's Wharf, 415 Main Street in historic downtown Gloucester. From Boston, follow Route 128 north to Gloucester. At Exit 10, bear right onto Eastern Avenue, then bear right onto Main Street. Rose's Wharf is about .2 mile on the left, opposite the Gibbs Gas Station.
Naturalist:	Naturalists from the Whale Conservation Institute.

Captain Jim Douglass notes, "All trips are research oriented and are led by members of the Whale Conservation Institute, headed by world-renowned Dr. Roger Payne, who was the host of The Discovery Channel's "In The Company of Whales."

"Also, we were the first whale-watching company in the Gloucester area and the second on the East Coast. We've been in this business since 1978."

A percentage of each fare is donated to the Whale Conservation Institute.

Seven Seas Whale Watch

Seven Seas Wharf, Gloucester, MA 01930
(800) 238-1776 or (978) 283-1776;
Web site www.cape-ann.com/7seas/whalewatch.html

Whales:	Humpback, finback, minke, right, pilot
Season:	May through mid-October

Boats: One boat carrying 149 passengers

Trips: Two 4-hour trips daily at 8:30 a.m. and 1:30 p.m. The 1:30 p.m. trip on weekends is the busiest.

Fare: Adults, $24; senior citizens, $19; children under 16, $15. Group rates available. Reservations strongly suggested.

Departure: Trips leave from the historic Seven Seas Wharf downtown on Route 127, next to the Gloucester House Restaurant. Take Exit 11 off Route 12 to downtown.

Naturalist: Naturalist on board from the Marine Education Center of Cape Ann.

"This is a spectacular ocean adventure not available in many places in the world, and is definitely not to be missed by anyone traveling in the area," notes Captain Paul Frontierro. "We offer guaranteed sightings, a warm and helpful crew, and naturalists with extensive experience in animal behavior worldwide."

Yankee Whalewatch

The Yankee Fleet, 75 Essex Avenue, Gloucester, MA 01930
(800) WHALING or (800) 942-5464 or (508) 283-0313;
Fax (508) 283-6089; Web site www.yankeefleet.com

Whales: Humpback, finback, minke, Atlantic white-sided dolphin, harbor porpoise

Season: May 1 through October 31

Boats: Seven boats; 70, 125, 144, or 150 passengers

Trips: Two or three 4-hour trips daily on weekdays, three to five trips on Saturdays, two to four on Sundays as demand warrants throughout the season. Generally, departure times are 8:30 a.m., 1:30 p.m., 2:30 p.m., and 5:30 p.m. The Saturday 1:30 p.m. trip is the busiest.

Fare: Adults, $24; senior citizens over 65, $19; children under 16, $15. Reservations advised. Package deal available for guests at the Cape Ann Marina Resort.

Departure: Trips leave from Cape Ann Marina complex. From Boston, take I-95 north to Route 128; go north to Exit 14 and head toward Gloucester, about 2 1/2 miles. Look for the Yankee Fleet office on the left.

Naturalist: Naturalists from the Center for Oceanic Research and Education Center narrate all trips.

"The Yankee Fleet has been family-owned and operated since 1944, and we use the newest, fastest vessels for whale watching in the area," says a spokesman. "In 1990, we instituted a general environment awareness program to educate passengers about things everyone can do to make a difference in protecting and cleaning up our environment."

Yankee Fleet has a guaranteed sightings policy with a 100 percent sighting record since 1986. From time to time, the Yankee Fleet offers extended whale-watch trips.

NANTUCKET

Nantucket Whale Watch

Straight Wharf, Nantucket, MA 02554
(800) WHALING or (800) 942-5464 or (508) 283-0313;
Fax (508) 283-6089; Web site www.yankeefleet.com

Whales:	Humpback, fin, minke, dolphins
Season:	Mid-July to mid-September
Boats:	The 100-foot *Yankee Spirit*
Trips:	One 8-hour trip at 9:30 a.m. on Tuesdays
Fare:	Adults, $75; children, $40. Reservations advised.
Departure:	Trips leave from the Hy-Line dock on Straight Wharf in downtown Nantucket.
Naturalist:	Naturalist on board from the Center for Oceanic Research and Education.

The Nantucket Whale Watch was started by the Yankee Fleet (out of Gloucester) and Seafarers Expeditions to provide cruises to the Great South Channel near Nantucket Shoals.

"These full-day excursions will allow you to appreciate the grace and beauty of the whales, dolphins, and seabirds of Nantucket's waters on a first-hand basis while contributing to ongoing marine studies," says a representative from the Nantucket Whale Watch.

PLYMOUTH

Captain John Boats

117 Standish Avenue, Plymouth, MA 02360
(800) 242-2469, (508) 746-2643; E-mail info@captjohn.com;
Web site www.captjohn.com

Whales:	Humpback, fin, minke, right, Atlantic white-sided dolphin
Season:	April 1 through October 31
Boats:	Eight boats, 65 to 250 passengers
Trips:	Two to five 4-hour trips daily, usually at 9 a.m., 11 a.m., 2 p.m., and 3:30 p.m. Departures vary according to demand. The 2 p.m. trip on weekends is the most popular.
Fare:	Adults, $24; senior citizens, $19; children under 12, $15. Group and family rates available. Reservations advised.
Departure:	Trips leave from Plymouth Town Wharf, at the end of Route 44 or via Route 3. (Captain John Boats also has a berth at Provincetown's MacMillan Wharf where they take interested ferryboat passengers on a whale watch.)
Naturalist:	Naturalist on board.

Doug Hall, director of sales, notes that Captain John Boats is "the largest fleet of whale-watching and fishing vessels in Massachusetts."

"Since 1977, Captain John Boats has logged sightings of whales and dolphins on more than 99 percent of the excursions, and sightings are guaranteed."

Captain Tim Brady & Sons, Inc.

254 Sandwich Street, Plymouth, MA 02360
(508) 746-4809

Whales:	Humpback, fin, right, minke, orca, Atlantic white-sided dolphin
Season:	April through November
Boats:	One boat, the *Mary Elizabeth*; 49 passengers
Trips:	One 4-1/2-hour trip daily at 2 p.m.; with one additional trip each Saturday and Sunday according to demand. Saturday is busiest.

Fare: Adults, $19; senior citizens, $17; children under 12, $11. Ten percent discounts for families.

Departure: Trips leave from Plymouth's historic Town Wharf, at the end of Route 44 or via Route 3.

Naturalist: Marine biologist serves as naturalist.

Captain Timothy C. Brady says, "We are the only 45-foot-long whale watcher in the area—new, modern, and fast. We usually take only about thirty-five passengers per trip so no one is crowded. And we can videotape your whale watch."

PROVINCETOWN

Cape Cod Cruises

58 Seven Hills Road, Plymouth, MA 02360
(508) 747-2400

Whales: Humpback, finback, minke, right, Atlantic white-sided dolphin

Season: May through October

Boats: One; 250 passengers

Trips: One 4-hour trip daily departs at midday from Provincetown. Weekends are busiest.

Fare: Adults, $24; senior citizens, $19; children under 12, $15; children under 8, free with parent. Reservations advised.

Departure: The cruise originates in Plymouth and the whale watch departs from Fisherman's Wharf in Provincetown, at the foot of Standish Street.

Naturalist: Naturalist on board.

"We are unique in that we pick up passengers from Plymouth as well as Provincetown," notes president Stan Tavares. "We give large groups with variable interests an option when their trip originates in Plymouth. Part of a group can get off in Provincetown, to shop or go to the beach, and the remaining passengers may stay aboard for a whale watch."

Dolphin Fleet of Provincetown

MacMillan Wharf, P.O. Box 243, Provincetown, MA 02657
(800) 826-9300 or (508) 349-1900

Whales: Humpback, fin, minke, right, dolphins

Season: April 15 through October

Boats: Three boats; each holds 300 passengers, but only 147 are allowed on board to ensure comfortable seating

Trips: Nine 3-1/2-hour trips daily in peak season, beginning at 8:30 a.m. and scheduled throughout the day until sunset. Tuesday afternoon is busiest.

Fare: Adults, $18; senior citizens and children 12 and under, $16; children under 7, free. Fares are lower in spring and fall. Group rates. Boats available for private charter in spring and fall. Reservations advised.

Departure: Trips leave from MacMillan Wharf, at the foot of Standish Street.

Naturalist: Naturalists from Provincetown's Center for Coastal Studies act as field guides.

Owner and Captain Albert J. Avellar, once referred to as "the patron saint of whale watching," notes, "We are in our third generation in our study of whales—we know the reproductive rate, etc. The scientists from the Center for Coastal Studies make ours educational trips, and we currently have the fastest whale-watch boats in Provincetown."

Portuguese Princess Whale Watch

P.O. Box 1469, MacMillan Wharf, Provincetown, MA 02657
(800) 442-3188 or (508) 487-2651; Fax (508) 487-6458

Whales: Humpback, finback, minke, right, Atlantic white-sided dolphin

Season: April through October

Boats: Two boats; each carries only 150 to avoid crowding

Trips: Three to six 3-1/2- or 4-hour trips daily, according to demand. Trips are in the morning, at midday, in the afternoon, and at sunset. In April, May, and early June, weekends are busiest; in summer weekends are not as busy and discounts are available. Tuesdays, Wednesdays, and Thursdays are busiest during the summer.

Fare: Fares range from $14 to $19, depending on the day and time. Reservations required during peak season and suggested in spring and fall.

Departure: Trips leave from the Provincetown Marina on MacMillan Wharf, at the foot of Standish Street in Provincetown.

Naturalist: Naturalist/whale experts as field guides on board.

"We serve homemade foods, including Portuguese specialties, and offer folk music on most trips," notes owner Suzanne Carter. We donate money to many whale conservation organizations, but we don't solicit money from customers during the trips. And we guarantee whale sightings."

The Portuguese Princess also owns and operates the Whale Watchers General Store at 309 Commercial Street in Provincetown.

Provincetown Whale Watch Inc.

MacMillan Pier, Provincetown, MA 02657
(800) 992-9333 or (508) 487-1582

Whales: Humpback, finback, minke, right

Season: Mid-May through mid-November

Boats: One boat, the *Ranger V*; 415 passengers

Trips: Three 3-1/2-hour trips daily at 9 a.m., 1 p.m., and 5 p.m. The midday trip on Tuesdays, Wednesdays, and Thursdays is the busiest.

Fare: Off-season rates (May through June and September through November): adults, $14; senior citizens, $12; children under 12, $10. In-season rates (July and August): adults, $18; senior citizens, $15; children, $12; children under 9 ride free. Discounts for AAA members.

Departure: Trips leave from MacMillan Wharf, at the foot of Standish Street in Provincetown.

Naturalist: Naturalist on board.

The Costa family, in the whale-watching business since 1988, brings a lifetime of experience on the sea and a rich family history, dating back to the early days of American whaling, says a spokeswoman.

SALEM

Salem Whale Watch

197 Derby Street, Salem, MA 01970
(978) 741-0434; Fax (978) 744-8718; E-mail eicc@shore.net;
Web site www.salemweb.com/biz/eicc

Whales: Humpback, finback, minke, dolphins

Season: May through October

Boats: *The Super Ranger*, which carries 149 passengers

Trips: In May, one trip at 11 a.m. on weekends. In June, one trip daily at 9 a.m. In July and August, two trips daily at 9 a.m. and 2 p.m. In September, one trip at 11 a.m. Monday through Friday and two trips at 9 a.m. and 2 p.m. on Saturday and Sunday. In October, one trip daily at 1 p.m. All trips last 4-1/2 hours.

Fare: Adults, $25; senior citizens, $20; students, $23; children 16 and under, $16. Group rates available. Reservations advised.

Departure: Trips leave from the Pickering Wharf Marina on Derby Street. Follow 128 north to 114 east and then follow "waterfront" signs to Pickering Wharf.

Naturalist: Naturalist from the Cetacean Research Unit of Gloucester.

"Our unique 'classroom-at-sea' program is designed to give passengers a first-hand knowledge and education of the marine environment, the special part whales play in that environment and man's impact on their survival," says a representative from Salem Whale Watch.

NEW HAMPSHIRE

HAMPTON BEACH

Al Gauron Deep Sea Fishing

State Pier, Hampton Beach, NH 03842
(603) 926-2469

Whales:	Humpback, finback, right, minke, Atlantic white-sided dolphin
Season:	April through October
Boats:	Four boats; three carry 77 passengers; one, 120
Trips:	Three 4- to 5-hour sunset whale-watch cruises each week as weather permits. Daily trips on demand in July and August. Boats available for private charter.
Fare:	Adults, $22; senior citizens, $20; children 12 to 18, $16; children 4 to 12, $12. Reservations advised.
Departure:	Trips leave from Hampton Harbor, by the Hampton River bridge in Hampton Beach.
Naturalist:	Captain narrates trips.

"We have four boats in our fleet and have one of the best reputations on the East Coast," says Captain Rocky Gauron. "We are family owned and operated, and all our captains have piloted their boats on at least one hundred whale watches. They are able to handle narrations very capably."

PORTSMOUTH

Oceanic Whale Watch Expeditions

Isles of Shoals Steamship Company, 315 Market Street, P.O. Box 311, Portsmouth, NH 03801
(800) 441-4620 or (603) 431-5500

Whales:	Humpback, fin, minke, right, sei, pilot, Atlantic white-sided dolphin

Season:	Late April through October 31
Boats:	Two boats; 149 and 349 passengers
Trips:	One 5-hour trip daily at 11:30 a.m. (Departure time may vary according to the season.) Saturday is the busiest day.
Fare:	Adults, $25; senior citizens, $24; children ages 3 to 12, $16. Reservations required on weekends; advised at all times. Guests at the Sheraton Hotel receive a discount on whale watch.
Departure:	Trips leave from Barker Wharf, 315 Market Street in Portsmouth. Off Interstate 95 (going north or south) take Exit 7 and turn toward downtown Portsmouth. Go about 1 mile. Office is across from the Sheraton Hotel.
Naturalist:	Naturalist aboard.

"We are the oldest whale-watch company in New England," notes Jennifer Hafner, senior naturalist. "On our Ocean Expedition Whale Watch, we guarantee that you will have the most fun-filled, educational experience possible. Our many hands-on activities, visual displays and our Honorary Naturalist Program will help you learn not only about whales, but about all the aspects of our rich marine environment." Trips also contribute valuable research data to the oldest whale behavior studies.

RYE

Atlantic Fleet

P.O. Box 678, Rye Harbor State Marina, Rye, NH 03870
(800)-WHALENH or (603) 964-5220

Whales:	Humpback, fin, minke, right
Season:	May 1 through early October
Boats:	One boat, the *M/V Atlantic Queen*, which carries 149 passengers
Trips:	One 4-hour trip daily at 1 p.m.
Fare:	Adults, $20; senior citizens, $18; children, $14. Reservations are advised.
Departure:	Trips leave from Rye Harbor State Marina.
Naturalist:	Yes

Owner Brad Cook notes, "Our naturalist provides a pre-cruise discussion and orientation, narration during the trip, and answers questions one-on-one on the return trip. Also, we have fast aluminum vessels, which provide more time on the whale grounds."

New Hampshire Seacoast Cruises

Rye Harbor State Marina, Box 232, Rye, NH 03870
(800) 964-5545 or (603) 964-5545

Whales:	Finback, humpback, minke, right, Atlantic white-sided dolphin, harbor porpoise
Season:	May 1 through mid-October
Boats:	One boat, the *Granite State*; 150 passengers
Trips:	Two 4-1/2-hour trips daily at 8:30 a.m. and 1:30 p.m. Abbreviated schedule during off-season.
Fare:	Adults, $20; senior citizens, $18; children, $15; under 5, free. Reservations recommended.
Departure:	Trips leave from Rye Harbor State Marina on Route 1A between Hampton Beach and Portsmouth, next to Saunders' Restaurant. Look for the giant American flag.
Naturalist:	Naturalist aboard.

"Every whale watch is led by an experienced professional research/naturalist, and the cruise is preceded by a lecture with graphics," says owner Leo Axtin. "Also, we are the nearest mainland port to the Isles of Shoals, the southernmost harbor seal nesting area in the western North Atlantic. Almost every whale trip takes us past these islands."

NEW JERSEY

CAPE MAY

Cape May Whale Watch and Research Center

1286 Wilson Drive, Cape May, NJ 08204
(609) 898-0055; Fax (609) 884-8602

Whales:	Humpback, finback, right, pilot, minke
Season:	April through December
Boats:	Two boats; 200 passengers each
Trips:	A 2-hour dolphin watch and breakfast cruise at 9:30 a.m. daily, a 3-hour trip at 9:30 a.m. weekends only, and a 3-hour sunset cruise at 6 p.m. weekends.
Fare:	For the 2-hour trip, adults, $22; senior citizens, $20; children 7 to 14, $8; children 6 and under, free. For the 3-hour trips, adults, $26; senior citizens, $24; children, $10. For the sunset cruise, adults, $18; senior citizens, $16; children, $8. Reservations advised.
Departure:	Trips leave from the end of Wilson Drive, off Route 109 at the Little Bridge.
Naturalist:	Naturalist on board.

"We offer the opportunity for the entire family and people of all ages to become better educated about environmental issues while enjoying the time spent doing so," says Captain Ron Robbins, who reports sighting as many as 600 whales each season. He's been in business since 1962, and publishes an annual newsletter.

MUSEUMS, AQUARIUMS, AND SCIENCE CENTERS

CONNECTICUT

The Maritime Center at Norwalk

10 North Water Street, Norwalk, CT 06854
(203) 852-0700

In historic South Norwalk, the Maritime Center features 25 marine habitats, a maritime history museum, a wooden boat shop and an IMAX theater. The Center houses more than 125 different species of marine life, including playful harbor seals, tiny brine shrimp and 10-foot sharks, all indigenous to Long Island Sound.

Summer hours at the Center (from July 1 through Labor Day) are from 10 a.m. to 6 p.m. In winter, the Center is open from 10 a.m. to 5 p.m. Closed Thanksgiving and Christmas. Admission to Aquarium and the Maritime Hall is $7.75 for adults, $6.50 for children. IMAX admission is $6.50 for adults, $4 for children. Combination admission is $12 for adults, $9.50 for children.

Each year, the Maritime Center at Norwalk schedules two three-day whale-watch trips off Cape Cod. For information, contact the Center.

Mystic Marinelife Aquarium

55 Coogan Boulevard, Mystic, CT 06355
(860) 572-5955; Fax (860) 572-5969

More than 6,000 sea life specimens, including beluga whales, are displayed in forty-nine living exhibits in the Mystic Marinelife Aquarium. Seal Island, a 2.5-acre outdoor exhibit, shows the natural habitats of seals and sea lions. Whale and dolphin shows daily.

From June 30 through Labor Day, the Aquarium is open 9 a.m. to 6 p.m.; the rest of the year, 9 a.m. to 5 p.m. Closed Thanksgiving, Christmas, New Year's Day, and the last week of January. Admission is $13 for adults, $8 for children 5 through 12, and $12 for senior citizens.

MAINE

Natural History Museum

College of the Atlantic, 105 Eden Street, Bar Harbor, ME 04609
(207) 288-5015; Fax (207) 288-2328

This small museum is part of the College of the Atlantic and features displays of Mount Desert Island flora and fauna. Daily participatory programs include assembling a 20-foot whale skeleton.

The Natural History Museum is open daily 9 a.m. to 5 p.m. Monday through Saturday from mid-June to Labor Day, and 10 a.m. to 4 p.m. Monday through Friday from Labor Day to June. Admission is $2.50 for adults, $1 for senior citizens and teens and $1 for children.

MARYLAND

National Aquarium in Baltimore

Pier 3, 501 East Pratt Street, Baltimore, MD 21202
(410) 576-3800

The main building of the National Aquarium is a seven-level building where more than 5,000 salt- and freshwater species are on display. Special exhibits include a South American tropical rain forest, an outdoor 70,000-gallon rock pool, and a 220,000-gallon ocean tank that houses sharks, rays, and large fish. The Marine Mammal Pavilion, which opened in December 1990, is primarily dedicated to dolphins but includes a life-size model of Scylla, a known humpback who lives in the Atlantic Ocean.

From May 15 to September 15, the Aquarium is open from 9 a.m. to 8 p.m. seven days a week. From September 16 through May 14, hours are 10 a.m. to 5 p.m. Saturday through Thursday and 10 a.m. to 8 p.m. on Friday. Closed Thanksgiving and Christmas Day. Admission is $14 for adults; $10.50 for senior citizens, $7.50 for children ages 3 to 11. Children under 3 are free.

MASSACHUSETTS

New Bedford Whaling Museum

18 Johnny Cake Hill, New Bedford, MA 02740
(508) 997-0046; Fax (508) 997-0018

This is the largest museum in the United States devoted to whaling in the age of sail. Exhibits include a humpback whale skeleton, a 98-foot mural of sperm whales painted by Richard Ellis, and galleries devoted to scrimshaw, whale boats, and whaling equipment. There also is an extensive collection of art related to whaling.

The focal point of the exhibits is a half-scale model of the whaling boat *Lagoda*, which visitors may board. A twenty-two-minute segment of a silent film showing the chase and capture of a whale is shown daily at 10:30 a.m. and 1:30 p.m. in July and August and at 2 p.m. on Saturday and Sunday the other months of the year.

The Whaling Museum is open 9 a.m. to 5 p.m. seven days a week. From June through September, the museum is open until 8 p.m. on Thursday. Closed Thanksgiving, Christmas, and New Year's Day. Admission is $4.50 for adults, $3.50 for senior citizens, $3 for children 6 through 14.

New England Aquarium

Central Wharf, Boston, MA 02119
(617) 973-5200 or (617) 973-5200 (recording)

More than seventy exhibits, with new displays each year, continue to delight visitors to the New England Aquarium on Boston's historic waterfront. The 187,000-gallon Giant Ocean Tank extends from floor to ceiling, and huge sea turtles, sharks, and moray eels swim alongside as you descend the spiral ramp around the tank. California sea lions perform daily aboard Discovery, a floating marine mammal pavilion.

From July 1 through Labor Day, the Aquarium is open 9 a.m.to 6 p.m. Monday, Tuesday, and Friday; 9 a.m. to 8 p.m. Wednesday and Thursday; 9 a.m. to 7 p.m. Saturday, Sunday and holidays. From Labor Day to June 30, the museum is open 9 a.m. to 5 p.m. Monday through Friday; 9 a.m. to 6 p.m. Saturday, Sunday, and holidays. Closed Thanksgiving and Christmas Day; open at noon on New Year's Day.

Admission is $11 for adults, $10 for senior citizens, $5.50 for children 3 to 11, $7.50 for senior citizens. During the summer, visitors receive a $1 discount from 4 to 7:30 p.m. on Wednesday and Thursday.

The New England Aquarium operates whale watches on its own boat. See listing under Boston, Massachusetts.

Peabody Essex Museum of Salem

East India Square, Salem, MA 01970
(978) 745-1876; Fax (978) 744-6776

Among the many treasures at the Peabody Essex Museum are exhibits on the natural resources, environment, and marine ecology of Essex County. Exhibits include birds, reptiles, fish, plants, mammals, and pond life. "Maritime New England," a permanent exhibit, includes paintings and artifacts documenting the history of maritime fishing and whaling industries. Special programs for children include classes on whale biology and Yankee whaling.

The Peabody Essex Museum is open 10 a.m. to 5 p.m. Monday through Saturday; and noon to 5 p.m. Sunday. Admission is $8.50 for adults; $7.50 for senior citizens and students; $5 for children 6 to 16.

NEW YORK

American Museum of Natural History

Central Park West at 79th Street, New York, NY 10024
(212) 769-5100

Said to be the largest museum of its kind, the American Museum of Natural History offers forty exhibit halls and numerous special display areas, with more than thirty million artifacts and specimens. The Hall of Ocean Life includes a 94-foot model of a diving whale.

The American Museum of Natural History is open 10 a.m. to 5:45 p.m. Sunday through Thursday and 10 a.m. to 8:45 p.m. Wednesday, Friday, and Saturday. Closed Thanksgiving and Christmas Day. Suggested admission is $8 for adults, $6 for senior citizens and students, and $4.50 for children.

The museum schedules an annual three-day whale watch off Cape Cod in May. The chartered trip includes a visit to the Mystic Aquarium. For more information, contact the museum's Department of Education.

MARINE SANCTUARIES

MASSACHUSETTS

Stellwagen Bank National Marine Sanctuary

14 Union Street, Plymouth, MA 02360
(508) 747-1691

Just 25 nautical miles east of Boston lies Stellwagen Bank, a submerged sand
bank in waters that support large populations of marine mammals and fish.
Three species of endangered whales (humpback, fin and right) use the area as
a nursery and feeding ground. Other cetaceans often spotted are Atlantic white-
sided dolphins, harbor porpoise, orcas, pilot whales and minke whales. Write
for a free brochure.

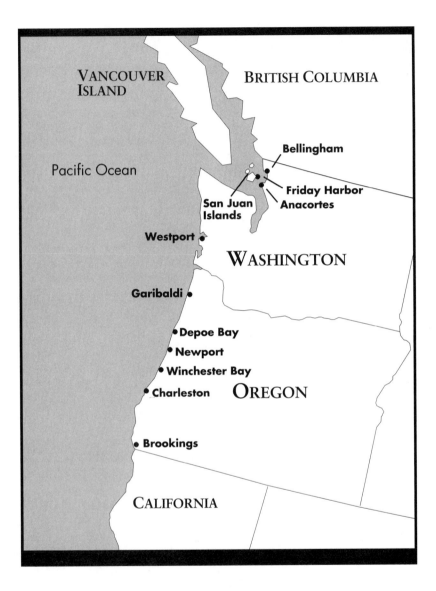

THE PACIFIC NORTHWEST

Whale watchers in Washington enjoy two seasons, in two different areas. Westport, on the Pacific Coast, boasts several tour operators who take whale watchers to see the annual migration of the gray whales. April and May are considered the best months; the weather has calmed sufficiently, and the whales swim more slowly as they head north to the Bering and Chukchi seas. The summer months, especially June and July, find whale watchers in search of three large populations of orcas and an abundance of minkes off the San Juan Islands.

Trips in the San Juan Islands, which depart from several cities, are available for one, two, three, or four days, on excursion boats, sailboats, and sea kayaks. Beginners are welcome on the kayak trips, which include instructions on maneuvering the craft. One tour operator notes, "Kayaking among whales is quite a thrill."

Oregon celebrates the annual migration of the gray whales and also welcomes those sperm whales, orcas, and humpbacks that are occasionally seen in the area. Like their colleagues on the Washington coast, whale-watch tour operators in Oregon all are at the mercy of the weather. Depoe Bay has the only "inside" whale watching, within the protection of the bay. Because of this geographical advantage, Depoe Bay bills itself as "The Whale-Watching Capital of the Oregon Coast." Trips are also available in other cities.

Gray whales traveling south reach Oregon early in December and are gone by mid-February. Whale watching peaks early in January. Heading north on the return trip, adult males and some females pass by Oregon from early March through mid-April; females with calves can be seen from early May through mid-June.

Even when the cold, rainy weather keeps the boats in their harbors, the state of Oregon has whale watchers in mind. Volunteers trained at the Extension Service at Oregon State University stand at lookout points at numerous locations along the Oregon coast. On duty from 10 a.m. to 1 p.m., December 26 through January 1 and again during the third week of March, the volunteers point out the passing whales and answer questions about the migration.

The lookout points, marked with signs that read "WHALE WATCHING SPOKEN HERE," include North Head, Fort Stevens State Park, Ecola State Park, Neahkahnie Mountain, Cape Meares State Park, Cape Lookout State Park, "D" River State Wayside, Boller Bay Wayside, Depoe Bay seawall, Rocky Creek Wayside, Cape Foulweather, Cape Perpetua overlook, Sea Lion Caves turnout, Umpqua Lighthouse State Park, Shore Acres State Park, and Harris Beach State Park.

TOURISM INFORMATION

OREGON

Central Oregon Coast Association

P.O. Box 2094, Newport, OR 97365
(800) 767-2064

Economic Development Department
Tourism Division

775 Summer Street N.E., Salem, OR 97310
(800) 547-7842 (outside Oregon)

Oregon Coast Visitors Association

P.O. Box 74, Newport, OR 97365
(888) 628-2101 or (541) 574-2679

Washington

Department of Trade and Economic Development
Tourism Development Division

101 General Administration Building, P.O. Box 42500, Olympia,
WA 98504
(800) 544-1800

Westport-Grayland Chamber of Commerce

2985 South Montesano Street, P.O. Box 306, Westport,
WA 98595
(800) 345-6223

WHALE-WATCHING TRIPS

OREGON

BROOKINGS

Tidewind Sportfishing

P.O. Box 6293, Brookings, OR 97415
(541) 469-0337; Fax (541) 469-0445

Whales:	Gray
Season:	December through March
Boats:	Three boats, the 43-foot *Super Star* that carries 28 passengers, the 38-foot *Leta J* that carries 14 passengers, and the 36-foot *Xtra Mile* that carries 6.
Trips:	Trips are arranged on request.
Fare:	$25 per person for a 2-hour trip. Reservations are appreciated.
Departure:	Trips leave from the port of Brookings Harbor just off Highway 101.
Naturalist:	No naturalist on board.

"Whales are near the shore just a short distance from the harbor," say Jim and Jan Pearce. "We provide literature on the whales for passengers."

CHARLESTON

Betty Kay Charters

P.O. Box 5020, Charleston, OR 97420
(800) 752-6303; Web site www.presys.com/ann/bettykay/

Whales:	Gray
Season:	January, March, April
Boats:	One boat; 30 passengers
Trips:	Trips are offered according to demand and the tide. Weekends are the busiest.
Fare:	$25 per person for a 3-hour trip. Minimum of 6 people. Reservations required.
Departure:	Trips leave from the Charleston boat basin. Cross the Charleston Bridge, turn right toward the small boat basin, and follow the signs.
Naturalist:	No naturalist on board.

Bill Whitmer, skipper and owner of Betty Kay Charters, has been going to sea since the early 1970s.

DEPOE BAY

Dockside Charters

P.O. Box 1308, 270 S.E. Coast Guard Place, Depoe Bay, OR 97341
(800) 733-8915 or (541) 765-2545; Web site www.newportnet.com/dockside

Whales:	Gray
Season:	Year 'round
Boats:	Two boats, carrying 30 and 6 passengers respectively
Trips:	Trips scheduled every hour from 10 a.m. until dark. Saturday is the busiest day.

Fare:	For the 1-hour trips on the big boat: Adults, $10, $6 for children 4 to 12. The 90-minute trip in the inflatable raft costs $25 per person. Reservations advised during holidays.
Departure:	Trips leave from the town harbor. Off Highway 101, turn east at Bay Street (the only stoplight in town) and follow the road past the Coast Guard station.
Naturalist:	No naturalist on board.

Co-owner James M. Tate says that Depoe Bay is the whale-watching capital "not only of Oregon, but may well deserve the title for the entire Pacific coast." Whales are present year 'round, feeding near the shore, providing great whale-watching.

Enterprise

P.O. Box 575, Depoe Bay, OR 97341
(503) 765-2245

Whales:	Gray
Season:	Year 'round
Boats:	One boat; 30 passengers
Trips:	Trips regularly scheduled from 9 a.m. until dark, according to demand and the tide. Weekends are the busiest days.
Fare:	Adults, $11 per hour; children: ages 7 to 12, $8 per hour; 7 and younger, free. Reservations advised.
Departure:	Trips leave from the town harbor. Off Highway 101, turn east at Bay Street (the only stoplight in town) and follow the road past the Coast Guard station. Dock is 100 feet from the parking lot.
Naturalist:	No naturalist on board.

"Depoe Bay is the World's Smallest Harbor, and whales come in close to shore," says owner Dave de Belloy. "We have seen whales feeding, mating, breaching, spyhopping, and cows with their calves. The spring is the best time, because the whales are slower."

Joan-E Charters

P.O. Box 388, 214 S.E. Highway 101, Depoe Bay, OR 97341
(800) 995-3866 or (541) 765-2222; Fax (541) 765-3197;
Web site www.netbridge.net/joan`e/

Whales:	Gray
Season:	February through October
Boats:	Three boats carrying 24 passengers, 46 passengers, and 99 passengers respectively.
Trips:	Six 1- or 2-hour trips scheduled from 10 a.m. until 5 p.m. daily, ocean permitting.
Fare:	Adults, $12 per hour; seniors and teens, $10 per hour; children 12 and under, $8 per hour. Reservations advised.
Departure:	Trips leave from the Joan-E Charters docks in Depoe Bay at 214 S.E. Highway 101.
Naturalist:	Knowledgeable skipper in the business since 1986 narrates trips.

Joan and Captain Andy, co-owners, say whale watching is a truly awe-inspiring experience. The 60-foot Grande is Depoe Bay's largest and only double-deck whale watching vessel.

Tradewinds Charters

P.O. Box 123, Depoe Bay, OR 97341
(800) 445-8730 or (541) 765-2345; E-mail rallyn@orednet.org;
Web site www.newportnet.com/tradewinds/

Whales:	Gray
Season:	All year
Boats:	Twelve boats; 180 passengers altogether
Trips:	Nine trips daily; some 1-hour and some 2-hour. Hourly trips leave from 9 a.m. until dark. The 2-hour trips leave at 11 a.m. and 1 p.m. Hourly trips on weekends are the most crowded.
Fare:	Adults, $11 an hour; children: ages 5 to 12, $6 an hour; 4 and younger, free. Some 90-minute Zodiac trips are available for $25 per person. Group rates available. Reservations advised. Custom packages through several local motels; write for information.

Departure: Trips leave from Tradewinds office on Highway 101 in downtown Depoe Bay at the north end of the bridge. Check-in is 30 minutes before departure.

Naturalist: Naturalist sometimes on board.

"Our crews are extremely friendly and make each trip a fun experience," owner Rich Allyn notes. "We have clean, modern vessels, and if a naturalist is not aboard, each of our crew is extremely knowledgeable and provides a very good talk about the whales."

GARIBALDI

Troller Deep Sea Fishing Charters

P.O. Box 605, 604 Mooring Basin Road, Garibaldi, OR 97118
(800) 546-3666 or (503) 322-3666

Whales: Gray

Season: February through April

Boats: Eight boats; 140 passengers altogether

Trips: Two 2-hour trips on weekdays and three on weekends, scheduled whenever the ocean permits. Saturday is the busiest day.

Fare: $15 per person. Reservations required.

Departure: Trips leave from the Garibaldi boat basin, just off Highway 101.

Naturalist: No naturalist on board.

Captain Jim Violette, the owner of Troller Deep Sea Fishing Charters, says his pelagic bird trips are as popular as his whale-watch trips.

NEWPORT

Bayfront Charters

1000 S.E. Bay Boulevard, Newport, OR 97365
(800) 828-8777 or (503) 265-7558

Whales:	Gray
Season:	December 1 through May 1
Boats:	Four boats, carrying between 20 and 48 passengers
Trips:	One 2-hour trip daily at 1 p.m.
Fare:	Adults, $15; children 6 to 12, $9. Reservations required.
Departure:	Trips leave from the Embarcadero Marina, on Bay Boulevard.
Naturalist:	Naturalist aboard.

"Location and friendly people," are what make Newport Sportfishing special, according to owners John and Roz Vostinak.

Sea Gull Charters

343 S.W. Bay Boulevard, Newport, OR 97365
(541) 265-7441; Fax (541) 265-3930;
Web site www.newportnet.com/seagull/

Whales:	Gray
Season:	Year 'round
Boats:	Four boats, carrying between 20 and 40 passengers
Trips:	Four 1/2- or 2-hour trips daily at 10:30 a.m., 12:30 p.m., 2:30 p.m., and 4:30 p.m., weather permitting. Whale watching is good every month except October and November.
Fare:	Adults, $16 for two hours, $12 for 1/2 hours; children 6 to 12, half price; 5 and under, free. Reservations required.
Departure:	Trips leave from Sea Gull docks on the Newport bayfront.
Naturalist:	Naturalist aboard.

"Our trips are very personal, as our boats are not crowded," says a representative from Sea Gull Charters.

WINCHESTER BAY

Strike Zone Marine & Charters

P.O. Box 1413, Winchester Bay, OR 97467
(800) 230-5350 or (541) 271-9706;
Web site www.pacific101.com/strikezone/

Whales:	Gray
Season:	December through May
Boats:	The 44-foot *Strike Zone*, which carries 22 passengers
Trips:	Trips scheduled according to demand. Trips last 2 to 3 hours.
Fare:	$30 per person. Reservations suggested.
Departure:	Trips leave from Dock A in Winchester Bay at Salmon Harbor.
Naturalist:	No naturalist on board.

Captain Scott Howard notes that *Strike Zone* is a family-owned and operated business founded in 1962.

WASHINGTON

ANACORTES

Elakah! Kayak Tours

P.O. Box 4092, Bellingham, WA 98227
(800) 434-7270 or (360) 734-7270

Whales:	Orca, porpoise
Season:	July through September
Boats:	Six kayaks; each holds two
Trips:	Trips lasting from one to four days, kayaking and camping in the San Juan Islands.
Fare:	Extended trips range from $69 to $395. Fare includes kayak instruction, guides, gear and meals on overnight trips. Reservations required. Custom trips for one to ten days are available for groups of four or more. Call for dates and prices.
Departure:	Kayaks leave from Lopez Island, a 45-minute ferry ride from Anacortes.
Naturalist:	Guides knowledgeable about the natural and cultural history of the area accompany each trip.

"Elakah! Kayak Tours has the capability of bringing nature and people together and producing a very special form of magic," says owner Jennifer Hahn. "The non-motorized aspect of Elakah! is enchanting in itself—what better way to see, feel, and enjoy nature than in a small, quiet boat not much above sea level."

Seattle Aquarium

Pier 59, Waterfront Park, Seattle, WA 98101
(206) 386-4353; Web site www.seattleaquarium.org

Whales:	Orca
Season:	Late May through early September

Boats: One boat; 40 passengers

Trips: Multiple 8-hour trips, all scheduled for 10 a.m. on Saturdays

Fare: Adults, $70; children, $65. Reservations required. Cost includes pretrip lecture scheduled for a day or two before each cruise.

Departure: Trips leave from Cap Sante marina in Anacortes. From Commercial Avenue (the main street), turn right on Eleventh Street. Cross the railroad tracks and go into the Cap Sante marina parking lot.

Naturalist: Naturalist aboard.

"The Seattle Aquarium offers boat trips for the general public to observe whales during two seasons of the year," says Leo J. Shaw, marine education specialist at the Aquarium. "During March and April, the Aquarium offers gray whale-watching trips from Westport, Washington, on weekends. During the months of June, July, and August, we offer cruises in the San Juan Islands of Washington state to search for the local killer whales."

BELLINGHAM

Island Mariner Cruises

#5 Harbor Esplanade, Bellingham, WA 98225
(360) 734-8866; Fax (360) 734-8867

Whales: Orca, minke

Season: Late May through mid-September

Boats: One boat; 149 passengers

Trips: One 7-1/2-hour trip every Saturday and Sunday from late May through mid-September; also one 7-1/2-hour trip every Tuesday and Thursday in July and August.

Fare: This 90-mile cruise through the San Juan Islands costs $55 for adults, $45 for senior citizens and $35 for children 15 and under. Reservations advised.

Departure: Trips leave from Squalicum Harbor in Bellingham. From Interstate 5, take the Meridian Street exit (Exit 256) and drive south for 0.5 miles. Turn right on Squalicum Way and drive 1.8 miles. Turn right on Coho Way and drive 2 blocks, to the Esplanade Building. The office is at the far east end.

Naturalist: Naturalist on board.

"We have been offering whale-watching cruises in the San Juan Islands since 1985, and our superb spotting service assures us the highest success rate," owner Terry Buzzard writes. "Our company has provided cruises for the National Audubon Society, National Wildlife Federation, Pacific Science Center and Greenpeace Northwest."

SAN JUAN ISLANDS

Blue Moon Explorations

476 Blank Road, Sedro-Woolley, WA, 98284
(800) 966-8806 or (360) 856-5622; E-mail bluemoon@xpressmail.net;
Web site www.home.cio.net/bluemoon

Whales: Orca

Season: May through August

Boats: Eight 2-person kayaks

Trips: Multiple 3-, 4- and 5-day trips in the San Juan Islands that include whale watching, bird watching, hiking and kayaking. Participants camp. Some trips are for women only.

Fare: Fares range from $100 to $125 a day, which includes kayaks, camping accommodations and meals, safety equipment, instruction and guides. Reservations required.

Departure: Trips begin on San Juan Island or at Alert Bay, British Columbia.

Naturalist: Naturalist aboard.

Owner Kathleen Grimbly says, "Blue Moon Explorations are designed to expand our awareness of the many intricate relationships in the web of life. Traveling by kayak, we experience the whales, and the web of life that supports them, more intimately and less intrusively. Our trips are designed for people of all ages and abilities."

Bon Accord Charters

P.O. Box 472, Friday Harbor, WA 98250
(360) 378-5921

Whales:	Orca, minke
Season:	Year 'round
Boats:	The 30-foot *Bon Accord*; six passengers
Trips:	One 5-hour trip daily at noon. Other trips available on request.
Fare:	$65 per person. Reservations advised.
Departure:	Trips leave from Slip M-8 at the main dock at the foot of town in Friday Harbor.
Naturalist:	The captain is a naturalist, trained by Earth Trust and The Whale Museum at Friday Harbor.

"We are the only operator that takes small groups for a custom, personalized tour," says Captain Richard Karon. "Our boat is a custom-built wood trawler with all comforts. In addition to whales, we see harbor seals, Dall's porpoise, sea lions, elephant seals, bald eagles and numerous seabirds on our wildlife cruises throughout the year."

Northwest Outdoor Center

2100 Westlake Avenue North, Seattle, WA 98109
(206) 281-9694

Whales:	Orca
Season:	May and June
Boats:	Kayaks
Trips:	Three-day trips in the San Juan Islands. Participants camp overnight.
Fare:	Adults, $295. Reservations required.
Departure:	Trips leave from Smallpox Bay, west of Friday Harbor on San Juan Island.
Naturalist:	Naturalist accompanies trips.

The Northwest Outdoor Center was founded by five "paddling enthusiasts/maniacs" in 1980. Herbie Meyer notes that classes, longer trips, and Christmas caroling by kayak are also available.

Resource Institute

2319 North 45th Street, #139, Seattle, WA 98103
(206) 784-6762

Whales:	Orca, minke, humpback
Season:	May through October
Boats:	65- to 72-foot classic wooden boats; 8 to 10 passengers
Trips:	Numerous trips, lasting from three to ten days, including several to Southeast Alaska. The San Juan Island trips go in search of orcas and minkes in May and October; humpbacks are seen in Alaska June through September. Participants live on board.
Fare:	Trips cost about $250 per day. Reservations required.
Departure:	Trips depart from Friday Harbor in Washington and also from Sitka, Petersburg, Juneau, and Ketchikan in Alaska.
Naturalist:	Naturalist aboard.

Seminars while afloat along the way (from the San Juan Islands to Alaska) range in subject matter, including natural history, marine biology, wood-carving, photography, music, poetry, anthropology and conservation.

"Groups live on board as we travel and study," says Paige Tyley. The Resource Institute is a non-profit educational organization.

San Juan Boat Rentals

P.O. Box 2281, Spring Street Landing, Friday Harbor, WA 98250
(800) 232-6722 or (360) 378-3499

Whales:	Orca, minke
Season:	May through September

Boats: Three boats, carrying from 12 to 50 passengers

Trips: Three 3-hour trips at 11:30 a.m., 12:30 p.m., and 1:30 p.m.

Fare: Fares range from $39 to $45 depending on the season, with discounts available for children, senior citizens, groups and charters. Reservations advised.

Departure: Trips leave from the Spring Street Landing in Friday Harbor, one block from the ferry landing.

Naturalist: Naturalist aboard.

Owner and skipper Darrell Roberts says the San Juan Islands are one of the best places in the world to see whales.

San Juan Excursions

P.O. Box 2508, Friday Harbor, WA 98250
(800) 80-WHALE or (360) 378-6636; Fax (360) 378-6652;
E-mail sanjuanex@watchwhales.com; Web site www.watchwhales.com

Whales: Orca, minke

Season: May through September

Boats: Two boats, the 64-foot motor yacht *Odyssey* that carries 75 passengers, and the 40-foot excursion boat *Malia Kai* that holds 25 passengers.

Trips: Two 3-1/2-hour trips daily, with a morning and an afternoon departure, depending on the ferry schedule. Call for times.

Fare: Adults, $45; children 12 and under, $32; children under 2, free. Reservations advised.

Departure: Trips leave from the Spring Street Landing in Friday Harbor, one block from the ferry landing.

Naturalist: Naturalists trained by the Whale Museum staff.

"We offer a comprehensive whale-watch/wildlife cruise, not a short whale glimpse as some operators do," says Lynn Danaher, president of San Juan Excursions.

San Juan Kayak Expeditions Inc.

P.O. Box 2041, Friday Harbor, WA 98250
(360) 378-4436

Whales:	Orca, minke, harbor porpoise
Season:	Late May through September 30
Boats:	Kayaks that hold two people each
Trips:	Three- and four-day trips available. Participants camp overnight. Weekends are busiest.
Fare:	Prices range from $305 for the three-day trip to $395 for the five-day trip. Reservations required.
Departure:	Trips leave from Friday Harbor, with transportation to the launch point.
Naturalist:	Naturalist accompanies trips.

Guide and founder Tim Thomsen notes, "Kayaking among whales is quite a thrill."

Sea Quest Expeditions/Zoetic Research

P.O. Box 2424R, Friday Harbor, WA 98250
(360) 378-5767; E-mail seaquest@pacificrim.net;
Web site www.sea-quest-kayak.com

Whales:	Orca, minke, Dall's porpoise, harbor porpoise
Season:	May through October
Boats:	Sea kayaks
Trips:	One-, two-, three-, and five-day kayak trips in the San Juan Islands. Participants camp overnight at small islands accessible only by boat.
Fare:	Depending on the length of the trip, fares range from $39 to $499 per person, including meals. Reservations required.
Departure:	Trips leave from the Ferry Terminal in Friday Harbor. Transportation is provided to the launch site, which varies according to the tides.
Naturalist:	A professional field biologist/educator serves as naturalist.

Mark Lewis, executive director, notes, "On numerous occasions, we have found our flotilla of kayaks completely infiltrated by orcas! We have never felt threatened during these exciting encounters. In fact, the whales are very careful about their movements when in close proximity to kayaks. We have even had participants be able to reach out and touch a wild orca that spy-hopped next to the kayak!"

Lewis says that beginners are welcome—90 percent of the participants have never been in a kayak before. He adds that no other kayak outfitter in the area operates trips designed specifically to see whales 100 percent of the time or uses biologists as naturalists.

Sea Quest Expeditions also offers research trips and will design custom trips. College credit is available for all programs.

Shearwater Adventures

P.O. Box 787, Eastsound, WA 98245
(360) 376-4699; Web site www.pacificrim.net/`kayak

Whales:	Orca, minke, harbor porpoise
Season:	April through October
Boats:	Sea kayaks, 65-foot sailing yawl
Trips:	Half-day, full-day and two-day kayak or kayak/sailing trips. No experience necessary.
Fare:	Fees vary. Reservations required.
Departure:	Participants meet at the ferry terminal on San Juan Island or Orcas Island. Transportation to launch site is provided.
Naturalist:	Trips are accompanied by a naturalist.

"We use sea kayaks and a sailboat to minimize our impact on the whales and because kayaks provide the most intimate contact with the water of any craft," says Tom Carter of Shearwater Adventures. "All of our trips integrate the natural history of Puget Sound as a whole, including marine mammals, birds, flora and fauna. Our whale trips additionally have the potential for memorable encounters with orcas and other whales."

Western Prince Cruises

P.O. Box 418, #2 Spring Street, Friday Harbor, WA 98250
(800) 757-6722 or (360) 378-5315; E-mail orca@rockisland.com;
Web site www.rockisland.com/`orca/

Whales:	Orca, minke, Dall's porpoise, harbor porpoise
Season:	Mid-April through mid-October
Boats:	Two boats; the 46-foot *Western Prince II*, which carries 30 passengers, and the 28-foot *Island Girl*, which carries 6 on custom charters
Trips:	One 4-hour trip daily (except Tuesday) at 1 p.m. through mid-June and after Labor Day or at 2 p.m. mid-June through Labor Day. Occasional morning trips.
Fare:	Adults, $45; children: 12 through 17, $32. Private charter rates available on request.
Departure:	Trips leave from the Port of Friday Harbor, 80 miles northwest of Seattle on Interstate 5 and via the San Juan ferry from Anacortes.
Naturalist:	Naturalist narrates each trip.

"We are the industry founder of orca whale watching based in the San Juan Islands and have specialized in these tours since 1986," says a spokesman.

Cachalot Whale Watch

2511 Westhaven Drive, P.O. Box 348, Westport, WA 98595
(360) 268-0323

Whales:	Gray
Season:	March through April
Boats:	One boat; 30 passengers
Trips:	One 2-1/2-hour trip daily at noon on weekdays; two trips daily at 11 a.m. and 2 p.m. on weekends

Fare: Adults, $25; children 12 and under, $15. Reservations advised.

Departure: Boat leaves from Float 12 in the Westport Marina.

Naturalist: Captain narrates.

Owners Darlene and David Camp are carrying on the family whale-watching business, and they guarantee sightings "or your next trip is on us."

Deep Sea Charters/Whale Watching Headquarters

Across from Float 6, Box 1115, Westport, WA 98595
(206) 268-9300; E-mail deepsea@seanet.com

Whales: Gray

Season: March through May

Boats: Nine boats; 6 to 20 passengers

Trips: Several 2-1/2-hour trips scheduled daily.

Fare: $25 per person. Family and school rates available. Reservations required. Deep Sea Charters and several local motels offer a package deal that includes a night's lodging and a whale watch.

Departure: Trips leave from Float 6 off Westhaven Drive, northeast of the Westport Maritime Museum.

Naturalist: Captain narrates.

Owner Larry Giese notes, "Before we leave the dock, we have an educational discussion about the gray whale and what you can expect. Gray whales are sighted 98 percent of the time." Free illustrated informational brochures are also available.

Seattle Aquarium

Pier 59, Waterfront Park, Seattle, WA 98101
(206) 386-4353; Web site www.seattleaquarium.org

Whales:	Gray
Season:	Mid-March through the end of April
Boats:	One boat that carries 75 to 100 passengers
Trips:	One 3-hour trip at 2 p.m. on Saturdays or Sundays.
Fare:	Adults, $28; children, $14.50. Reservations required. Fee includes pretrip educational program scheduled a few days in advance and on day of trip.
Departure:	Trips leave from Westport dock, at the foot of Dock Street at Westhaven Drive.
Naturalist:	Naturalist on board from the Aquarium staff.

The Seattle Aquarium offers boat trips for the general public to observe whales during two seasons of the year: from Westport during March and April, to observe gray whales, and from Anacortes in June, July, and August, to search for orcas in the San Juan Islands.

"The Seattle Aquarium does not display whales, dolphins, or porpoises," notes Leo J. Shaw, marine education specialist. "Our marine mammals on display are harbor seals, northern fur seals, and sea otters."

Westport Whale Watch/Ocean Charters Inc.

2315 W. Westhaven Drive, P.O. Box 548, Westport, WA 98595
(800) 562-0105 or (360) 268-9144; Fax (360) 268-1223

Whales:	Gray, sometimes orca
Season:	March 1 through mid-May
Boats:	Six boats, all 50 feet or longer; from 6 to 90 passengers
Trips:	Two 2-hour trips daily at 11 a.m. and 2 p.m. (Times may vary with the tides.) Saturday is the busiest day.
Fare:	Adults, $21.50; children ages 6 to 12, $12.50; 5 and under, free. Group rates available. Reservations required.
Departure:	Trips leave from Float 6 at the Westport Marina. In the dock area, turn left at the blinking light. Look for the only two-story building on the block.

Naturalist: Naturalist sometimes on board.

"Westport Whale Watch/Ocean Charters was the pioneer in establishing whale-watch tours out of Westport in 1979," notes the owner. "Our tour includes a seminar, presented by knowledgeable narrators, to familiarize you with the history, migration, and social habits of the gray whales."

MUSEUMS, AQUARIUMS, AND SCIENCE CENTERS

OREGON

Oregon Coast Aquarium

2820 S.E. Ferry Slip Road, Newport, OR 97365
(541) 867-3474; Fax (541) 867-6846

Opened in May of 1992, the Oregon Coast Aquarium sits on 32 bayfront acres. Indoors, three galleries focus on plant and animal communities living near shore and marine environments along the Oregon coast. A large changing exhibit area houses exciting new displays each year. A theater presents a program on the gray whale migration and another on sharks. The outdoor exhibits include a walk-through seabird aviary, an undersea coastal cave and landscaped habitats where sea otters, seals and sea lions are on display.

In summer, the Aquarium is open daily from 9 a.m. to 6 p.m. Winter hours are 10 a.m. to 5 p.m. daily. Closed Christmas Day. Adults, $8.50; senior citizens and students, $7.50; children ages 4 to 13, $4.25.

Oregon State University

Mark O. Hatfield Marine Science Center, 2030 South Marine
Science Drive, Newport, OR 97365
(541) 867-0100

Aquarium tanks and interpretive exhibits draw nearly half a million people each year to the Science Center, where visitors may observe and touch sea creatures. Special exhibits include sculptures of thirteen different whales, with accompanying text in Braille, and the skeletons of a minke whale and a harbor porpoise. Special school programs are also available.

The public area is open daily, 10 a.m. to 4 p.m.; summer hours are 10 a.m. to 6 p.m. Admission is free, though donations are accepted.

The Extension Service of Oregon State University also trains volunteers who are posted along the Oregon coast from December 26 through January 1 and again during the third week in March, at sites from Astoria to Brookings. Signs at the staffed lookouts read "WHALE WATCHING SPOKEN HERE," and volunteers are available from 10 a.m. to 1 p.m., rain or shine. They hand out educational materials and answer questions for the more than 20,000 people who visit the lookouts each year.

Indoor programs also are available. A free talk and film are presented daily at 2 p.m. during whale-watch season. Call (541) 563-2002 for more information.

WASHINGTON

Seattle Aquarium

Pier 59, Waterfront Park, Seattle, WA 98101
(206) 386-4320; Fax (206) 386-4328

The Seattle Aquarium features exhibits on sea life, a tide pool, a discovery lab, a salt marsh, and the Underwater Dome, where visitors may see salmon, sharks, octopus, and numerous other marine marvels that live in Puget Sound. In addition to permanent and special exhibits, the Aquarium also offers tours, classes, and lecture series.

The aquarium is open from 10 a.m. to 7 p.m. daily in the summer and from 10 a.m. to 5 p.m. in the winter. Admission is $7.75 for adults, $7 for senior citizens over 65, $5.15 for children 6 to 18, and $1.95 for children age 3 to 5. Under 2, free.

The Whale Museum

62 First Street North, Friday Harbor, WA 98250
(360) 378-4710

A research and development institution as well as a museum, the Whale Museum collects and disseminates information on the marine environment, with special emphasis on whales, dolphins, and porpoises. Programs include exhibits, workshops, field courses in whale biology, a teaching curriculum, lab work, and educational programs as well as whale-watch trips. The Whale Museum is open seven days a week, 10 a.m. to 6 p.m. Memorial Day weekend through September and 11 a.m. to 4 p.m. October through May. Admission is $5 for adults, $4 for senior citizens, $2 for students with ID and children under 18. Children under 5 get in free. Group rates are available.

Westport Maritime Museum

2201 Westhaven Drive, P.O. Box 1074, Westport, WA 98595
(360) 268-0078

Housed in a former Coast Guard Station, the Westport Maritime Museum reflects Westport's ties to the bounty of the sea, forests and Gray Harbor. Adjacent to the station sits a Whale House, which contains marine mammal skeletons, including complete gray and minke whales.

Hours are noon to 4 p.m. on weekends in April and May, 10 a.m. to 4 p.m. Wednesday through Sunday from June through September, and tours by request from noon to 4 p.m. in the winter months. Admission is $2 for adults, $1 for children, and $5 for families with two adults and three children. Donations to the Westport-South Beach Historical Society are heartily welcomed.

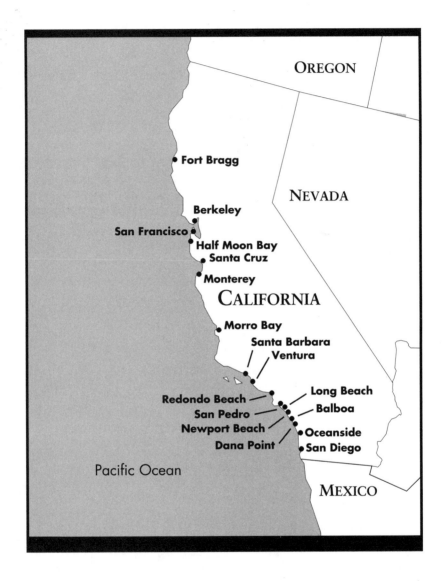

CALIFORNIA

You may choose from nearly fifty whale-watch trip operators off the coast of California. In southern California, competition is lively in areas where several trip operators in some towns vie for passengers.

In northern California, where the tides and the weather are less consistent than in the southern part of the state, whale watching is less popular—but entirely possible.

If you plan to be in California sometime during the annual gray whale migration, between late December and April, you will have no trouble booking a whale-watch trip in most coastal towns. Yet surprisingly few companies offer trips from June to October, when blue whales, orcas, and humpbacks are in the area. If you plan to be in California then, call or write to ask about "off-season" whale-watch trips or private charters.

Many of the trip operators on the California coast are primarily sportfishing charter companies that turn their attention to whale watching during the early months of the year. Their commitment to customer service has kept them in business for fifteen or twenty years or even longer, and most of them strive to provide enjoyable, educational whale-watch trips.

Because it's so unusual not to see gray whales during the annual migration, many trip operators guarantee sightings and offer a "whale check" for a free trip in the unlikely event that whales are nowhere to be found.

Tourism Information

CALIFORNIA
California Division of Tourism
801 K Street, Suite 1600, Sacramento, CA 95814

(800) 862-2543

WHALE-WATCHING TRIPS

BALBOA

Davey's Locker Sportfishing

400 Main Street, Balboa, CA 92661
(714) 673-1434; Web site www.daveyslocker.com

Whales:	Gray, Pacific white-sided dolphin, common dolphin
Season:	December 26 through April 1
Boats:	Five boats; up to 148 passengers each
Trips:	Weekdays, two trips at 10 a.m. and 1 p.m. Saturdays and Sundays, three trips at 9 a.m., noon, and 2:30 p.m. All trips are 2-1/2 hours long. Weekends are the busiest times.
Fare:	Adults, $14, senior citizens, $12, children 4 to 12, $8. Reservations required.
Departure:	Trips leave from Balboa Pavilion. Take the 55 Freeway south to Newport Boulevard; follow to Main Street and turn left.
Naturalist:	Naturalist from the American Cetacean Society.

BODEGA BAY, HALF MOON BAY, SANTA CRUZ, SAUSALITO

Shearwater Journeys

P.O. Box 190, Hollister, CA 95024
(831) 637-8527;
Web site www.alink.net/`shearwater/shearwaterjourneys.html

Whales:	Blue, fin, sperm, humpback, gray, orca, minke
Season:	Whale watches all year
Boats:	Four boats; 50 to 60 passengers each
Trips:	Trips are scheduled year 'round to Cordell Bank, Pioneer Canyon, Monterey Bay and the Farallon Islands. Weekend trips are busiest.
Fare:	Half-day and full-day whale watches range from $28 to $90 per person, depending on the destination and the point of departure. Group rates available. Reservations required.
Departure:	Trips leave from several ports, depending on the destination. Call for specific information.
Naturalist:	One naturalist from the American Cetacean Society is on board for every ten passengers.

Owner Debra Love Shearwater, in this business since 1978, specializes in natural history trips. Her video, "Through the Seasons," provides a 36-minute trip in Monterey Bay featuring 24 species of seabirds and 17 species of marine mammals. To order, send your name and address with $25 plus $3 shipping and handling for VHS format. Send $30 plus $5 shipping for PAL format.

BERKELEY

Dolphin Charters

1007 Leneve Place, El Cerrito, CA 94530
(800) 472-9942 or (510) 527-9622; Fax (510) 525-0720;
E-mail dolphin3@earthlink.net; Web site www.dolphincharters.com

Whales: Gray in winter, humpback and blue in spring and fall

Season: January through May

Boats: The 50-foot *Delphinus*; 40 passengers

Trips: Selected day-long trips on weekends, some overnight trips and week-long trips in summer to various destinations, including Point Reyes, San Francisco Bay, and to the Farallon Islands. Saturday is the busiest day.

Fare: Trips range from $49 to $69. Reservations advised.

Departure: Trips leave from the Berkeley marina, at the foot of University Avenue, just off 1-80.

Naturalist: Naturalist aboard.

Dolphin Charters, in business since 1978, specializes in whale-watch trips worldwide. "We have had nearly 100 percent success in seeing gray whales on trips to Point Reyes in January and March," says owner and marine biologist Ronn Patterson.

The Farallon Islands cruises provide an opportunity to see a variety of whale species, including blue and humpback, as well as sharks, pinnipeds (seals, sea lions, walruses, etc.), and other sea life.

DANA POINT

Dana Wharf Sportfishing

34675 Golden Lantern, Dana Point, CA 92629; (949) 496-5794; Web site www.danawharfsportfishing.com

Whales: Gray

Season: November 28 through March 31

Boats: Ten boats; 6 to 99 passengers each

Trips: Weekdays, three trips at 10 a.m., noon, and 2 p.m.; Saturdays and Sundays, five trips at 8 a.m., 10 a.m., noon, 2 and 4 p.m. Nine trips daily during the annual Dana Point Festival of Whales, which includes educational programs and cultural events as well as whale-watch trips. All trips last 2 hours. Early morning trips on Saturdays are the busiest.

Fare: Adults, $14; senior citizens, $8; children 12 and under, $8 on weekdays. Reservations required. Discounts on whale-watch trips are available for guests at Laguna Cliffs Marriott and the Doubletree Guest Suites of Dana Point.

Departure: Trips leave from the Dana Wharf Docks in Dana Point Harbor. From the Pacific Coast Highway, follow Golden Lantern down to the water.

Naturalist: Naturalist aboard.

The Dana Point Festival of Whales is held each year in February and March to celebrate the arrival of the gray whales. Mike Hansen, general manager of Dana Wharf Sportfishing, notes, "Emphasis is placed on the local marine environment, but the whales are the center of attention."

FORT BRAGG

Lady Irma II

P.O. Box 103, Fort Bragg, CA 95437
(707) 964-3854

Whales: Gray, occasional orca, humpback, finback

Season: January 1 through April 15

Boats: One boat; 22 passengers

Trips: One 2-hour trip daily at 1 p.m.

Fare: Adults and children, $25. Reservations advised.

Departure: Trips leave from the Wharf Restaurant on the Noyo River. As you travel north on Highway 2, make the first right after the Noyo River Bridge.

Naturalist: No naturalist on board.

"There is a whale festival in this area that starts in Mendocino the second weekend in March and ends in Fort Bragg the following weekend. On those weekends, we run four whale-watch trips a day. A wine tasting, whale run, and arts and crafts shows are all part of the festival," says owner Rick Thornton.

HALF MOON BAY

Huck Finn Sportfishing

P.O. Box 1432, El Granada, CA 94018
(800) 572-2934 or (415) 726-7133

Whales:	Gray
Season:	Mid-December through April
Boats:	Quite A Lady, 22 passengers; *Hull Cat* and *Captain Pete*, 38 passengers each; *Queen of Hearts*, 46 passengers
Trips:	Trips by request only on weekdays; two or three on Saturdays and Sundays at 10 a.m. and 1:30 p.m. All trips are 2-1/2 to 3 hours long. Saturday afternoon trips are the most popular.
Fare:	$20 for adults, $18 for children ages 5 to 12. No children under 5, please. Reservations advised.
Departure:	Trips leave from Pillar Point Harbor at Half Moon Bay, 25 miles south of San Francisco on Highway 1 or 4 miles north of Half Moon Bay on Highway 1.
Naturalist:	No naturalist on board.

"Our primary income is from fishing, but whale watching is something that is a thrill for both my husband, Bill, and me. If the whales were here all the time, we could easily do it every day," says co-owner Peggy Beckett.

"We do provide written information on the whales for passengers to take home, books to look at on board, a running commentary on what we are looking for and seeing, and whale certificates for those days we are successful."

Oceanic Society Expeditions

Fort Mason Center, Building E, San Francisco, CA 94123
(800) 326-7491 or (415) 441-1106; Fax (415) 474-3395;
Web site www.oceanic-society.org

Whales:	Gray
Season:	December 26 through April
Boats:	The 56-foot *Salty Lady*; carries 48 passengers
Trips:	Every Saturday and Sunday and select Fridays at 9 a.m. and 1 p.m. Trips are 3 hours long.

Fare: On Fridays, adults, $30; children 5 through 15 and senior citizens over 60, $28. On weekends, adults, $33; children 5 through 15 and senior citizens over 60, $31. No one under 5 permitted on the boat. Group rates available. Reservations required.

Departure: Trips leave from Pillar Point Harbor in Half Moon Bay.

Naturalist: Naturalists on board from Oceanic Society Expeditions.

Oceanic Society Expeditions was founded in 1972 to create educational worldwide nature programs. The organization's whale-watch program strives to increase public awareness of the importance of protecting our fragile marine environment.

LONG BEACH

Catalina Cruises

320 Golden Shore Boulevard, Long Beach, CA 90802
(800) CATALINA or (562) 436-5006

Whales: Gray

Season: December 26 through early April

Boats: Three boats; 700-passenger capacity each, but whale-watch cruises are limited to 450 passengers

Trips: One 3-hour trip at 10 a.m. most weekdays; two 3-hour trips on Saturday and Sunday, at 10 a.m. and 1:30 p.m. Saturday morning trips are the most popular.

Fare: Adults, $15; senior citizens 55 and older, $12; children: ages 3 through 11, $11; under 3, free. Group rates available. Reservations are required.

Departure: Trips leave from the Catalina Landing, 320 Golden Shore Boulevard in downtown Long Beach, at the south end of the Long Beach Freeway 710.

Naturalist: Naturalist from Cabrillo Aquarium/American Cetacean Society.

Marketing director Mindy Griffin says, "We have the largest whale-watching vessels on the West Coast, and the most comfortable, too, with three levels of outside viewing and two spacious interior cabins with large windows."

Long Beach Sportfishing at Berth 55

555 Pico Avenue, Long Beach, CA 90802
(562) 432-8993

Whales:	Gray, pilot, occasional orca
Season:	December 26 through early April
Boats:	Five boats; 497 passengers total
Trips:	Three 3-hour trips daily at 9 a.m., 11 a.m. and 2 p.m. The 11 a.m. trip is the most popular.
Fare:	Adults, $12; children ages 2 to 15 and senior citizens, $9. Group rates. Reservations required.
Departure:	Trips leave from Berth 55 at the Long Beach marina. Take the 710 Freeway south to the off-ramp at 7th Avenue and Pico. The marina is across from the ramp.
Naturalist:	Captains serve as naturalists.

Between them, owners Veronica Wegner and Don Ashley have two decades in the sportfishing business. "All our captains have been running whale watches for years and have extensive knowledge of gray whales' physical and biological features, of their migration habits and feeding habits," Wegner says.

Spirit Cruises

429 Shoreline Village Drive, Suite N, Long Beach, CA 90802
(562) 495-5884

Whales:	Gray
Season:	December 26 through mid-April
Boats:	Four boats, a 50-foot cruiser, a 90-foot sailing ship, a 65-foot motor yacht and a 90-foot motor yacht; 49, 103, 125 and 150 passengers respectively
Trips:	Weekdays, one trip at 11:30 a.m.; two trips on Saturday and Sunday at 11 a.m. and 1:30 p.m. Trips are about 2-1/2 hours long. The Sunday afternoon trip is the busiest.
Fare:	Adults, $15; children ages 2 to 12, $8. Twenty percent discount on weekday trips. Reservations required.
Departure:	Trips leave from Long Beach and San Pedro, depending on which trip you book. Call for details and directions.
Naturalist:	Captain serves as naturalist.

Staff member Kristin Wilson notes, "We guarantee a whale sighting. And we use charter boats with seating for everyone, not old fishing boats."

Star Party Cruises

140 Marina Drive, Long Beach, CA 90803
(562) 799-7000; Web site www.reggae-boat.com

Whales:	Gray
Season:	January through mid-April
Boats:	A 100-foot yacht; 300 passengers
Trips:	One 2-1/2-hour trip at 10 a.m. on weekdays and two 2-1/2 hour trips at 10 a.m. and 1 p.m. on weekends. Weekends are the busiest.
Fare:	Adults, $13; senior citizens, $12; children under 12, $10. Reservations required.
Departure:	Trips leave from Seaport Village in Long Beach.
Naturalist:	Naturalist on board.

Whale sightings guaranteed. The yacht, new in 1997, has a whale museum on board and shows educational videos.

MONTEREY

Chris' Fishing Trips

48 Fisherman's Wharf, Monterey, CA 93940
(408) 375-5951

Whales:	Gray in winter; blue, minke, orca in summer and fall
Season:	December 25 through late March
Boats:	Four boats; 49 to 75 passengers each
Trips:	Weekday trips at 10 a.m., noon and 2 p.m. according to demand. Four 2-hour trips on weekends, at 9 a.m., 11 a.m., 1 p.m., and 3 p.m. Saturday is busiest day.
Fare:	Adults, $25; children, $20. Reservations advised.
Departure:	Trips leave from Fisherman's Wharf in Monterey, just off the Pacific Grove/Del Monte exit off Highway 1, going south.
Naturalist:	Skipper narrates trips.

Todd Arcoleo, an office staff member, says, "Enjoy an outing with family and friends on Monterey Bay with the gray whales."

Monterey Sport Fishing
and Princess Monterey Cruises

96 Old Fisherman's Wharf #1; Monterey, CA 93940
(800) 200-2203 or (408) 372-2203; Fax (408) 372-3708;
Web site www.sealifetours.com

Whales:	Gray, humpback, blue, orca and dolphins
Season:	Mid-December through April for gray whales; May through October for humpback, blue, orcas
Boats:	Two boats; 80 and 100 passengers
Trips:	Hourly gray whale trips daily in season, starting at 9 a.m. for a minimum of 10 passengers. Trips are 2 to 3 hours long. Two 3- to-4 hour trips daily in summer, at 10 a.m. and 1 p.m. Early trips on weekends are the busiest.
Fare:	Fares vary from $15 to $28 for adults and $12 to $25 for children under 12, depending on length of trip. Group rates available. Reservations required. Discount coupons for whale watches given to guests at Doubletree Hotel, Gosby House Inn, Hyatt Regency, Monterey Plaza, the Sheraton Monterey and local inns.
Departure:	Trips leave from Monterey's Fisherman's Wharf, just off the Pacific Grove/Del Monte exit off Highway 1, going south.
Naturalist:	Naturalist from the American Cetacean Society.

"Our boats provide excellent opportunities for close-up viewing of one of the world's largest animals in a special and diverse habitat," says a spokesman.

Oceanic Society Expeditions

Fort Mason Center, Building E, San Francisco, CA 94123
(800) 326-7491 or (415) 441-1106; Fax (415) 474-3395;
Web site www.oceanic-society.org

Whales:	Humpback, blue
Season:	July, August, September, October
Boats:	The 55-foot *Point Sur Clipper*. Participants sleep in comfortable lodges.
Trips:	Six 7-day research expeditions in Monterey Bay and adjacent areas, with 5 days spent on the water observing and photo-identifying Pacific white-sided dolphins and humpbacks and possibly blue whales and other cetaceans.

Fare: $990 per person, which includes accommodations, most meals, boat charter, and leadership. Does not include airfare or transfers.

Departure: Trips begin and end in Monterey, California.

Naturalist: Oceanic Society Expeditions researchers.

"Monterey Submarine Canyon and adjacent waters support one of the highest diversities of marine mammals in the world—26 different species have been observed here," says a spokeswoman. "This expedition offers a special opportunity to observe a variety of dolphins and whales, and to contribute to a scientific project."

Randy's Fishing and Whale-Watching Trips

66 Fisherman's Wharf #1, Monterey, CA 93940
(408) 372-7440; Fax (408) 372-7445; E-mail randysfish@email.msn.com;
Web site www.randysfishingtrips.com

Whales: Gray; occasionally orca, blue

Season: January through March

Boats: Three boats; 48, 48, and 68 passengers

Trips: Three trips each weekday, at 9:30 a.m., 11:30 a.m. and 1:30 p.m. Six trips on Saturday and Sunday, beginning at 9:30 a.m. All trips last about 2 hours. The busiest day is Saturday.

Fare: Adults, $15; children 12 and younger, $10.

Departure: Trips leave from Fisherman's Wharf, off the Pacific Grove/Del Monte exit off Highway 1, going south.

Naturalist: Crew members narrate trips on weekdays; a marine biologist is on board every weekend.

Owner Peter Bruno, in recognition of the "immeasurable assistance the Society for the Prevention of Cruelty to Animals offers our sea life," donates 50 cents for each passenger.

MORRO BAY

Virg's Sportfishing & Whale Watching

1215 Embarcadero, Morro Bay, CA 93422
(800) 932-3473 or (805) 772-1222; Fax (805) 772-2921;
Web site www.virges.com

Whales:	Gray
Season:	Mid-December through April or early May
Boats:	Six boats; 35 to 75 passengers each
Trips:	One or two trips, according to demand, on weekdays. Three trips on Saturday and Sunday at 8:30 and 11:30 a.m. and 2:30 p.m. Trips are 2 to 2-1/2 hours long. The busiest day is Saturday.
Fare:	Adults, $16; children under 12, $10; children under 5, $5. Discounts for groups. Reservations required.
Departure:	Trips leave from the dock, across from Pacific Gas and Electric.
Naturalist:	Naturalist on some trips.

"Sail alongside the gray whale on its way to its winter quarters, and learn about the whales from the experts," says a spokesman from Virg's Sportfishing. "Our knowledgeable sea captains narrate each cruise. Bring your camera!"

NEWPORT BEACH

Newport Landing Sportfishing

309 Palm, Suite F, Balboa, CA 92661
(949) 675-0550

Whales:	Gray, minke, several species of dolphin
Season:	December 26 through early April
Boats:	Four boats; 116, 88, 48, and 45 passengers
Trips:	Two trips each weekday at 10 a.m. and 1 p.m.; three trips on Saturdays and Sundays at 9 a.m., noon, and 2:30 p.m. All trips last 2 to 2-1/2 hours.

Fare: Adults, $14; senior citizens, $8; children 12 and younger, $8, on weekdays. Group rates for schools, churches, and community groups. Reservations advised. Newport Beach Meridian Hotel guests receive discounts on Newport Landing Sportfishing whale watches.

Departure: Trips leave from Newport Landing Sportfishing dock between Adams and Palm Street, just off Balboa Boulevard next to the auto ferry.

Naturalist: Skipper serves as naturalist.

"Since the gray whale can be readily found within a few miles off the coast, a simple cruise of a few hours lets thousands of people view not only the whales in their natural habitat, but also many species of resident marine animals, such as the common dolphin, bottlenose dolphin, sea lions, birds, and occasionally killer whales and sharks," says staff member George Eddy.

OCEANSIDE

Helgren's Oceanside Sportfishing

315 Harbor Drive South, Oceanside, CA 92054
(760) 722-2133; Fax (760) 433-4804

Whales: Gray

Season: December 26 through March 31

Boats: Two boats; 125 and 135 passengers

Trips: Weekdays, two trips at 10 a.m. and 1 p.m.; Saturdays and Sundays, three trips at 9 a.m., 11:30 a.m. and 2 p.m. All trips are 2 hours long. Saturday midday trip is the busiest.

Fare: Adults, $14; senior citizens, $12; children, $10. Group rates available. Reservations recommended.

Departure: Trips leave from Oceanside Harbor. Take Harbor Drive exit off I-5; follow to the boat harbor.

Naturalist: Captain narrates trips.

Helgren's has been a family-owned business since 1978. All information provided during the captain's narration is from Dr. Raymond Gilmore at the American Cetacean Society.

REDONDO BEACH

Redondo Sport Fishing

223 North Harbor Drive, Redondo Beach, CA 90277
(310) 372-2111; Fax (310) 376-4764

Whales:	Gray, orca, blue, pilot
Season:	December 26 through April 1
Boats:	The *Voyager*; 125 passengers
Trips:	Two 3-hour trips daily: 10 a.m. and 1:30 p.m. on weekdays, 9:30 a.m. and 1:30 p.m. on Saturdays and Sundays. Saturday is the busiest day.
Fare:	Adults, $12; children under 12, $8. Group rates available, and ride two-for-one on weekday afternoons.
Departure:	Trips leave from the Redondo Sport Fishing Pier. From the 405 Freeway, go west on 190th Street to Harbor Drive and then turn south. Pier is across from the Holiday Inn.
Naturalist:	Naturalist from the Cabrillo Aquarium/American Cetacean Society aboard each trip.

Owner John Glackin notes that the *Voyager* is a double-deck excursion boat designed specifically for whale watching, with ample seating for all passengers. "This is not a fishing boat, which often has limited seating. Also, we are just minutes from the open ocean, which increases our whale-watching time. We guarantee whales!"

SAN DIEGO

Classic Sailing Adventures

2051 Shelter Island Drive, San Diego, CA 92106
(619) 224-0800

Whales:	Gray
Season:	December 15 through March 15

Boats: The 38-foot sailing yacht *Soul Diversion*, 6 passengers

Trips: Two trips daily, 8:30 a.m. to 12:30 p.m. and 1 to 5 p.m.

Fare: $150 per person. Price includes beverages and snacks. Reservations required.

Departure: Trips leave from Shelter Island Marina Inn.

Naturalist: Knowledgeable captain narrates.

Owner M.J. Moore says, "With only six passengers on each excursion, there is a more personalized experience for everyone. If wind permits, we sail as much as possible. Passengers may participate in the sailing or relax and enjoy the whale-watching experience."

H&M Landing

2803 Emerson Street, San Diego, CA 92106
(619) 222-1144

Whales: Gray

Season: December 15 through March 15

Boats: Twenty boats; 6 to 100 passengers; limited passenger loads on whale watches

Trips: Two 3-hour trips daily at 10 a.m. and 1:30 p.m.; 5-hour trips Thursday through Sunday at 10 a.m. The busiest day is Saturday.

Fare: Adults, $17 for 3 hours and $25 for 5 hours; senior citizens, $12 and $20; children 17 and under, $12 and $15. Reservations required.

Departure: Trips leave from San Diego Bay, on Emerson, which is off Rosecrans, just before Shelter Island Drive.

Naturalist: Narrative provided by staff.

"We guarantee whale sightings or you get a free reride," notes the manager. "We run every day, weather permitting."

Hornblower/Invader Cruises Inc.

1066 North Harbor Drive, San Diego, CA 92101
(619) 686-8700; Fax (619) 686-8733; Web site: www.hornblower.com

Whales:	Gray
Season:	Mid-December through April
Boats:	The 151-foot luxury yacht *Lord Hornblower*; 500 passengers
Trips:	Two 3-1/2-hour trips daily at 9:30 a.m. and 1:30 p.m. The busiest day is Saturday.
Fare:	Adults, $19.50; senior citizens, $17.50; children ages 3 through 12, $9.75. Reservations advised.
Departure:	Trips leave from 1066 North Harbor Drive, on the Embarcadero, next to the cruise ship terminal.
Naturalist:	All trips narrated.

Built in 1984 and patterned after the classic steamers of the early 1900s, *Lord Hornblower* has three decks, two dining salons, two parquet dance floors, three bars and an expansive sundeck for viewing whales. Whale sightings are guaranteed.

Islandia Sportfishing

1551 West Mission Bay Drive, San Diego, CA 92109
(619) 222-1164

Whales:	Gray, finback, Pacific white-sided dolphin
Season:	Late December through late March
Boats:	The 85-foot *Dolphin*; 147 passengers
Trips:	Two trips daily at 10 a.m. and 1 p.m. Trips last 2 to 3 hours. Saturday midday trips are the busiest.
Fare:	Adults, $14; senior citizens and children, $10. Guaranteed sighting or ride again free. Reservations advised.
Departure:	Trips leave from the dock by the Islandia Hyatt Hotel, off West Mission Bay Drive.
Naturalist:	Captain narrates trips.

Owner John Taylor, in the business for more than a decade, says, "We like people and we love whales—that's the Islandia difference."

Orion Charters Inc.

Sheraton San Diego Hotel & Marina
1380 Harbor Island Drive, San Diego, CA 92101
(619) 574-7504; Fax (619) 692-2257;
E-mail ocaptkeith@msn.com; Web site www.orionsailing.com

Whales:	Gray, finback, Pacific white-sided dolphin
Season:	December 15 through March 31
Boats:	Two boats; the 64-foot sailing yacht *Orion* that carries up to 20 passengers and a 32-foot *Fancy Parts* that holds up to 6 passengers
Trips:	Two trips daily on weekdays; two on Saturdays and Sundays. Weekend days are the busiest.
Fare:	Adults, $45; children, $25 for 4-hour personalized sailing and whale-watching trip. Reservations suggested.
Departure:	Trips leave from Slip C at the Sheraton San Diego Hotel & Marina, just across the street from the San Diego International Airport.
Naturalist:	The owner, who holds a degree in marine biology with a special emphasis on oceanography, serves as naturalist.

"Whale watching is a special experience aboard a sailing vessel—quiet, smooth," notes Captain Keith Korporaal. "We quite literally sail alongside these wonderful animals, and we'd love to have you come with us. Our small groups lend themselves to personalized trips."

Point Loma Sportfishing

1403 Scott Street, San Diego, CA 92106
(619) 223-1627

Whales:	Gray
Season:	December 26 through March 31
Boats:	One boat, 107 passengers
Trips:	One 3-1/2-hour trip daily on weekdays, at 1 p.m.; two 3-1/2-hour trips on weekends, at 9 a.m. and 1 p.m. The afternoon trip on the weekends is the most popular.
Fare:	Adults, $17; children under 15, $12. Reservations required.
Departure:	Trips leave from the office, on San Diego Bay, just two miles west of the airport.
Naturalist:	No naturalist on board.

Owner Ross Hecht has been taking people out to sea since 1947.

San Diego Harbor Excursion

1050 North Harbor Drive, San Diego, CA 92101
(619) 234-4111

Whales:	Gray; occasional fin, orca, pilot, blue
Season:	December 26 through the end of March
Boats:	One boat, the 65-foot *Morning Star*, 103 passengers
Trips:	Two 3-hour trips daily at 10 a.m. and 1:30 p.m. The most popular day is Saturday.
Fare:	Adults, $19.95; children, half price. Reservations required only for large groups.
Departure:	Trips leave from San Diego Harbor Excursions, at the foot of Broadway on the waterfront.
Naturalist:	Captain serves as naturalist.

Ben Griffith, the owner and captain of the *Morning Star,* has been in the sport-fishing business since 1960. "We completely narrate the whale-watch trips, including information on the harbor and the history of San Diego. We also show a gray whale video on the return trip," he said. "I personally try to see that one and all enjoy themselves. We're run more like a family operation than a large company operation."

An open-ended rain check is issued if no whales are sighted.

San Diego Natural History Museum

Balboa Park, P.O. Box 1390, San Diego, CA 92112
(619) 232-3821 ext. 203; Fax (619) 232-0248

Whales:	Gray; occasionally fin, blue, orca, humpback
Season:	January
Boats:	One boat, the 88-foot *Pacific Queen,* 60 passengers
Trips:	Several day trips from 8 a.m. to 5 p.m. that circle the Coronados Islands.
Fare:	Museum members, $56; non-members, $66. Minimum age is 12. Call for schedule. Reservations required.
Departure:	Trips leave from Fisherman's Landing in San Diego Bay. Call for directions.
Naturalist:	Naturalist from the San Diego Natural History Museum.

"Dr. Raymond Gilmore, a former museum staff member, was instrumental in starting whale-watching programs in southern California and Baja California," notes a museum spokeswoman.

Seaforth Sportfishing Corp.

1717 Quivira Road, San Diego, CA 92109
(619) 224-3383

Whales:	Gray
Season:	December through mid-March
Boats:	Three boats; 105, 118, and 149 passengers
Trips:	Two 2-1/2-hour trips on weekdays at 10 a.m. and 1 p.m. Three trips on Saturdays, Sundays, and holidays at 9 a.m., 11:30 a.m., and 2 p.m. Weekends are busiest days.
Fare:	Adults, $14; children, senior citizens, and military, $10. Reservations advised.
Departure:	Trips leave from Seaforth Landing at 1717 Quivira Road in Mission Bay. From the east and south, take I-8 west to the Sports Arena Boulevard turnoff. Exit right and follow the "TO WEST MISSION BAY" signs to the cloverleaf. Exit on West Mission Bay Drive, turn left at Quivira Road. From the north, take I-5 to Sea World Drive exit. Pass Sea World and follow the "TO WEST MISSION BAY" signs to the cloverleaf. Then repeat as above.
Naturalist:	Naturalist aboard.

"We invite you to journey with us and experience these magnificent creatures in their natural habitats," notes an employee at Seaforth Sportfishing. "Guaranteed whale sighting, or ride again free!"

SAN FRANCISCO

Oceanic Society Expeditions

Fort Mason Center, Building E, San Francisco, CA 94123
(800) 326-7491 or (415) 441-1106; Fax (415) 474-3395;
Web site www.oceanic-society.org

Whales:	Gray
Season:	December 26 through April
Boats:	The 63-foot *Super Fish*; 49 passengers

Trips: Every Saturday and Sunday and select Fridays at 9:30 a.m. Trips are 6-1/2 hours long.

Fare: On weekends, adults, $50; children 10 through 15 and senior citizens 60 or older, $48. On Fridays, adults, $48; children 10 through 15 and senior citizens 60 or older, $46. No one under 10 permitted on the boat. Group rates available. Reservations required.

Departure: Trips leave from San Francisco Yacht Harbor/Marina Green.

Naturalist: Naturalist on board from Oceanic Society Expeditions.

Oceanic Society Expeditions also sponsors eight-hour trips to the Farallon Islands on selected dates from June through mid-November. Blue and humpback whales often are spotted on these trips, which cost $65 per person. Write for more information.

SAN FRANCISCO, SAUSALITO, MONTEREY BAY, AND BODEGA BAY

Footloose Forays/Michael Ellis

P.O. Box 175, Sebastopol, CA 95473
(707) 829-1844; E-mail mjnature@aol.com

Whales: Gray in winter and spring; blue and humpback in summer and fall

Season: Year-round

Boats: Two boats, about 50 passengers each; one whale watch conducted from shore.

Trips: Trips scheduled at various times in winter and spring to see gray whales and in summer and fall to see blue whales and humpbacks. Summer trips to the Farallon Islands are the most popular. Land-based trips also available.

Fare: Range is from $23 to $55 per person, depending on length of trip. Reservations required.

Departure: Depending on destination, trips leave from San Francisco, Sausalito, Monterey Bay and Bodega Bay.

Naturalist: Naturalist aboard.

Owner Michael Ellis is a well-versed naturalist, and he accompanies every trip. Ellis also writes a syndicated nature column for several Northern California newspapers and is a commentator on KQED-FM in San Francisco.

SAN PEDRO

L.A. Harbor Sportfishing

1150 Nagoya Way, Berth 79, San Pedro, CA 90731
(310) 547-9916

Whales:	Gray, orca, dolphins
Season:	December 26 through March 31
Boats:	*First String*, a 93-foot boat with an upper sundeck that carries 150 passengers
Trips:	Two trips on weekdays at 11:30 a.m. and 2 p.m.; three trips on Saturdays and Sundays at 9 a.m., 11:30 a.m. and 2 p.m. Trips last about 2-1/2 hours. The morning trip on Saturdays is the most popular.
Fare:	Adults, $15; senior citizens, $13; children 12 and under, $10. Reservations advised.
Departure:	Trips leave from L.A. Harbor Sportfishing, located at Berth 79 in the Ports O'Call Village at San Pedro.
Naturalist:	The captain serves as naturalist.

"We use a spotter plane to further our success rate," says a spokeswoman. "The plane locates marine life and we are able to go directly there, giving the passengers more viewing time than ever."

Skipper's 22nd Street Landing

141 West 22nd Street, San Pedro, CA 90731
(310) 832-8304

Whales:	Gray
Season:	January through March
Boats:	Two boats; 96 and 122 passengers
Trips:	Two trips on weekdays at 10 a.m. and 1 p.m.; three trips every Saturday and Sunday at 9 a.m., 11:30 a.m. and 2 p.m. Trips last 2 to 2-1/2 hours. Saturday morning is the busiest time.
Fare:	Weekdays: adults, $13; children 12 and under and seniors 62 and over, $10. Weekends: adults, $14; children 12 and under and seniors 62 and over, $11. Reservations required.
Departure:	Trips leave from Cabrillo Marina. Take the Harbor Freeway south to the end. Turn left onto Gaffey Street; go to 22nd Street and turn left. Drive 4-1/2 blocks. The Landing is on the right; free all-day parking on the left.
Naturalist:	Naturalist on board from Cabrillo Aquarium/American Cetacean Society.

"Join us and observe the greatest creatures on Earth as they make their way to the breeding grounds off Mexico's coast," says a spokeswoman.

Spirit Cruises and Whale Watch

Ports O'Call, Berth 77, San Pedro, CA 90731
(310) 548-8080

Whales:	Gray
Season:	December 26 through mid-April
Boats:	Four boats; 49, 100, 125, and 150 passengers
Trips:	One trip on weekdays at 11 a.m.; two trips on Saturday and Sunday at 11 a.m. and 1:30 p.m. Trips last 2-1/2 to 3 hours. The Sunday afternoon trip is the most popular.
Fare:	Adults, $15; children ages 2 through 12, $8. Reservations required. With advance reservations, you get a discount on weekday trips.

Departure: Trips leave from Ports O'Call in San Pedro and Shoreline Village in Long Beach; call for directions.

Naturalist: Naturalist on board.

Owner Jayme S. Wilson says, "We use sailing ships and motor yachts—the nicest boats in southern California. Guaranteed whale sightings or you get a free pass for another trip!"

SANTA BARBARA

Capt. Don's Coastal Cruises

219 Stearns Wharf, Box G, Santa Barbara, CA 93101
(805) 969-5217

Whales: Gray, blue, humpback, common dolphin

Season: Mid-February to mid-April for grays, June through September for blues and humpbacks

Boats: Two boats; 49 passengers and 149 passengers

Trips: Three 2-1/2-hour gray whale trips daily at 9 a.m., noon, and 3 p.m. For blues and humpbacks, one 6-hour trip daily at 8 a.m. Weekends are busiest.

Fare: Gray whale trips: Adults, $24; senior citizens, $20; children 12 and under, $15. Blue whale trips: Adults, $55, seniors, $50, children, $35. Reservations required.

Departure: Trips leave from Stearn's Wharf, at the base of State Street in Santa Barbara.

Naturalist: Captain serves as naturalist.

Captain Donald L. Hedden notes, "Over 22,000 gray whales migrate through the Santa Barbara Channel during our season, within 5 miles from shore."

Condor Cruises

677 Miramonte Drive, Santa Barbara, CA 93109
(888) 77WHALE or (805) 963-3564; Fax (805) 965-0942;
Web site www.condorcruises.com

Whales:	Gray, humpback, blue, common dolphin, Pacific white-sided dolphin
Season:	February through April for grays, June through September for blues and humpbacks
Boats:	The 88-foot *Condor*; 125 passengers
Trips:	Three 2-1/2-hour trips daily at 9 a.m., noon, and 3 p.m. February through April. Full-day trips all summer and on weekends in the fall.
Fare:	Adults, $65, children 12 and younger, $35 in winter and summer. Spring fares for the shorter trips cost $24 for adults and $14 for children. Reservations required.
Departure:	Trips leave from SEA Landing in the Santa Barbara Harbor.
Naturalist:	Qualified naturalists aboard all trips.

Captain Fred Benko has been providing whale-watching trips since 1973, and now provides all trips sponsored by the Santa Barbara Museum of Natural History. The Whale Corps, trained naturalists from the museum, accompany the trips. Sightings are guaranteed.

Oceanic Society Expeditions

Fort Mason Center, Building E, San Francisco, CA 94123
(800) 326-7491 or (415) 441-1106; Fax (415) 474-3395;
Web site www.oceanic-society.org

Whales:	Blue, humpback
Season:	July and August
Boats:	*Spike Africa*, a 70-foot schooner that sleeps 12. Participants live aboard.
Trips:	Two 7-day trips working with researchers documenting the occurrence of blue whales and humpback whales.
Fare:	$1,390 per person. Fare includes accommodations, all meals and guides. Reservations required.
Departure:	Trips leave from Santa Barbara.

135

Naturalist: Naturalists on board from Oceanic Society Expeditions.

California's Santa Barbara Channel is one of the few places in the world where large numbers of blue whales—the largest animal ever to live on Earth—gather to feed, says a spokeswoman.

SANTA CRUZ

Stagnaro Original Fishing Trips

Box 1340, Santa Cruz, CA 95061
(408) 427-2334; E-mail fun@stagnaros.com; Web site www.stagnaros.com

Whales:	Gray
Season:	December through April
Boats:	Two boats; 35 and 73 passengers
Trips:	One trip on weekdays by request; two 3-hour trips on Saturdays and Sundays at 11 a.m. and 2 p.m. Please call to confirm times.
Fare:	Prices vary. Please call for current price. Reservations advised, but not required.
Departure:	Trips leave from Santa Cruz Wharf, at the foot of Washington Street on Beach Street.
Naturalist:	No naturalist on board.

"Set off with us for a morning or afternoon trip on the waters of Monterey Bay to enjoy sightings of one of the greatest wonders of our coast, the gray whale," says the Stagnaro family.

VENTURA

Island Packers

1867 Spinnaker Drive, Ventura, CA 93001
(805) 642-1393; Fax (805) 642-6513; E-mail ipco@isle.net;
Web site www.isle.net`ipco

Whales:	Gray, minke
Season:	December 26 through March 31
Boats:	Four boats; 25, 48, 48, and 80 passengers
Trips:	One or two trips on weekdays; two on Saturdays and two on Sundays. According to demand, trips are offered at 9:30 and 11 a.m. or 1:30 p.m. Saturday is the busiest day.
Fare:	Half-day excursions: adults, $21; children, $14. Anacapa Island whale-watch trips: adults, $39; children, $22. Whale-watch trips to Santa Cruz Island: adults, $50; children, $40. Reservations required. The Doubletree Hotel in Ventura offers guests discount coupons for Island Packers whale watches.
Departure:	Trips leave from Ventura Harbor. Take the Seaward off-ramp south on Harbor Boulevard and turn right on Spinnaker Drive in the Ventura Harbor.
Naturalist:	Crew members, most of whom have degrees in environmental science or biology, serve as naturalists.

"Island Packers is a family-owned and operated business," notes owner William Mark Connally, the son of the founder. "We are the concessionaire to the Channel Islands National Park and provide transportation to the park and interpretive services for the National Park Service."

MUSEUMS, AQUARIUMS, AND SCIENCE CENTERS

CALIFORNIA

Aquarium of the Pacific

P.O. Box 20268, Long Beach, CA 90801
(562) 590-3100

Opened in June of 1998, the Aquarium of the Pacific is a celebration of the world's largest and most diverse body of water. In 156,735 square feet, seventeen major habitats and 30 small exhibits showcase more than 550 different species of the inhabitants of the Pacific Ocean. Educational programs are available.

The Aquarium is open from 10 a.m. to 6 p.m. every day except Christmas. Admission is $13.95 for adults, $11.95 for senior citizens, and $6.95 for children 3 to 11.

Cabrillo Marine Aquarium

3720 Stephen White Drive, San Pedro, CA 90731
(310) 548-7562

The Cabrillo Marine Aquarium has more than thirty aquariums and exhibits, which provide a close-up look at a wide variety of sea creatures of the Southern California area. Among the exhibits is one on the migration of the gray whales. Recreational and educational programs are available, including whale-watch trips from January through April.

Open noon to 5 p.m. Tuesday through Friday; 10 a.m. to 5 p.m. Saturday and Sunday. Closed on Mondays. Admission is free, but beach parking is $6.50 per car, with reduced rates from December through February.

California Academy of Sciences

Golden Gate Park, San Francisco, CA 94118
(415) 221-5100; Fax (415) 750-7346

The Academy is a natural history museum, aquarium, and planetarium all rolled into one. Classes on marine mammals, including whales, are held periodically for adults and children. For information on adult education classes, call (415) 750-7100.

Open daily 10 a.m. to 5 p.m.; extended hours in the summer. Adults, $8.50; senior citizens and students 12 to 17, $5.50; children ages 4 through 11, $3. Admission is free on first Wednesday of each month.

Long Marine Laboratory

100 Shaffer Road, Santa Cruz, CA 95060
(408) 459-4308; Fax (408) 459-3383

Long Marine Laboratory serves as the marine research and instructional facility of the University of California at Santa Cruz. Exhibits include an 85-foot skeleton of a blue whale, tidepool animals in touch tanks, an aquarium, and displays related to current research.

Open 1 to 4 p.m. Tuesday through Sunday; closed on Mondays and holidays. Group tours available at expanded hours by appointment.

Monterey Bay Aquarium

886 Cannery Row, Monterey, CA 93940
(408) 648-4800

More than 120,000 specimens representing 525 species are housed in the aquarium. Special features are several undersea habitats, including a three-story kelp forest and a 90-foot-long exhibit of Monterey Bay habitats. From the public entrance, a parade of life-size marine mammals, including a 43-foot gray whale and her 22-foot calf, wends its way overhead into the Marine Mammals gallery.

Open daily from 9:30 a.m. to 5:30 p.m. Adults, $14.95; students and senior citizens, $11.95; children, $6.95.

San Diego Natural History Museum

P.O. Box 1390, Balboa Park, San Diego, CA 91112
(619) 232-3821

Exhibits on marine life, shells, desert ecology, and the Foucault pendulum are on display. Open 9:30 a.m. to 5:30 p.m. seven days a week in summer, from 9:30 a.m. to 4:30 p.m. in winter. Adults, $6; seniors, $5; children 6 through 17, $3; children 5 and younger, free. Free admission once a month on Tuesday. For dates call (619) 239-0512. The museum also sponsors whale watches.

Santa Barbara Museum of Natural History

2559 Puesta del Sol Road, Santa Barbara, CA 93105
(805) 682-4711

Marine life exhibits include a 72-foot skeleton of a blue whale and several marine life and habitat displays in Marine Hall. A research laboratory, library, observatory, and planetarium are on the museum grounds.

Open 9 a.m. to 5 p.m. Monday through Saturday; 10 a.m. to 5 p.m. Sunday and some holidays. Closed Thanksgiving, Christmas, and New Year's. Admission $5 for adults, $4 for youths and seniors, $3 for children under 12.

A lifesize model of a gray whale is on display at the Sea Center, #211 Stearns Wharf, which is affiliated with the Museum. The Sea Center has a touch tank and other marine displays and is open every day from 10 a.m. to 5 p.m. from June 1 to Labor Day and noon to 5 p.m. weekdays and 10 a.m. to 5 p.m. weekends and some holidays from Labor Day to May 31. The touch tank is closed until noon. Adults, $3; senior citizens and teens, $2, children 3 to 12, $1.50.

Stephen Birch Aquarium

Scripps Institution of Oceanography, 2300 Expedition Way,
LaJolla, CA 92093
(619) 534-3474; Fax (619) 534-7114

In addition to displays of oceanic wonders, the Stephen Birch Aquarium sponsors occasional whale-watch cruises, snorkel and scuba expeditions, tidepooling trips, and classes for children and adults. Write for a brochure and calendar of events.

Open daily 9 a.m. to 5 p.m. Closed on Thanksgiving and Christmas. Admission is $7.50 for adults, $6.50 for seniors, $5 for students, $4 for children ages 4 to 12, and free for kids under 4.

NATIONAL PARKS AND MARINE SANCTUARIES

CALIFORNIA

Channel Islands National Park

1901 Spinnaker Drive, Ventura, CA 93001
(805) 658-5700

Channel Islands National Marine Sanctuary

113 Harbor Way, Santa Barbara, CA 93109
(805) 966-7107

Five of the eight Channel Islands make up Channel Islands National Park. The islands are Anacapa, Santa Cruz, Santa Rosa, San Miguel, and Santa Barbara plus 125,000 acres of submerged lands. The Marine Sanctuary encompasses 1,252 square nautical miles of near-shore and offshore waters. Boat trips, diving, fishing, visits to the Sea Center, and wildlife watching are all available.

Write for a free map and brochures about island life, ecology, and activities.

Gulf of the Farallones National Marine Sanctuary

National Oceanic and Atmospheric Administration, GGNRA,
Fort Mason, Building 201, San Francisco, CA 94123
(415) 561-6622

The Gulf of the Farallones National Marine Sanctuary encompasses 948 square nautical miles of water off the California coastline north of San Francisco. Designated in 1981, the sanctuary consists of an offshore marine region of the Gulf of the Farallones and the nearshore waters of Bodega Bay, Tomales Bay, Drakes Bay, Bolinas Bay, Estero San Antonio, Estero de Americano, Duxbury Reef, and Bolinas Lagoon. Write for a free brochure and map of the area.

Monterey Bay National Marine Sanctuary

299 Foam Street, Suite D, Monterey, CA 93940
(408) 647-4201

The Monterey Bay National Marine Sanctuary—which covers 4,024 square nautical miles—is a haven for sea otters, seals, shorebirds, squid, sardines and thousands of other species, including many that are threatened or endangered. The sanctuary was so designated in 1992. Write for a free brochure.

Point Reyes National Seashore

Point Reyes, CA 94956
(415) 663-1092

The Point Reyes National Seashore, about 50 miles north of San Francisco, has a rich cultural and natural heritage to explore. Visitors centers, hiking trails, exhibits, and stationary whale watching from several points are all available in the 73,000-acre recreational area. From December 30 through February, free shuttle bus service for whale watchers is available. Ask at the Bear Valley Visitor Center for the pick-up point. Rangers are always on hand to answer questions. Write for a free brochure, map, and calendar of events.

MONUMENTS

Cabrillo National Monument

P.O. Box 6670, San Diego, CA 92106
(619) 557-5450

Cabrillo National Monument is located at the southern end of Point Loma, within the city limits of San Diego. Whale Watch Weekend, held annually in January, includes informal lectures and presentations and displays as well as opportunities to sight the migrating gray whales from a sheltered overlook. Educational materials about whales are available all year.

Open every day, 9 a.m. to 5:15 p.m.; extended hours in summer. Admission is $5 per vehicle or $2 per person on foot.

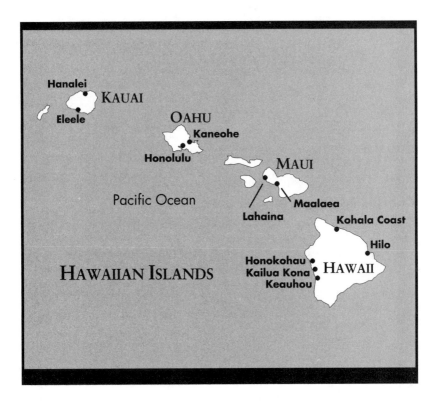

Hanalei
KAUAI
Eleele

OAHU
Kaneohe
Honolulu

MAUI
Maalaea
Lahaina
Kohala Coast

Pacific Ocean

Hilo

HAWAIIAN ISLANDS

Honokohau
Kailua Kona
Keauhou

HAWAII

HAWAII

Lahaina, on the island of Maui, was once the capital of the American Pacific whaling fleet. Today whale-watch tour boats stand in the harbor, waiting to carry passengers to see the whales that swim in Hawaiian waters each year from December to April.

Just a few years ago, the only whale-watch tours in the Hawaiian Islands operated out of Lahaina, though some sport and fishing boats based on other islands were available for private charter. Today, wherever you succumb to the seductive languor of Hawaii, you can book passage on a whale-watch trip. Excursion boats, sailboats, and inflatable rafts are all available, with departure points from Kauai, Maui, Oahu, and the "Big Island," Hawaii. (Can Lanai be far behind?)

The attraction is primarily humpback whales, which come to Hawaii each year to mate and give birth. Some areas are so replete with mothers and calves that they have been dubbed "nurseries" and declared sanctuaries. In addition to the frolicsome humpbacks, other smaller cetaceans such as pilot whales and bottlenose dolphins are frequently seen in Hawaiian waters.

If you miss the boat, so to speak, and happen to be lying on a beach on the northwestern coast of Maui at the right time of year, you may think that you see whales breaching along the shore of Lanai.

That's probably more than just a Mai Tai-induced illusion.

TOURISM INFORMATION

HAWAII
Hawaii Visitors Bureau
2270 Kalakaua Avenue, Suite 801, Honolulu, Oahu, HI 96813
(808) 924-0266

WHALE-WATCHING TRIPS

HAWAII

HONOKOHAU, KAILUA, AND KEAUHOU

Dan McSweeney's Whale Watching Adventures

P.O. Box 139, Holualoa, Hawaii, HI 96725
(888) WHALES6 or (808) 322-0028; Fax (808) 322-2732;
E-mail dmcswwa@interpac.net; Web site www.ilovewhales.com

Whales:	Humpback, pilot, sperm, dolphins
Season:	All year, except May and June
Boats:	*Lady Ann*, a 38-foot motor yacht that carries 42 passengers
Trips:	One 3-1/2-hour trip at 8 a.m. Monday through Friday from July 1 to December 19; Two 3-hour trips daily at 8 a.m. and 12:30 p.m. from December 20 to April 30.
Fare:	Adults, $44.50 plus tax; children 11 and under, $29.50 plus tax; infants under 1, free. Reservations recommended.
Departure:	Trips leave from Honokohau Harbor in Kailua-Kona. Please call for directions to the boat.
Naturalist:	Narration by Captain Dan McSweeney, a whale scientist.

"You can see whales here any day, any season," says Dan McSweeney. "I guarantee a whale sighting, and also that participants' experience will be valuable as they see, learn about, and appreciate these intriguing animals." McSweeney, the founder of the Wild Whale Research Foundation, has studied Hawaii's whales since 1974 and logged 25,000 hours of whale watching.

Living Ocean Adventures

P.O. Box 1622, Kailua-Kona, Hawaii, HI 96745
(808) 325-5556; Fax (808) 325-0502; E-mail bottrell@kona.net

Whales: Humpback, pilot, dolphins

Season: Mid-December through mid-April for humpbacks

Boats: *Spinner*, a 31-foot custom Bertram sportfisher, 6 passengers

Trips: Two 3-1/2-hour trips daily at 8:30 a.m. and 12:30 p.m.

Fare: $54.50 for adults, $39.50 children 12 and under

Departure: Trips leave from Honokohau Harbor.

Naturalist: Skipper narrates all trips.

"We provide a personal and uncrowded experience with humpback whales," says owner and skipper Thomas Bottrell, who has degrees in oceanography and ecology and experience on Kona waters since 1975. Living Ocean Adventures also provides whale watching and sportfishing year 'round.

KOHALA COAST

Ocean Sports Waikoloa

69-275 Waikoloa Beach Drive, Waikoloa, HI 96743
(808) 886-6666; Fax (808) 886-5863; E-mail seasmoke@usa.net;
Website www.hawaiioceansports.com

Whales: Humpback

Season: December 15 to April 15

Boats: Five boats; 6, 18, 25, 36 and 49 passengers

Trips: Four trips daily. Three-hour snorkel and whale watch at 8:30 a.m.; a 1-1/2-hour motor/sail cruise at 12:30 p.m. and 2 p.m.; a 1-1/2-hour sunset sail at 4:30 p.m. Saturday is busiest day.

Fare: Early trip: adults, $59; children under 12, $31. Midday trip: adults, $39; children, $20. Sunset trip: adults, $49. Reservations advised.

Departure: Boat leaves from Anaehoomalu Bay Beach, in front of the Royal Waikoloan Hotel and Waikoloa Beach Resort.

Naturalist: Naturalist on most trips.

"Ocean Sports' approach to whale watching is unique in that the captains and crews are as excited and enthusiastic about seeing these gentle creatures as are our guests, and all have a genuinely good time," says Rick Conners. "Some groups are treated to an unofficial initiation as honorary crew members as they learn our whaling song:"

> Yo ho, yo ho, a sailor's life for me!
> Yo ho, yo ho, a sailor's life for me!
> We sail this ship upon the sea
> in search of humpback whales.
> We see them breach,
> We see them splash,
> We see them wave their tails!
> Oh . . . ooooh, yo ho, yo ho, a sailor's life for me!

KONA

Blue Moon Explorations

P.O. Box 2568WW, Bellingham, WA 98227
(206) 966-8805

Whales:	Humpback
Season:	February and March
Boats:	Eight 2-person kayaks
Trips:	Several 5- to 10-day trips to the Big Island, including whale watching, snorkeling, kayaking, and hiking. Accommodations include a retreat center and camping. Some trips are for women only.
Fare:	Fares range between $600 and $1,200, which includes kayaks, camping accommodations, most meals in Hawaii, accessories, group camping equipment, a VHF radio, safety equipment, guides and instruction. Reservations required.
Departure:	Trips begin in Kona.
Naturalist:	Naturalist aboard.

Owner Kathleen Grimbly says, "Blue Moon Explorations are designed to expand our awareness of the many intricate relationships in the web of life. Traveling by kayak, we experience the whales and the web of life that supports them more intimately and less intrusively. Our trips are designed for people of all ages and abilities."

Hawaii Sailing Company

P.O. Box 1813, Honokaa, Hawaii, HI 96727; (808) 326-1986; E-mail hawshop@gte.net

Whales: Humpback

Season: November to May

Boats: A 38-foot sailing yacht; 6 passengers each

Trips: Two- to six-day sailing trips around the "Big Island" of Hawaii. Participants live on board.

Fare: $160 per person per day includes meals, whale watching, snorkeling, body surfing, and cruising. Reservations required.

Departure: Boat leaves from Kona, Hawaii.

Naturalist: None on board.

"Up until April, the humpback whales will be arriving in Hawaii for the mating season. Sailing is the perfect way to enjoy this yearly migration," notes Captain Bill Chambers.

"The anchorages range from the peaceful out-of-the-way harbors to active resort areas. The beaches are some of the finest in the world, the waters clear and warm for snorkeling and body surfing, and the scenery pure Hawaii."

KAUAI

ELEELE

NaPali Explorer Whale Watching Adventure

9600 Kaumualii Highway, Waimea, Kauai, HI 96796
(808) 335-9909; Web site www.napaliexplorer.com

Whales:	Humpback
Season:	January 1 to April 30
Boats:	The *NaPali Explorer*, an inflatable raft that carries 49 passengers
Trips:	Three 2-1/2-hour trips at 9 a.m., noon and 3 p.m. Tuesday and Thursday. One 2-1/2-hour trip at 2 p.m. other days. Morning trip includes snorkeling off coral reefs, weather permitting.
Fare:	Adults, $60; children, $30. Reservations advised.
Departure:	Boats leave from Port Allen, the boat harbor in Eleele on the west shore of Kauai. Meet at The Exploration Company in the Eleele Shopping Center.
Naturalist:	Naturalists trained by marine biologists.

"Some 600 humpback whales visit our islands from January through April," says a spokesman. "These 50-ton giants migrate to Hawaii's warm waters to calve and mate before returning to their summer home off Alaska."

HANALEI

Captain Zodiac Raft Expeditions

P.O. Box 456, Hanalei, Kauai, Hi 96714
(800) 422-7824 or (808) 826-9371; Fax (808) 826-7704;
E-mail captain@aloha.net; Website www.planet-hawaii.com/zodiac

Whales:	Humpback
Season:	January to mid-April
Boats:	Inflatable rafts; 16 passengers each
Trips:	Trips range from 3 to 5 hours, depending on demand. Trips include snorkeling off coral reefs, weather permitting. Wednesday is busiest day.
Fare:	Adults, $55 to $105. Beverages, brunch or lunch provided. Reservations advised.
Departure:	Boats leave from Hanalei Harbor and Nawiliwil. Check in at the Captain Zodiac office on Highway 56, just before the Ching Young Shopping Village.
Naturalist:	Knowledgeable captains narrate all trips.

"We use 23-foot Zodiac rafts popularized by Jacques Cousteau," says manager Clarence H. Greff Jr. "We are the pioneer rafting company in Hawaii, having started the rafting tour business here in 1974. We have two locations in Hawaii—Kauai and the Big Island—and we are the largest rafting company in the islands."

Hanalei Sea Tours

P.O. Box 1437, Hanalei, Kauai, Hi 96714
(800) 733-7997 or (808) 826-7254; Fax (808) 826-7747

Whales:	Humpback
Season:	December to April
Boats:	Eight boats; rigid-hull inflatable rafts, 15 passengers; power-driven catamarans, 16 passengers
Trips:	Trips for 2-1/2, 4, and 5 hours daily, with morning and afternoon departures.

Fare: $55 for adults and $35 for children 12 and under for 2 1/2-hour trip; $75 for adults and $55 for children 12 and under for 4-hour trip (includes snorkeling and snacks); $100 for adults and $80 for children for 5-hour trip (includes hike, beach picnic, snorkeling and beverages). Group rates available. Reservations required.

Departure: Boats leave from Hanalei Bay. Meet at Hanalei Sea Tours office, the second building on the left after the first one-lane bridge in Hanalei.

Naturalist: Captain serves as naturalist.

"Hanalei Sea Tours operates year round offering scenic cruises of the beautiful NaPali coastline," says Ronnie Grover, general manager. "During these adventures, we enjoy viewing marine life, including dolphins, sea turtles, and the humpback whales in season."

A portion of all fares is donated to save the whales.

"NaPali is our objective—to get our passengers out to explore the majestic cliffs that are so rich in Hawaiian history, cruise through sea caves and lava tubes, and experience seeing marine life in their natural habitat."

MAUI

LAHAINA

Maui Nui Explorer Whale Watching Adventure

330 Hukilike Street, Kahului, Maui, HI 96732
(808) 873-3475

Whales: Humpback

Season: December 15 through April 15

Boats: One boat, the *Maui Nui Explorer*, which holds 49

Trips: One 2-hour trip at 1:30 p.m. daily. Snorkel cruises also available.

Fare: Adults, $29, children ages 2 to 11, $21. Reservations advised. Portion of proceeds benefits Hawaii Wildlife Fund.

Departure: Boat leaves from Lahaina Dock, just off Front Street.

Naturalist: Naturalists from Hawaii Wildlife Fund.

"Some 600 humpback whales visit our islands from January through April," says a spokesman. "These 50-ton giants migrate to Hawaii's warm waters to calve and mate before returning to their summer home off Alaska."

Maui Princess/Lahaina Princess

113 Prison Street, Lahaina, Maui, HI 96761
(800) 275-6969 or (808) 661-6165; Fax (808) 661-5792;
E-mail ismarine@maui.net; Website www.maui.net/`ismarine

Whales: Humpback

Season: Mid-December to May

Boats: The 188-foot *Maui Princess* and the 65-foot *Lahaina Princess*; carrying 149 passengers each

Trips:	Three 2-1/4-hour trips daily at 8:30 a.m., 11:30 a.m. and 2:30 p.m.
Fare:	Adults, $31; children ages 3 to 12, $17.50; infants, free. Special rates on first and last trip of the day. Portion of fare goes to Maui Whale Aid, a private foundation established to fund whale research and education in Hawaii. Reservations advised.
Departure:	Boats leave from Slip 3 in Lahaina Harbor, just across the street from the banyan tree and the Pioneer Inn.
Naturalist:	Naturalist accompanies all trips.

"Our two vessels are the most comfortable whale-watch vessels on Maui," notes Andrew Wood. "Whale-cam, our state-of-the-art underwater video system and large-screen televisions allow views of whale behavior previously unavailable." Passengers may participate in research by photographing and collecting critical information such as pod configuration, latitude and longitude of sightings, whale behavior, and whale identification. Photos and other data are made available to researchers around the world.

Ocean Riders

P.O. Box 967, Lahaina, Maui, HI 96767
(808) 661-3586

Whales:	Humpback
Season:	December through April
Boats:	Two rigid-hull inflatable rafts; 13 and 18 passengers
Trips:	Four 2-hour trips daily at 8:30 a.m., 10:45 a.m., 1 p.m., and 3:30 p.m.; one 3-hour trip daily at 7:30 a.m. that includes snorkeling.
Fare:	Adults, $45; children, $30. Add $10 for the snorkeling trip. Includes beverage, light snack, snorkeling equipment, and snorkeling instruction. Reservations required.
Departure:	Boats leave from Mala Wharf in Lahaina. Turn off Front Street near the Safeway, the cannery, and the "JESUS IS COMING" sign.
Naturalist:	Captains and crew are trained by researchers.

"We operate state-of-the-art rigid-hull inflatables that are the safest, fastest and most fun boats in Pacific waters—the boat ride alone is worth the fare," says owner Sherrill Jeter. "We offer guaranteed whale sightings from January 5 through April 30, or your money back."

Pacific Whale Foundation's Eco-Adventures

101 North Kihei Road, Suite 25, Kihei, Maui, HI 96753
(800) 942-5311 or (808) 879-8811; Fax (808) 879-2615;
E-mail ecoadventures@pacificwhale.org; Web site www.pacificwhale.com

Whales:	Humpback, pilot and false killer, dolphins
Season:	Late November through May
Boats:	Two boats; *Manutea*, a 50-foot sailing catamaran that carries 409 passengers and *Whale II*, a 50-foot sailing ketch that carries 26 passengers
Trips:	Several 2-hour whale-watch cruises daily, departing at almost every hour of the day.
Fare:	Prices start at $19.80 for adults, half price for children ages 4 to 12 and free for children under 4. Reservations required. Proceeds benefit whale research.
Departure:	Boats leave from Slip 11 in Lahaina Harbor, just off Front Street.
Naturalist:	Naturalists on board have marine field research experience.

"Pacific Whale Foundation is recognized worldwide for our pioneering research, education and conservation efforts on behalf of the endangered hump-back whale," says Greg Kaufman, president and founder. "Our marine research efforts in Hawaii and throughout the Pacific span nearly two decades."

Scotch Mist Sailing Charters

P.O. Box 831, Lahaina, Maui, HI 96767
(808) 661-0386; Fax (808) 667-2113

Whales: Humpback

Season: Mid-December to mid-April

Boats: One sailing yacht, *Scotch Mist II;* 25 passengers

Trips: Four 2-hour trips daily at 8 a.m., 11 a.m., 2 p.m., and
4:30 p.m.

Fare: Adults, $35; children under 12, $25. Beer, wine, and soft
drinks included. Reservations required. Charters available.

Departure: Boat leaves from Slip 9 in Lahaina Harbor, just off Front Street
by the Pioneer Inn.

Naturalist: No naturalist on board.

"Slip into whale country and see the humpbacks up close from the deck of a private yacht," says staff member Leslie Ferguson. The *Scotch Mist II* was first to finish in the 1982 Victoria-to-Maui Yacht Race. It is available to visitors for sailing, snorkeling, champagne sunset cruises, and whale watching.

Ultimate Rafting Maui

P.O. Box 1773, Lahaina, Maui, HI 96767
(808) 667-5678; Fax (808) 874-8527; E-mail ecoraft@maui.net;
Web site www.maui.net/`ecoraft

Whales: Humpback

Season: December through April

Boats: One 30-foot aluminum-hulled, inflatable raft that carries
24 passengers

Trips: Three 2-hour trips daily at 7:30 a.m., 1 p.m. and 3:30 p.m.
A snorkel trip/whale watch also is available.

Fare: Adults, $29 for the 7:30 a.m. and 3:30 p.m. trips; $39 for the
mid-day trip. Reservations advised.

Departure: Trips leave from Lahaina Harbor.

Naturalist: Marine biologists accompany all trips.

"At Ultimate Rafting, we sincerely strive to make your tour with us a truly memorable experience. Our vessel was designed with marine viewing in mind and our knowledge of animal behavior and the ability to transport small personal groups quickly to remote areas to view wildlife has no equal," says Ted Mickowski, marine biologist and founder.

Windjammer Cruises

283 Wili Ko Place, Suite 1, Lahaina, Maui, HI 96761
(800) SEA-HULA or (808) 667-2179

Whales: Humpback

Season: Mid-December through April

Boats: *Spirit of Windjammer*, a 70-foot three-masted schooner that carries 93 passengers

Trips: Three 2-hour cruises daily at 9 a.m., 11:30 a.m. and 2 p.m. Dinner cruise and whale watching at 5:30 p.m.

Fare: Adults, $34.95 for daytime cruises, $69 for dinner; children under 12, free during the day and $36.62 for dinner cruise. Reservations required.

Departure: Boat leaves from Slip 1 in Lahaina Harbor, just off Front Street, near the banyan tree.

Naturalist: Naturalist aboard.

"Help the whales by whale watching on a vessel that supports education and research on Hawaii's humpback whale," says a spokesman for Windjammer Cruises.

MAALAEA

Navatek II Whale Watching Adventure

330 Hukilike St., Kahului, Maui, HI 96732
(808) 873-3475

Whales: Humpback, pilot and false killer, dolphins

Season: December 15 through April 15

Boats: One boat, the *Navatek II*, which holds 140

Trips: One 2-hour cruise at 2:30 p.m. daily except Friday. Snorkel and dinner cruises also available.

Fare: Adults, $39; children ages 2 to 11, $26.50. Reservations advised. Portion of proceeds benefits Hawaii Wildlife Fund.

Departure: Boat leaves from Maalaea Harbor just off Highway 30.

Naturalist: Naturalists from Hawaii Wildlife Fund.

"Some 600 humpback whales visit our islands from January through April," says a spokesman. "These 50-ton giants migrate to Hawaii's warm waters to calve and mate before returning to their summer home off Alaska."

Pacific Whale Foundation's Eco-Adventures

101 North Kihei Road, Suite 25, Kihei, Maui, HI 96753
(800) 942-5311 or (808) 879-8811; Fax (808) 879-2615;
E-mail ecoadventures@pacificwhale.org; Web site www.pacificwhale.com

Whales: Humpback, pilot and false killer whales, dolphins

Season: Late November through May

Boats: Two boats; *Ocean Spirit*, a 65-foot power catamaran that carries 142 passengers, and *Pacific Whale*, a 41-foot expedition boat that carries 34.

Trips: Several 2-hour whale-watch cruises daily, departing at almost every hour of the day.

Fare: Prices start at $19.80 for adults, half price for children ages 4 to 12 and free for children under 4. Reservations required. Proceeds benefit whale research.

Departure: Boats leave from Slip 52 in Maalaea Harbor just off Highway 30.

Naturalist: Naturalists on board have marine field research experience.

"Pacific Whale Foundation is recognized worldwide for our pioneering research, education and conservation efforts on behalf of the endangered humpback whale," says Greg Kaufman, president and founder. "Our marine research efforts in Hawaii and throughout the Pacific span nearly two decades."

MAUI, MOLOKAI, AND LANAI

Oceanic Society Expeditions

Fort Mason Center, Building E, San Francisco, CA 94123
(800) 326-7491 or (415) 441-1106; Fax (415) 474-3395;
Web site www.oceanic-society.org

Whales: Humpback, pilot, false killer, spinner dolphins

Season: March

Boats: Small private boats

Trips: Eight-day land-based trips, sailing the waters of Maui, Lanai, and Midway Atoll.

Fare: $1,990 per person. Price includes meals, accommodations, boat trips, guides. Reservations required.

Departure: Trip begins upon arrival at Lahaina Harbor on Maui and ends in Honolulu.

Naturalist: Marine biologist.

"With a marine biologist/naturalist, we sail the less-touristed waters," says a spokeswoman. "We'll observe humpback whales in more secluded breeding areas. On the Midway Atoll boat trips, we can expect to see a herd of 200 or more spinner dolphins, sea turtles, monk seals and seabirds."

Oceanic Society Expeditions has conducted natural history tours since 1972.

OAHU

HONOLULU

Navatek I Whale Watching Adventure

P.O. Box 29816, Honolulu, Oahu, HI 96820
(808) 848-6360

Whales: Humpback

Season: January through April

Boats: The *Navatek I*, 380 passengers

Trips: Two 2-hour trips daily at 8:30 a.m. and noon

Fare: For the early trip, adults, $39; children 5 to 12, $19. For the deluxe luncheon cruise, adults, $47; children, $24.50. Reservations advised.

Departure: Trips leave from Pier 6 in the Honolulu Harbor.

Naturalist: Naturalist from the University of Hawaii narrates trips.

"Some 600 humpback whales visit our islands from January through April," says a spokesman. "These 50-ton giants migrate to Hawaii's warm waters to calve and mate before returning to their summer home off Alaska."

KANEOHE AND HONOLULU

Honolulu Sailing Company

47-335 Lulani Street, Kaneohe, Oahu, HI 96744
(800) 829-0114 or (808) 239-3900; Fax (808) 836-0008

Whales: Humpback, pilot

Season: January to May

Boats: Two 50-foot sailing yachts; 8 passengers each

Trips: Two half-day trips at 8 a.m. and 1 p.m. One all-day trip at 9 a.m. Overnight trips also available. Weekends are the busiest times.

Fare: $50 per person for half day, $90 for full day, $260 for overnight (two days). Reservations required.

Departure: Boats leave from Kaneohe Bay or from Honolulu Harbor. Call for directions.

Naturalist: No naturalist on board.

"We have been observing humpback whales on our cruises longer than anyone," says Mike Mickelwait, one of the captains. "Quiet sailboats are much better for not disturbing whales."

MUSEUMS

Whalers Village Museum

2435 Kaanapali Parkway, G-8, Lahaina, Maui, HI 96761
(808) 661-5992

The museum's whale pavilion features the skeleton of a 40-foot sperm whale. The history of the whaling industry in Hawaii is portrayed through an extensive artifact and photo collection, along with a re-created ship's fo'castle and a model of a whaling boat.

New is "Hale Kohala,"—House of the Whale, an educational exhibit featuring whale models, including a 16-foot baby humpback whale.

The museum is in the Whalers Village Shopping Complex. Take the elevator or stairs to the Third Level of Building G. Hours are 9:30 a.m. to 10 p.m. daily. Admission is free.

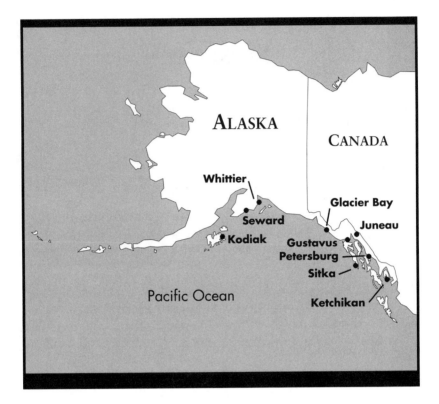

ALASKA

CANADA

Whittier

Glacier Bay

Seward

Juneau

Kodiak

Gustavus

Petersburg

Sitka

Pacific Ocean

Ketchikan

ALASKA

Alaska—"The Great Land"—has its share of great whales. Humpback, fin, gray whales, and orcas all swim off Alaskan shores. Still, the whale-watch industry is developing relatively slowly, although the many sportfishing charters and wilderness lodges have always considered sighting whales a normal occurrence.

The little town of Gustavus, just outside of the glorious Glacier Bay National Park and Preserve, probably offers the most whale-watch tours in Alaska. Trips also originate in Juneau, Ketchikan, Kodiak, Petersburg, Seward, Sitka, Valdez and Wrangell. Extended tours visit several destinations in southeast and south-central Alaska, and most originate from points outside Alaska.

Some of the best serendipitous whale watching takes place aboard the Alaska State ferries that operate in southeast and south-central Alaska. The U.S. Forest Service provides Forest Interpreters on board to conduct programs on whales, marine mammals, and the special features of the Chugach and Tongass National Forests. All programs are free to ferry passengers. Cruiseship passengers who keep a careful watch also may see whales. The scenery in Alaska is so magnificent that you're guaranteed a breathtaking backdrop for any whale sightings.

WHALE-WATCHING TRIPS

ALASKA

GLACIER BAY

Alaska's Glacier Bay Tours and Cruises

520 Pike Street, Suite 1400, Seattle, WA 98101
(800) 451-5952 or (206) 623-7110; Fax (206) 623-7809;
E-mail gbinfo@cruisetours.com; Web site www.glacierbaytours.com

Whales:	Humpback, orca, minke
Season:	Early May to mid-September
Boats:	Two boats; 150 and 300 passengers
Trips:	One 9-hour glacier cruise daily at 7 a.m. and one 3-hour whale-watch cruise at 2 p.m.
Fare:	For the glacier cruise, adults, $156.50; children 11 and younger, half fare. Lunch included. For the nature cruise, $78 per person. Reservations required.
Departure:	Trips leave from the lodge's dock in Bartlett Cove, Glacier Bay National Park, which is accessible by plane or ferry. Packages are available that include flight to Bartlett Cove, flight and lodging, or flight and multiday cruise.
Naturalist:	National Park Service naturalist on board.

Alaska's Glacier Bay Tours and Cruises is the concessionaire at Glacier Bay National Park in southeastern Alaska, about 60 miles northwest of Juneau. Jerre Fuqua, director of marketing, says that the park is famous for whale watching. "It is the dream trip for nature photographers and those who love to see wildlife, including whales."

Fuqua adds, "Glacier Bay is also famous for its glaciers, with over one hundred alpine glaciers and with sixteen tidewater glaciers calving icebergs into the picturesque fjords."

GUSTAVUS

Alaska Discovery Inc.

5449-4 Shaune Drive, Juneau, AK 99801
(800) 586-1911 or (907) 780-6550; Fax (907) 780-4220;
E-mail akdsico@alaska.net; Web site www.akdiscovery.com

Whales:	Humpback, minke, orca
Season:	May through August
Boats:	Six kayaks; 2 people each
Trips:	One-, three-, six-, and eight-day sea kayaking and camping trips along Point Adolphus and Glacier Bay.
Fare:	The one-day trip is $119, the three-day costs $625, the six-day is $1,500 and eight-day trips range from $2,350 to $2,600. All trips include pre-trip lodging, floatplane charters and entrance to Glacier Bay National Park.
Departure:	Trips leave from and conclude in Gustavus, which is accessible only by boat or plane.
Naturalist:	Naturalist guides accompany trips.

"Sea kayaking with whales is absolutely unforgettable" says manager Susan Warner. "I never tire of camping along the wilderness shores, listening to the whales frolic as I fall asleep at night." People of any experience level are welcome to travel with Alaska Discovery.

Fairweather Fishing and Guide Service

June-August: P.O. Box 164, Gustavus, AK 99826
(907) 697-2335

September-May: P. O. Box 1335, Homer, AK 99603
(907) 235-5291 or (907) 235-3844

Whales:	Humpback, minke, orca
Season:	May 30 to September 15
Boats:	One boat, *Tomten;* 6 passengers
Trips:	One trip a day on demand, 7 a.m. to 3:30 p.m.

Fare: $90 per person for half day; $160 for full day, which includes lunch. Reservations required. For information on a package offer, contact P.O. Box 1335, Homer, AK 99603.

Departure: Boat leaves from the dock in Gustavus, which is accessible by boat or by air.

Naturalist: Naturalist aboard.

Says skipper Wayne Clark, "We have chartered trips with National Geographic, Audubon, National Wildlife, and International Wildlife organizations. The boat trip is a short twenty-minute ride to an area that has had whale numbers consistent from May to September anywhere from six to twelve humpbacks feeding right up against the shoreline. Eagles, seals, porpoises, and sea lions, also!"

Clark formerly worked as a rural bush teacher in the area.

Glacier Bay Puffin Charters

P.O. Box 3, Gustavus, AK 99826
(907) 697-2260; Fax (907) 697-2258; E-mail puffin@compuserve.com;
Web site www.puffintravel.com

Whales: Humpback

Season: May 15 to September 15

Boats: Two boats, 42-foot *Gusto* and 60-foot *Sea Wolf*; 6 passengers each. Other boats available.

Trips: One or two 4-hour trips a day at 7 a.m. and 1 p.m.; one 8-1/2-hour trip at 7 a.m. or by custom charter.

Fare: Adults, $180 for a full-day trip, $100 for half day. (Full-day trips preferred.) Children 12 and younger, free. Reservations advised. Packages available at Puffin's Bed and Breakfast, same address as above.

Departure: Boat leaves from Gustavus's dock. Gustavus is accessible only by plane or boat.

Naturalist: Naturalist or narrator aboard.

Glacier Bay—Your Way!

P.O. Box 5, Gustavus, AK 99826
(907) 697-2288; Fax (907) 697-2289.

Whales:	Orca, humpback
Season:	May 1 to September 15
Boats:	Two boats, *Pacific* and *Frolic*; 6 passengers each
Trips:	Full- or half-day charters daily at 7:30 a.m. and noon. Overnight charters also available. Packages available at Glacier Bay Country Inn, at above address.
Fare:	$160 for full day (about 8 hours), $90 for half day (about 4 hours). Reservations advised.
Departure:	Boats leave from dock in Gustavus. Access to Gustavus is by boat or plane.
Naturalist:	Captain serves as naturalist.

Owners Ken and Sandy Marchbanks have put together a number of tour options, but guests are not limited to these exact tour options.

Glacier Guides Inc.

Summer: P.O. Box 66, Gustavus, AK 99826
(907) 697-2252 or (907) 463-1591

Winter: P.O. Box 460, Santa Clara, UT 84765
(435) 628-0973

Whales:	Humpback, orca, minke
Season:	April to October
Boats:	A 72-foot yacht, *Alaskan Solitude*; 12 passengers, and the 40-foot *Alaskan Hunter*, 6 passengers
Trips:	One- to six-day trips, during which participants live on board, or daily charters from a lodge in Gustavus.
Fare:	Charter cost for the *Alaskan Solitude* is $15,900 for 6-day trip for up to 6 passengers, $2,850 per additional person. Full-day charter for the *Alaskan Hunter* is $250 per passenger, with a minimum of two. Half-day charter costs $150 per passenger, with a minimum of two. Reservations required.

Departure: Longer trips leave from the dock in Glacier Bay, which is accessible by ferry or plane. Half- and full-day trips leave from Gustavus.

Naturalist: The naturalist has been a licensed Alaska Master Guide/Outfitter since 1978.

"Glacier Bay National Park's sixteen glaciers calving into the sea is one of nature's major spectacles," says Jimmie C. Rosenbruch, a licensed Alaska Master Guide. "Less than two hundred years ago, Glacier Bay was a great ice-field. Today, ice has receded nearly 100 miles, leaving a magnificent bay full of all manner of wildlife and serving as summer feeding grounds for whales." Rosenbruch notes that most tour operators do not have permits for the calm, inside waters of Glacier Bay.

Gustavus Inn at Glacier Bay

P.O. Box 60, Gustavus, AK 99826
(800) 649-5220 or (907) 697-2254; Fax (907) 697-2255

Whales: Humpback, orca, minke, dolphin

Season: May 1 through September 15

Boats: Six boats that carry from 2 to 120

Trips: Short trips, half-day trips, full day and overnight trips available throughout the season via cabin cruiser, kayak or sailboat.

Fare: Short trips, $78. Chartered boat trips cost $125 per person for half days and $210 per person for full-day trips. Daily 8-hour trip to Glacier Bay on catamaran that carries 120 costs $175 for adults and $88 for children. A one-day kayak trip costs $119. Reservations advised.

Departure: Boats leave from Gustavus dock one mile from Gustavus Inn or from Bartlett Cove.

Naturalist: Naturalists from the National Park Service narrate the trips to Glacier Bay. Skippers narrate other trips.

"Since 1966, we have been hosting visitors to Glacier Bay in our unique home-stead," say owners JoAnn and David Lesh. "Humpback whales feed here in rich tidal currents at the mouth of Glacier Bay." The Leshes offer several packages that include whale-watch trips and a few days at their 14-room inn.

Gustavus Marine Charters

P.O. Box 81W, Gustavus, AK 99826
(907) 697-2233; E-mail gmc@mars.he.net;
Web site www.gustavusmarine charters.com

Whales:	Humpback, orca, minke
Season:	May 15 to September 15
Boats:	Two boats; 30 and 40 feet, 6 passengers each
Trips:	Single- or multi-day charters.
Fare:	For party of four, $1,200 a day. Or $900 each for three days, two nights on board, with four-person minimum. Reservations required.
Departure:	Boats leave from the dock in Gustavus. Access to Gustavus is by plane or boat.
Naturalist:	The captain, a former park ranger in Glacier Bay National Park, narrates.

"Cruise the icy fjords in the comfort and privacy of your own diesel-powered yacht," owner Mike Nigro says. "Enjoy photography, birding, whale watching, and tidewater glaciers, plus the finest saltwater fishing Alaska has to offer. Spend three or four days getting to know this special part of the Great Land."

SeaWolf Wilderness Adventures

P.O. Box 97, Gustavus, AK 99826
(907) 697-2416

Whales:	Humpback, minke, orca
Season:	May 1 through October 1
Boats:	The 65-foot *M/V SeaWolf* that carries 30 passengers, plus 2-person sea kayaks
Trips:	Half-day, full-day, dinner cruises and overnight adventures.
Fare:	Adults, $100 to $300, depending on trip. Discounts for children. Reservations advised.
Departure:	Boats leave from Gustavus, which is accessible only by boat or plane. Pick-up available.

Naturalist: Naturalist aboard.

Co-owners/captains John "Rusty" Owen and Pamela Miedtke offer custom trips so guests may whale watch from the boat or at whale-eye level in a kayak. Overnight trips explore Glacier Bay and other remote areas. At anchor at night, whales can be heard breathing and splashing. Other sightings include sea otters, seals, sea lions, puffins, bears and wolves.

Spirit Walker Expeditions

P.O. Box 240W, Gustavus, AK 99826
(800) KAYAKER or (907) 697-2266; Fax (907) 697-2211;
E-mail kayak@he.net; Web site www.he.net/`kayak

Whales:	Humpback, orca, minke, gray
Season:	May 1 to October 1
Boats:	Two-person kayaks
Trips:	Two, five and seven-day trips kayaking in Icy Strait and camping on Chichagof Island.
Fare:	From $550 to $1,488 per person, which includes charter transportation from Gustavus, all meals and equipment.
Departure:	Trips leave from the dock in Gustavus, which is accessible by plane or limited tour boat access.
Naturalist:	Naturalist accompanies trip.

"Sea kayaking is probably the most exciting way to see whales," says Nathan Borson, president. "We have seen humpback whales on every "WHALES! Trip" we have done. We get close, without chasing or disturbing whales. There is no engine noise, so we hear the whales breathing and slapping the water clearly. There is no prop noise to interfere with our hydrophone.

"Drifting right at the surface of the water, we see other life, too—sea lions, seals, much bird life, even plankton and kelp. We get a feeling of what it's like for a whale to live here. We camp on a beach that whales swim past at night, breathing noisily."

JUNEAU, KETCHIKAN, AND PETERSBURG

Outdoor Alaska

P.O. Box 7814, Ketchikan, AK 99901
(907) 225-6044; Fax (907) 225-8636

Whales:	Humpback
Season:	June through September
Boats:	Three boats, *Misty Fjord*, *Emerald Fjord*, and *Crystal Fjord*; up to 32 passengers each
Trips:	One-day or multi-day charters.
Fare:	$118 to $200 per person per day depending on number of passengers. Reservations required.
Departure:	Trips leave from Juneau, Ketchikan and Petersburg, all of which are accessible by air or boat.
Naturalist:	Skipper is marine biologist.

"Admiralty Island in southeast Alaska has surrounding it one of the largest populations of humpback whales in Alaska," says native Alaskan Captain Dale Pihlman. "These whales are concentrated for convenient viewing in the inland waters of Stephens Passage, Seymour Canal and Frederick Sound."

KODIAK

Kodiak Nautical Discoveries

P.O. Box 95, Kodiak, AK 99615
(907) 486-5234

Whales:	Gray, humpback, orca
Season:	May to November
Boats:	One boat, the *Sea Surgeon*; 6 passengers
Trips:	One trip daily at 8 a.m.

Fare: $150 per person for 8-hour trip.

Departure: Boat leaves from Slip 52 in the main boat harbor in Kodiak, on Marine Way at Shelikof Street.

Naturalist: Skipper narrates trip.

Ron Brockman, the skipper, was born and raised on Kodiak Island. He has operated a charter boat in Kodiak waters since 1970, has fished commercially and taught outdoor courses at the Kodiak College, and holds a degree in biology from Alaska Methodist University.

Brockman is a semiretired orthopedic surgeon and a captain in the Naval Reserve. Brockman's partner, Tom Stick, is a former dentist who spent many months off the coasts of Alaska and Siberia in a U.S. Navy nuclear submarine. Off the boat, Stick guides hunts and has managed a fishing lodge.

Kodiak Western Charters

P.O. Box 4123, Kodiak, AK 99615
(907) 486-2200; E-mail info@tenbears.com; Web site www.tenbears.com

Whales: Fin, humpback, minke, orca, gray

Season: April 1 through December

Boats: One 50-foot boat, *Ten Bears*; 14 passengers

Trips: Single full-day trips or multi-day charters.

Fare: Fares vary—write or call for information.

Departure: Boat departs from St. Herman's Boat Harbor on Near Island, just across the bridge from Kodiak.

Naturalist: Naturalist on board.

Owner and operator Eric Stirrup has sailed Kodiak Island waters for 12 years. He has a degree in marine biology and the oceans have been his interest and avocation since 1973.

"The rich shelf waters of the Gulf of Alaska are home to many resident and migrating whales. March brings the gray whales, and fin and humpbacks are common visitors during the summer. Minke and orcas are seen throughout the year."

SEWARD

Kenai Fjord Tours

P.O. Box 1889, Seward, AK 99664
(800) 478-8068 or (907) 224-8068; Fax (907) 224-8934

Whales:	Orca, humpback, gray
Season:	March through November
Boats:	The 95-foot *Coastal Explorer* plus eight others
Trips:	Three full-day trips daily at 8 a.m., 10 a.m. and 11:30 a.m. Two half-day trips daily at 8:30 a.m. and 1 p.m.
Fare:	For full day trips, $99. For half-day trips, $59. Reservations requested.
Departure:	Boats leave from Seward Boat Harbor; the office is on the boardwalk. Via highway, Seward is 125 miles south of Anchorage. You can also get there by train, bus, or plane.
Naturalist:	Captains narrate cruises.

The Chiswell Islands, in Kenai Fjords National Park, are a designated marine wildlife refuge. "As we cruise the rugged coastline, you'll see large seabird rookeries and up to 1,000 vocal sea lions in one of the largest concentrations of marine wildlife anywhere," a spokeswoman says.

Mariah Tours and Charters

P.O. Box 1309, Seward AK 99664
(800) 270-1238 or (907) 224-8623

Whales:	Orca, humpback, gray, minke, fin
Season:	April 20 to September 30
Boats:	Two boats; 16 passengers each
Trips:	Two 9-hour trips daily at 8 a.m. and 10 a.m. Saturday is busiest day. Exclusive charters available.
Fare:	Adults, $120.75; children 11 and younger, $59.85. Lunch is included. Reservations advised.

Departure: Boats leave from Slip D6 and D10 in the Seward Boat Harbor. Via highway, Seward is 125 miles south of Anchorage. You can also get there by train, bus, or plane.

Naturalist: Captains serve as naturalists.

Mariah Tours shows you a unique natural setting in and around Kenai Fjords National Park and the Chiswell Islands National Wildlife Refuge, says a spokeswoman. Trips offer unsurpassed opportunities for close-up viewing of whales; a large sea lion colony; over fifty species of birds; huge concentrations of puffins, kittiwakes, and murres; and numerous bald eagles, plus a visit to an active tidewater glacier.

SITKA

Alaska Wyldewind Charters

617 Katlian, B-33, Sitka, AK 99835
(907) 747-5734

Whales: Humpback; occasionally gray, orca, minke

Season: Late April to late September

Boats: One boat, the *Wyldewind*; 6 passengers

Trips: Numbers and times of trips depend on demand, accessibility of whales, and captain's availability.

Fare: Boat charter is $60 for half day; $85 for full day; $96 for 24 hours, sharing purchase and preparation of food; $140 for 24 hours, including meals. Minimum two passengers. Reservations advised. Special room rate available at Westmark Shee Atika, P.O. Box 318, Sitka, AK 99835; (907) 747-6241.

Departure: Boat leaves from Sitka, which is accessible by plane or ferry.

Naturalist: Skipper serves as naturalist.

Skipper Jerry Dzugan says, "We also combine other activities with whale watching, such as sailing, other wildlife viewing, hot springs, hiking, and exploring. We have no set schedule of arrivals/departures but plan trips around our clients' schedules, interests, and budgets.

"Our whale-watching activities for the public emphasize nonintrusive observation techniques so as to cause the least amount of stress and disturbance to marine mammals' natural behavior. The ability to sail noiselessly along while observing the rich wildlife and spectacular scenery helps create a unique experience for those who appreciate unspoiled wilderness and rich wildlife viewing."

VARIOUS DESTINATIONS

Audubon Nature Odysseys

700 Broadway, New York, NY 10003
(212) 979-3067; Fax (212) 353-0190; E-mail travel@audubon.org;
Web site www.audubon.org/market/no/

Whales:	Humpback
Season:	June
Boats:	The *Sea Lion*; 36 cabins for 70 passengers plus small inflatable landing craft for short expeditions
Trips:	An 8-day cruise at least once a season to Misty Fjords, Le Conte Bay, Tracy Arm, Haines, Point Adolphus, Glacier Bay National Park and the islands of southeast Alaska.
Fare:	$3,070 to $4,470 per person. Price includes cabin, meals, transfers, excursions, permits, tips, and taxes. Airfare not included. Reservations required.
Departure:	Group gathers in Seattle and flies to Sitka, where the cruise begins.
Naturalist:	Naturalist is Audubon senior staff member.

In June 1989, the National Audubon Society sponsored its first excursion along the coast of southeast Alaska. A spokeswoman notes, "I wish I could share with you all the wonderful responses of those who sailed together. Even our seasoned, world-traveling Audubon staff guides come back with stories of unbelievable beauty and magnificent wildlife."

Dolphin Charters

1007 LeNeve Place, El Cerrito, CA 94530
(800) 472-9942 or (510) 527-9622; Fax (510) 525-0720;
E-mail dolphin3@earthlink.com; Web site www.dolphincharters.com

Whales:	Orca, humpback, minke, gray, depending on trip
Season:	June through mid-September
Boats:	The 50-foot *Delphinus*; 8 passengers in three double staterooms and a four-person berth
Trips:	Multiple 5- to 11-day cruises on various routes in southeastern Alaska. Some trips include journeys to whale-watching sites in British Columbia. Participants live aboard.
Fare:	Fares range from $1,795 to $2,795, depending on itinerary. Price includes meals, accommodations, and transportation during the program. Reservations required.
Departure:	Boat departs from various ports in Alaska and British Columbia, depending on the trip.
Naturalist:	Naturalist accompanies each trip.

"Are you inquisitive? Do you love nature? Do you dream of an unrivaled adventure?" says Ronn Patterson, a leading authority on whales who has been offering trips since 1976. "Our natural history vacations are designed just for you. We provide a penetrating view of the world. Delight you with uncommon experiences. Enrich your understanding. Reawaken the sense of wonder and excitement you felt as a child!"

Oceanic Society Expeditions

Fort Mason Center, Building E, San Francisco, CA 94123
(800) 326-7491 or (415) 441-1106; Fax (415) 474-3395;
Web site www.oceanic-society.org

Whales:	Humpback
Season:	July
Boats:	The 65-foot *Snow Goose*, which sleeps 12. Participants live aboard
Trips:	One 9-day cruise in Southeast Alaska.
Fare:	$2,550 per person, which includes accommodations, meals and guides. Reservations required.

Departure: Trip begins in Petersburg and ends in Sitka

Naturalist: Naturalist from Oceanic Society Expeditions

"Every summer, almost 100 humpback whales gather in Frederick Sound to feed on krill," says a a spokeswoman. "It is one of the best places in the world to observe humpback whales feeding. It was here that 'bubble netting' was first observed, and the whales can be seen lunging into schools of fish with their mouths agape."

Other sights include bears at Anan Bay, the tidewater glacier at Le Conte Bay, plus porpoise, seals, dolphins, eagles and seabirds.

Sea Quest Expeditions/Zoetic Research

P.O. Box 2424, Friday Harbor, WA 98250
(360) 378-5767; E-mail info@sea-quest-kayak.com;
Web site www.sea-quest-kayak.com

Whales: Humpback, orca, porpoises

Season: Late June through early September

Boats: Sea kayaks. Participants camp in the wilderness.

Trips: Several 9-day trips of kayaking and camping in tents.

Fare: $1,549 per person, which includes everything except airfare to Alaska. Reservations required.

Departure: Trips begin and end in Petersburg, Alaska.

Naturalist: A professional educator with a degree in the natural sciences serves as naturalist.

Participants will kayak in the waterways where humpback and orca whales are found in summer and also will glide by tidewater glaciers, wilderness islands, and stunning mountain views, says a spokesman.

MUSEUMS

Alaska Sea Life Center

P.O. Box 1329, Seward, AK 99664
(800) 224-2525 or (907) 224-6300; Fax (907) 224-6320;
Web site www.alaskasealife.org/

Built on a seven-acre lot on the edge of Resurrection Bay, the Alaska Sea Life Center has a threefold mission: research, wildlife rehabilitation, and public education. The three main exhibits hold Steller sea lions, harbor seals, and a variety of sea birds. The exhibits are replicas of the animals' natural habitats.

The Center is open from 9 a.m. to 9:30 p.m. daily from early May through early September, from 9 a.m. to 7 p.m. daily the month of September, and from 9 a.m. to 6 p.m. daily from October through April. Admission is $12.50 for adults and $10 for children ages 4 to 16.

Pratt Museum

3779 Bartlett Street, Homer, AK 99603
(907) 235-8635; Fax (907) 235-2764

The Pratt Museum, run by the Homer Society of Natural History, collects, preserves, and interprets the history of the Kenai Peninsula. The whale exhibit includes a sperm whale skeleton, a beluga skeleton, a Bering beaked whale skeleton, a fin whale skull, and a Cuvier's beaked whale skull.

Hours are 10 a.m. to 6 p.m. daily in summer and noon to 5 p.m. Tuesday through Sunday in winter. The museum is closed Thanksgiving, Christmas and in January. Admission for nonmembers is $4 for adults, $3 for senior citizens, $2 for teens, and $1 for children ages 6 to 12.

University of Alaska Museum

907 Yukon Drive, Fairbanks, AK 99775
(907) 474-7505; Fax (907) 474-5469

The mission of the museum is to collect, interpret, and teach the natural and cultural history of the circumpolar area. Included in the exhibit on whales are the skull and lower jaw of a bowhead whale and paraphernalia related to the Eskimos' whale hunting. One such item is a twelve-person umiak, a boat made of split walrus hide with waterproof stitching.

From June through August, the museum is open daily 9 a.m. to 7 p.m.; in May and September, 9 a.m. to 5 p.m.; from October through April, noon to 5 p.m. weekdays. Adults, $5; seniors, $4.50; children ages 7 to 17, $3; children under 7, free. No admission is charged on Fridays during the winter.

NATIONAL PARKS

ALASKA

Glacier Bay National Park and Preserve

P.O. Box 140, Gustavus, AK 99826
(907) 697-2230

Glacier Bay National Park and Preserve was completely covered by ice just two hundred years ago. Today the park has sixteen tidewater glaciers, remnants of a general ice advance—the Little Ice Age—that began four thousand years ago. Wildlife in the park and preserve, which cover 3,328,000 acres, include humpback, minke, and orca whales. Write for a free brochure and map.

Kenai Fjords National Park

National Park Service, P.O. Box 1727, Seward, AK 99664
(907) 224-3175

Glaciers, seabirds, marine mammals, and a rugged coast are the special features of the Kenai Fjords National Park, which covers 567,000 acres. Write for a free map and brochure.

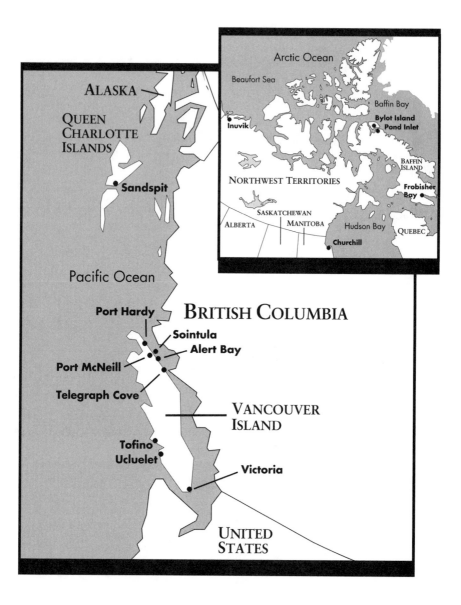

ALASKA

QUEEN
CHARLOTTE
ISLANDS

● Sandspit

Pacific Ocean

Arctic Ocean

Beaufort Sea

Inuvik

Baffin Bay

Bylot Island
Pond Inlet

NORTHWEST TERRITORIES

BAFFIN
ISLAND

Frobisher
Bay ●

SASKATCHEWAN

ALBERTA   MANITOBA   Hudson Bay   QUEBEC

Churchill

Port Hardy   BRITISH COLUMBIA

Sointula
Alert Bay

Port McNeill

Telegraph Cove

VANCOUVER
ISLAND

Tofino
Ucluelet

Victoria

UNITED
STATES

WESTERN CANADA AND NORTHWEST TERRITORIES

When it comes to whales, Canada has something for everyone.

The mighty blues, rare right whales, finbacks, humpbacks, almost-mythical bowheads, grays, tusked narwhals, pilot whales, orcas, and belugas swim in the seas off both coasts, inhabit arctic waters, and populate at least two rivers. Whales are also in Canada's gulfs, bays, and sounds, and at the right time of year, you can watch the whales of your choice from shore.

British Columbia can count on gray whales in March and April; orcas and minkes in July, August, and September; and maybe some finbacks and humpbacks later in the year. In response, tour operators sponsor trips from several cities on Vancouver Island and in the Queen Charlotte Islands. Some tour operators offer extended trips departing from various locations in British Columbia to better watch Canada's whales.

Every July and August, special expeditions leave Churchill, Manitoba, to see belugas in Hudson Bay and the Churchill River. The popular belugas can also be seen off Inuvik, in the Northwest Territories, in July and August. Trips to see the tusked narwhal and the seldom-observed bowhead originate from Baffin Island.

Basically, you can count on whales wherever there are whale-watch tour operators; but given the vast coastal exposures of Canada, don't be surprised if you encounter them elsewhere, too.

TOURISM INFORMATION

BRITISH COLUMBIA
Tourism British Columbia
Parliament Buildings, Victoria, British Columbia, V8V 1X4 Canada

(800) 663-6000

MANITOBA
Travel Manitoba
Dept. 6020, Seventh Floor, 155 Carlton Avenue, Winnipeg, Manitoba R3C 3H8 Canada

800 (665-0040)

NORTHWEST TERRITORIES
Arctic Tourism
P.O. Box 610, Yellowknife, Northwest Territories, XlA 2N5 Canada

(800) 661-0788

WHALE-WATCHING TRIPS

ALERT BAY, ALDER BAY, AND PORT MCNEILL

Sea Smoke/Sail with the Whales

P.O. Box 483, Alert Bay, British Columbia, V0N 1A0 Canada
(800) 668-ORCA or (250) 974-5225; Fax (250) 974-2266;
E-mail seaorca@island.net; Web site www.island.net/`seaorca

Whales:	Orca, minke, dolphins, porpoise
Season:	June to October
Boats:	*Tuan*, a 44-foot sailboat that carries 14 passengers and *Cetacea*, a 40-foot motor launch that carries 30.
Trips:	Two 5-hour trips daily to upper Johnstone Strait and Blackfish Sound, leaving Alert Bay at 8 a.m. and 1:30 p.m. and Alder Bay at 8:15 p.m. and 1 p.m. Two 3-hour trips daily leaving Alert Bay at 10 a.m. and 2 p.m. and Alder Bay at 10:15 a.m. and 1:45 p.m. Call for updated information on trips out of Port McNeill.
Fare:	For the 5-hour trips, $75 (Canadian) plus for adults, $70 for senior citizens, $60 for children 5 to 14, $40 for children 2 to 4. Devonshire tea is included in the fare. For the shorter trips, $60 for adults, $55 for senior citizens, $45 for children 5 to 14, and $35 for children 2 to 4. Reservations required.
Departure:	Boat leaves from Alert Bay, Alder Bay and Port McNeill on occasion.
Naturalist:	Naturalist aboard.

David and Maureen Towers established their company in 1986, and they endeavor with each tour to provide personalized care, quality service and a lasting impression of the uniqueness of the area. "Tours are educational and capture the exhilarating essence of being right there," they say.

PORT HARDY

Oceanic Society Expeditions

Fort Mason Center, Building E, San Francisco, CA 94123
(800) 326-7491 or (415) 441-1106; Fax (415) 474-3395;
Web site www.oceanic-society.org

Whales:	Orca, minke
Season:	August and September
Boats:	One 68-foot ketch, *Island Roamer*; 16 passengers
Trips:	One-week trip living on board and sailing off Vancouver Island.
Fare:	$1,670 (U.S.) per person. Price includes meals, accommodations, and guides. Reservations required.
Departure:	Trip begins at Port Hardy, on north Vancouver Island.
Naturalist:	Naturalist aboard.

"Johnstone Strait is absolutely the best place in the world to see killer whales," says a spokeswoman for Oceanic Society Expeditions. "Nowhere else can you expect to experience such close encounters with these majestic mammals.

"Approximately 330 individual whales have been identified in the waters off British Columbia and Washington. Pods can contain up to 50 animals. Our expedition combines whale watching with sailing and exploring the shores of an island wilderness."

Sea Quest Expeditions/Zoetic Research

P.O. Box 2424R, Friday Harbor, WA 98250
(360) 378-5767

Whales:	Gray, humpback, orca, dolphins
Season:	Late June through early September
Boats:	Sea kayaks
Trips:	Several 7-day trips kayaking and tent camping in remote wilderness.
Fare:	$999 (U.S.) per person. Price includes all expenses except travel to the departure point. Reservations required.

Departure: Trips begin at Port Hardy, on north Vancouver Island.

Naturalist: A professional educator with a degree in the natural sciences serves as naturalist.

Gray whales are so abundant here that a research camp has been established, says executive director Mark Lewis. "Other marine mammals, including orcas, humpback whales, two species of porpoise, white-sided dolphins, harbor seals, and the threatened Steller's sea lion are found. Overhead, bald eagles seem to perch on every point of land as they patiently await migrating salmon. Marine birds, such as puffins and murres, gather to nest in noisy rookeries."

PORT MCNEILL

Discovery Charters & Tours

#205-7134 Vedder Road, Chilliwack, British Columbia, V2R 4G4 Canada
(888) 468-6877 or (604) 824-1460; Fax (604) 824-1470;
E-mail rfahr@uniserve.com; Web site www. discovery charters.bc.ca

Whales: Orca, gray, minke, humpback, dolphins

Season: June to October for orcas, other whales between March and May

Boats: A tour boat that carries 6 to 10, a fishing boat that carries 4 or 5, and an inflatable boat

Trips: One 10-hour trip daily at 8 a.m.

Fare: Adults, $260 (Canadian) plus tax; children 12 and younger, $100 plus tax. Reservations required. Charter trips for two or three days also available.

Departure: Trips leave from Port McNeill. Shuttle service is available from Vancouver International Airport or hotels in Vancouver.

Naturalist: Knowledgeable captain and staff serve as naturalists.

"We have encountered as many as 50 whales in one sighting and often enjoy a gracious display of their many different behaviors such as spyhopping, tail slapping and breaching," says Nicole Schubert, tour coordinator.

Ecosummer Expeditions

5640 Hollybridge Way, #130, Richmond, British Columbia, V7C 4N3 Canada
(800) 465-8884 or (604) 7484; Fax (604) 214-7485;
Web site www.ecosummer.com

Whales:	Orca, gray, minke
Season:	Late June to late September
Boats:	Six 2-person kayaks; 10 participants and 2 guides
Trips:	Seven-day trips paddling and camping along the Inside Passage off Vancouver Island.
Fare:	$895 (U.S.) per person. Reservations required.
Departure:	Trips start at Port McNeill.
Naturalist:	Guides are naturalists.

"Although we have operated sea kayak adventures since the 1970s, the concept is still new to many people, who may have visions of paddling in the small unstable kayaks typically used for river trips," says a spokesman.

"However, in actuality, we use very stable craft especially designed for ocean environments. These boats demand no previous experience, and all persons adapt very quickly to the paddling and sailing skill required."

Orca Watch, a land-based program, is also available. Write for information.

Founded in 1976, Ecosummer Expeditions began as an adventure company that promoted environmental education, working primarily with high school students. Founder Jim Allan was soon deluged with requests from adults who wanted activity-oriented, natural history trips, and so Ecosummer Expeditions evolved.

Ecosummer Expeditions

5640 Hollybridge Way, #130, Richmond, British Columbia, V7C 4N3 Canada
(800) 465-8884 or (604) 7484; Fax (604) 214-7485;
Web site www.ecosummer.com

Whales:	Orca
Season:	July through September
Boats:	Sea kayaks

Trips:	Three-, 4- and 7-day trips to a base camp in Johnstone Strait where participants camp and go kayaking among the whales.
Fare:	Fare ranges from $415 (U.S.) to $895 per person. Reservations required.
Departure:	Trips begin and end in Port McNeill.
Naturalist:	Guides are naturalists.

"Utilizing a well-appointed base camp environment, these trips offer itineraries for those interested in the magic of kayaking with orcas while enjoying all the comforts of home," says Steve Booth, expedition director.

Northern Lights Expeditions

P.O. Box 4289, Bellingham, WA 98227
(800) 754-7402 or (360) 734-6334; E-mail slim@seakayaking.com;
Web site www.seakayaking.com

Whales:	Orca, minke
Season:	June to September
Boats:	Kayaks for 13 participants and 3 guides
Trips:	Kayaking and camping for 6 days along the Inside Passage off Vancouver Island.
Fare:	$1,095 (U.S.) per person. Price includes food, kayak, and camping gear. Minimum age 16 for most trips. Reservations required.
Departure:	Trips leave from Port McNeill and Prince Rupert.
Naturalist:	Guides are naturalists.

"Participants have a chance to live on the shores of the whale's environment for a week," says founder and head guide David Arcese. "You can hear the whales passing in the night, close to the beach. You can paddle within a few feet of the whales because the kayaks are silent and slow-moving, thereby not causing anxiety among the whales."

The trips are intended for people who have no experience kayaking, and the pace is relaxed, he says.

Viking West Lodge & Charter

P.O. Box 113, Port McNeill, British Columbia, V0N 2R0 Canada
(250) 956-3431; E-mail vikingwest@capescott.net;
Web site www.iigi.com/os/bc/vwest/whale.htm

Whales:	Orca, minke, humpback, gray
Season:	Mid-June through October
Boats:	Two boats; a 36-foot twin diesel that carries up to 12 passengers, and a 16-foot Zodiac raft that carries four passengers
Trips:	One or two trips daily to Robson Bight area, leaving between 8 and 10 a.m. and returning by 1 to 3 p.m.
Fare:	$60 per person. Multi-day packages available with lodging on the boat. Write or call for details.
Departure:	From Port McNeill and Telegraph Cove.
Naturalist:	Skipper serves as naturalist.

The skipper, Dennis Richards, says, "Whale watching is the neatest thing on the water, except maybe swimming with them." Richards was the area's first full-time professional guide, and has been in the business since 1984. "On day charters," he says, "I cook fresh-caught crab or fish—it's dellcious," he says.

SOINTULA

WAYWARD WIND CHARTERS

P.O. Box 300, Sointula, British Columbia, V0N 3E0 Canada
(604) 973-6307

Whales:	Orca, sometimes minke
Season:	July through early October
Boats:	One 28-foot sailboat; 8 passengers
Trips:	One 8-hour trip daily, possibly to Robson Bight, a marine preserve set aside for orcas. Seafood luncheon and home-baked sweets served.
Fare:	Adults, $70 (Canadian); seniors and children 5 to 12, $45. Reservations advised. Waterfront log cottage available for accommodations.

Departure: Trips leave from Sointula, on Malcolm Island. Regular ferry service runs from Port McNeill to Sointula; the trip takes 30 minutes. Transportation from the ferry dock is provided, if necessary.

Naturalist: Skipper serves as naturalist on board.

John and Vilma Gamble say, "We feel our business is unique because of its personalized service. Depending on the group and time, a little fishing or sightseeing may be done." Wayward Wind's skipper has been sailing on the Pacific since the 1970s and gladly shares his extensive knowledge.

TELEGRAPH COVE

Raven Kayak Experiences

501 Harris, Bellingham, WA 98225
(206) 671-4528

Whales: Orca, minke, gray, harbor porpoise

Season: Mid-March through mid-October

Boats: Six 2-person kayaks

Trips: Several 1- to 8-day trips, kayaking and camping in the San Juan Islands, Knight Inlet or Barkley Sound. The Knight Inlet trip is the most popular.

Fare: Trips in the San Juan Islands range from $89 for one day to $449 for five days. Knight Inlet and Barkley Sound, both 8-day trips, cost $850. Meals prepared by a gourmet chef are part of the package. Reservations required.

Departure: Trips leave from Telegraph Cove. Transportation from Bellingham is provided.

Naturalist: Naturalist aboard.

"My guides and I are bridges to the natural world," says owner Jeff Albin. "We provide safe access to the wild places within and outside of us all. In these places, people learn much about themselves and their connection to the Earth."

The trip storyteller tells traditional tales about the origin of whales, tales from indigenous cultures in the area of Vancouver, and the naturalist provides whale etiquette.

Stubbs Island Charters Ltd.

P.O. Box 2-2, Telegraph Cove, British Columbia V0N 3J0 Canada
(250) 928-3185 or 928-3117; Fax (250) 928-3102; E-mail stubbs@island.net;
Web site www.stubbs-island.net

Whales:	Orca
Season:	June to mid-October
Boats:	Two 60-foot motor vessels
Trips:	Up to five trips daily, depending on the month. Call or write for times.
Fare:	$65 (Canadian) per person, with discounts for senior citizens and children. Reservations recommended.
Departure:	Trips leave from the end of the boardwalk in Telegraph Cove, south of Port McNeill.
Naturalist:	Knowledgeable skipper serves as naturalist.

Operating since 1980, Stubbs Island Charters were the first whale-watching company established in British Columbia. The vessels are Coast Guard certified and equipped with hydrophones to listen to the whale vocalizations.

TOFINO

Blue Moon Explorations

476 Blank Road, Sedro-Woolley, WA 98284
(800) 966-8806 or (360) 856-5622; E-mail bluemoon@xpressmail.net;
Web site www.home.cio.net/bluemoon

Whales:	Gray
Season:	August and September
Boats:	Eight 2-person kayaks
Trips:	Multiple 5-day trips to Vancouver Island, B.C. and Long Beach Peninsula. Participants camp. Some trips are for women only.
Fare:	$625 per person, which includes kayaks, accommodations and meals, safety equipment, and guides. Reservations required.
Departure:	Trips begin and end at Tofino, B.C.
Naturalist:	Naturalist aboard.

Owner Kathleen Grimbly says, "Blue Moon Explorations are designed to expand our awareness of the many intricate relationships in the web of life. Traveling by kayak, we experience the whales more intimately and less intrusively. Our trips are designed for people of all ages and abilities."

Jamie's Whaling Station

P.O. Box 129, Tofino, British Columbia, V0R 2Z0 Canada
(800) 667-9913 or (250) 725-3919; Fax (250) 725-2138;
E-mail jamies@island.net; Web site www.jamies.com

Whales:	Gray, orca, minke, humpback
Season:	February 15 to October 30
Boats:	Three rigid-hull inflatable Zodiacs; 12 passengers each; a 65-foot cabin cruiser, *Lady Selkirk*, 47 passengers; two cabin cruisers, carrying 12 passengers each; and a 65-foot glass-bottom boat
Trips:	Two to four trips a day. Zodiacs go on 2-hour trips at 9:30 a.m., noon and 3 p.m. Large boats go on 2- to 3-hour trips at 11 a.m. and 1:30 p.m. February 15 through April 30 and 3-hour trips May 1 through October 1.
Fare:	Zodiacs: adults, $50 (Canadian); students, $45; children ages 6 to 12, $35. Children under 6 not permitted on Zodiacs. Large boats: adults; $70; senior citizens, $65; children ages 6 to 12, $48; children 1 to 5, $20. Reservations advised. Packages offered with Whalers' Retreat Bed and Breakfast. Some trips also available with pick-up at hotels on the east coast of Vancouver Island. Call for information.
Departure:	Boats depart from Tofino's Whaling Wharf, 606 Campbell in Tofino.
Naturalist:	Knowledgeable skippers provide narration.

Watching whales off Vancouver Island's west coast in a rigid hull inflatable raft is "ideal for those who enjoy life in the fast wave," says president Jamie Bray.

"On our whale-watching cruises, you'll enjoy tall tales and local legends as we cruise past the islands and inlets that housed many a colorful character. Whale sightings guaranteed—whales you'll see or your next trip is free!

"Wild about wildlife? We've got more than whales to show you."

Remote Passages Marine Excursions

P.O. Box 624, Tofino, British Columbia, V0R 2Z0 Canada
(604) 725-3330; Fax (604) 725-3380

Whales:	Gray, orca, humpback, minke
Season:	March 1 to October 31
Boats:	Four rigid-hull inflatables; 12 passengers each; "cruiser" flotation suits, gloves, hats and rubber boots provided.
Trips:	Three 2-1/2-hour whale watch trips daily at 9 a.m., noon, and 3 p.m. A 6-1/2-hour trip that leaves early in the afternoon includes a visit to Hot Springs Cove. Sunset tours in summer.
Fare:	For whale watch trips, adults, $55 (Canadian); students, $50; children under 12, $38. The *Hot Springs Explorer* costs $80 for adults, $75 for students and $55 for children. Reservations advised.
Departure:	Trips leave from Meares Landing boathouse at Main and Wharf streets in Tofino.
Naturalist:	Naturalist aboard.

Remote Passages has been running programs since 1986. "We introduce you to the whales in their natural environment," says owner Don Travers. "We are respectful guests in the home of the grays, friendliest of the great whales." Also, a population of humpback whales appears to be establishing a summer presence off the coast near Tofino.

UCLUELET

Canadian Princess Resort

P.O. Box 939, Ucluelet, British Columbia, V0R 3A0 Canada
(800) 663-7090 or (604) 726-7771; Fax (604) 726-7121

Whales:	Gray and occasionally orca
Season:	March 1 to September 31
Boats:	Ten boats; 18 to 22 passengers each
Trips:	Two 3-hour trips daily at 9 a.m. and 1:30 p.m.

Fare: Adults, $39 (Canadian); children 12 and under, $25. Family and group rates. Rates higher on weekends. Reservations advised on weekdays, required on weekends. Accommodations available at the resort's center, a 235-foot ship, *Canadian Princess,* or on the shore.

Departure: Trips leave from Ucluelet Harbor.

Naturalist: No naturalist on board.

Lorena Ikle, service manager, says, "The mainstay of this resort and the reason we have so many return guests is our crew, who are the backbone of this operation. That is what makes us special. They really do care about the guests."

She adds, "The drive from Nanaimo to Ucluelet is very scenic, with lots of stops along the way. Traveling along the Pacific Rim Highway is breathtaking."

Subtidal Adventures

P.O. Box 78, Ucluelet, British Columbia, V0R 3A0 Canada
(250) 726-7336; Fax (250) 726-1292

Whales: Gray, humpback, orca

Season: March 1 to October 31

Boats: A 36-foot ex-rescue boat, *Dixie IV*, and a 24-foot rigid hull inflatable Zodiac; 24 passengers total

Trips: Two to four trips daily of different durations to various destinations in Barkley Sound to see the gray whales or off shore to see humpbacks and orcas.

Fare: Fares for gray whale trips in the spring are $40 (Canadian) for adults, $20 for children 6 to 12, and $10 for children under 6. For humpback or orca trips, $60, $40 and $30, respectively. Reservations advised. You may make them at the office at #1-1950 Peninsula Road in the West Ucluelet Mall.

Departure: Boats depart from Ucluelet Boat Basin on Vancouver Island.

Naturalist: Skipper serves as naturalist.

"We are the oldest charter boat company here and have tailored our cruises to provide the best possible experience to our guests," says owner Brian Congdon. "Whichever cruise you choose, we know you will go home with memories to last a lifetime."

VICTORIA

Great Pacific Adventures

P.O. Box 8173, Victoria, British Columbia, V8W 3R8 Canada
(250) 386-2277; Fax (250) 386-3370;
E-mail whales@greatpacificadventures.com;
Web site www.greatpacificadventures.com

Whales:	Orca, minke, humpback, gray
Season:	Year 'round, though May to September is peak season for whales
Boats:	Three rigid-hull inflatable boats; each carries12 passengers. Cruiser suits provided.
Trips:	From May to September, eight 3-hour trips at 9 a.m., 10 a.m., 10:30 a.m., 1 p.m., 2 p.m., 2:30 p.m., 5 p.m., and 5:30 p.m. From October to April, three 2-hour trips on demand, typically at 10:30 a.m., noon and 2:30 p.m.
Fare:	From May to September: Adults, $75 (Canadian) plus tax; children 16 and under, $45. From October to April: Adults, $55 plus tax; children 16 and under, $45. Reservations advised.
Departure:	Boats depart from pier near the booking office at 811 Wharf Street by the Tourist Information Center.
Naturalist:	Naturalist on board.

"Great Pacific Adventures works with a network of spotters to ensure a sighting on almost every trip," says Jane Victoria King, marketing director. "Each customer is catered to with assistance in suiting up. We supply sunscreen, and the full-length cruiser suits plus gloves on the cold days and towels on the wet days."

Orca Spirit Adventures

P.O. Box 5441, Station B, Victoria, British Columbia, V8R 6S4 Canada
(888) 672-6722 or (250) 383-8411; Fax (250) 383-4666;
E-mail whales@orcaspirit.com; Web site www.orcaspirit.com

Whales:	Orca, minke, humpback, gray
Season:	Year 'round
Boats:	The 45-foot *Orca Spirit*, which carries up to 40 passengers

Trips:	Three 3-hour trips daily at 9 a.m., 1 p.m. and 5 p.m.
Fare:	Adults, $79 (Canadian) plus tax; children under 16, $49 plus tax. Reservations required.
Departure:	Boat departs from the marina behind the Coast Victoria Harbourside Hotel at 146 Kingston Street.
Naturalist:	Three naturalists on board.

"The best time of year for whale watching and marine wildlife tours is April through October," say owners Nadene Inouye and John Douglas. "The *Orca Spirit* is one of the fastest whale-watching vessels in Victoria, which provides less travel time and more time to enjoy the surrounding wildlife. The boat also has a library of whale books and nature books and shows wildlife videos on board. Tours are suitable for all ages."

Seacoast Expeditions Ltd.

1655 Ash Road, Victoria, British Columbia, V8N 2T2 Canada
(800) 386-1525 or (250) 383-2254; Fax (250) 383-4383;
E-mail seacoast@islandnet.com; Web site www.islandnet.com/`seacoast

Whales:	Orca, minke
Season:	May 1 to October 30; highest frequency of sightings is during June and July
Boats:	Three rigid-hull inflatable boats; each carries 12 passengers. Full-length cruiser suits provided.
Trips:	Five 3-hour trips daily at 9 a.m., 10 a.m., 1 p.m., 2 p.m. and 5 p.m. May through September. One trip daily at 1 p.m. in March, April, and October.
Fare:	Adults, $79 (Canadian) plus tax; youths 13 to 17, $59; children under 12, $39. Guaranteed sightings cost $10 more per person. Reservations advised.
Departure:	Boats depart from Ocean Pointe Resort, 45 Songhees Road at the west end of the Johnson Street Bridge.
Naturalist:	Naturalist on board.

"Our naturalists have expertise on whales, dolphins, porpoises, birds, seals, and sea lions. Naturalists stimulate discussion, provide some commentary, and invite questions," says owner Alex Rhodes.

Spyhopper Whale Watching

950 Wharf Street, Victoria, British Columbia, V8W 1T3 Canada
(250) 388-6222; Fax (250) 388-6886;
Web site www.island.net.com/`spyhop

Whales:	Orca, humpback, minke, gray
Season:	Year 'round
Boats:	Two 27-foot, aluminum-hull inflatable boats; each carries 12 passengers
Trips:	Five 3-hour trips at 9 a.m., 10 a.m., 1 p.m., 2 p.m. and 5 p.m. during peak season (May through October) to see orcas. Marine wildlife tours, 2-hour trips to see grays, minkes and humpbacks are scheduled according to demand and weather conditions from November through April.
Fare:	Peak season: Adults, $75 (Canadian) plus tax; children ages 6 to 16, $45 plus tax. Off-season: Adults, $55 plus tax; children ages 6 to 16, $35 plus tax. Reservations advised.
Departure:	Boats depart from the Victoria Marine Adventure Center in downtown Victoria at 950 Wharf Street.
Naturalist:	Naturalist on board.

"Spyhopper Whale Watching prides itself in offering the highest percentage of whale sightings out of the Victoria area," says owner Bill McEwen. "Our aim is to provide our customers with an extraordinary experience that will be a memorable part of their trip."

VARIOUS DEPARTURE POINTS

Bluewater Adventures

#3-252 East First Street, North Vancouver, British Columbia, V7L 1B3 Canada
(604) 980-3800; Fax (604) 980-1800; E-mail blueh2o@istar.ca;
Web site www.home.istar.ca/`blueh2o

Whales:	Orca, gray, humpback, minke
Season:	April to October

Boats: Two boats, *Island Roamer,* a 68-foot ketch that carries 16 passengers, and *Snow Goose,* a 65-foot boat that carries 12 passengers. Participants live on board.

Trips: Five- to 11-day trips to the San Juan and Gulf Islands, the Queen Charlotte Islands, Johnstone Strait or southeast Alaska.

Fare: Sample fares: $900 (U.S.) per person for 5 days in the San Juan and Gulf Islands; $1,575 for 7 days in Johnstone Strait; $1,995 for 9 days in the Queen Charlotte Islands, and $2,450 for 10 days in southeast Alaska. Reservations required.

Departure: Trips leave from Port Hardy, Sandspit, Prince Rupert and Sidney, British Columbia or Petersburg and Sitka, Alaska, depending on the destination.

Naturalist: Naturalist aboard.

"*Island Roamer*'s crew has been running quality natural history and sailing adventures since 1973," a spokesman says. "We have operated cruises for many well-known educational institutions and were privileged to be chosen by World Wildlife of Canada to run a whale-watching trip for His Royal Highness Prince Philip.

"You can rely on our experienced crew to offer you the finest wildlife and wilderness adventure possible. Their knowledge of marine biology, whales, native Indian culture, birds, and ecology will make your trip interesting and educational."

MANITOBA

CHURCHILL

Churchill Nature Tours

P.O. Box 429, Erickson, Manitoba, R0J 0P0 Canada
(204) 636-2968; Fax (204) 636-2557; Web site www.churchillnaturetours.com

Whales:	Beluga whales and assorted seals
Season:	June 1 to August 30
Boats:	Aluminum boats or rigid-hull inflatable rafts; 10 to 30 passengers each; all Coast Guard certified
Trips:	Several multi-day tours of Manitoba each year include at least two boat trips for whale watching. Tours also include a half-day tundra tour.
Fare:	A 4-day tour of tundra, including whale watching, costs $695 (U.S.). Includes food, lodging, and guides. Reservations required.
Departure:	Participants fly to Churchill from Winnipeg.
Naturalist:	Naturalist accompanies tour.

"We are Manitoba's finest nature tour company and one of the only," says Daniel Weedon, owner and tour leader. "We have complete package tours—deluxe design."

Sea North Tours Ltd.

P.O. Box 222, Churchill, Manitoba, R0B 0E0 Canada
(204) 675-2195; Fax (204) 675-2198

Whales:	Beluga
Season:	June 25 to August 28
Boats:	Coast Guard-certified tour boats and inflatable boats, carrying from 10 to 30 passengers

Trips: Daily trips on Churchill River and Hudson Bay, weather and tides permitting. Trips last 2-1/2 or 4 hours.

Fare: Fares start at $49 (Canadian) for adults, $24.50 for children 12 and younger. Reservations advised. Most whale watching package tours to Churchill include Sea North's services.

Departure: Trips leave from 39 Franklin Street in center of Churchill.

Naturalist: Captain serves as naturalist.

Mike and Doreen Macri say, "Our boats are frequently surrounded by hundreds of belugas during a tour. All boats are hydrophone-equipped to listen to their incredible vocalizations."

NORTHWEST TERRITORIES

BAFFIN ISLAND

Atlantic Marine Wildlife Tours Ltd.

227 Wright Street, Fredericton, New Brunswick, E3B 2E3 Canada
(506) 459-7325; Fax (506) 453-3589; E-mail jelewis@unb.ca

Whales: Narwhal, bowhead, beluga

Season: May through August

Boats: The *Cape Islander*

Trips: Two 10-day trips by plane, sled, and snowmobile to Baffin Island in the Arctic Circle, with stops at Frobisher Bay, Pond Inlet, and Bylot Island. Also, one 10-day trip in August to view narwhals from a boat. Food and lodging in hotels and tents. Trips conclude in Ottawa.

Fare: $4,125 (U.S.) per person. Price includes airfare from Ottawa to Baffin Island, room, board, guides, tours, entertainment. Reservations required.

Departure: Trips leave from Ottawa.

Naturalist: Naturalist accompanies trip.

"The adjacent waters around Baffin Island and Bylot Island contain the richest profusion of marine mammals in the eastern Arctic including concentrations of narwhal, bowhead, and beluga whales," says Dr. Eugene Lewis, president of Atlantic Marine Wildlife Tours.

"There are also many harp, bearded, and ring seals along with wandering polar bears, arctic foxes, and migratory birds en route to their summer nesting grounds."

The inlets and waterways are still frozen in May and June, but there are twenty-four hours of daylight and the temperatures are above freezing. In July, the ice melts and by August, navigation by boat is possible.

Churchill Nature Tours

P.O. Box 429, Erickson, Manitoba, R0J 0P0 Canada
(204) 636-2968; Fax (204) 636-2557; Web site www.churchillnaturetours.com

Whales: Narwhal, bowhead, beluga

Season: June

Boats: No boats—camping on the ice floe edge where the open waters of Baffin Island meet the land-locked ice pack.

Trips: One 10-day trip in early June that includes touring, hotel stays, traveling by sled and 5 nights camping on the ice floe.

Fare: $4,125 (U.S.). Reservations required.

Departure: Trip begins and ends in Ottawa.

Naturalist: Naturalist accompanies tour.

In addition to whales, tour leader Daniel Weedon notes that participants on this "easy adventure" also may expect to see seals, polar bears, walrus, migratory birds and spectacular scenery.

INUVIK

Arctic Tour Company

P.O. Box 2021, Inuvik, Northwest Territories, X0E 0T0 Canada
(867) 777-4100; Fax (867) 777-2259

Whales:	Beluga
Season:	July and August
Boats:	Boats are sometimes used for tours; sometimes not.
Trips:	Several beluga-watching trips sold as add-ons to other tours of the Northwest Territories.
Fare:	$99 (Canadian) plus tax per person, which does not include the cost of the other tours. Write or send a Fax for more information. Reservations required.
Departure:	Tours leave from Inuvik.
Naturalist:	Guide is native Inuit.

The Arctic Tour Company is located in Inuvik, 150 miles north of the Arctic Circle. Owner Roger Gruben offers a variety of tours and services within the Western Arctic year 'round.

MUSEUMS, AQUARIUMS, AND SCIENCE CENTERS

BRITISH COLUMBIA

Vancouver Aquarium

P.O. Box 3232, Vancouver, British Columbia, V6B 3X8 Canada
(604) 685-3364 or 682-1118 (recording); Fax (604) 631-2529

Situated downtown in Stanley Park, the aquarium showcases aquatic life from the Arctic Ocean to the Amazon jungle, the tropical Pacific Ocean to British Columbia's own waters. Two orcas inhabit a four-million-litre re-creation of a west coast Gulf Islands habitat. Five belugas live in a similar-sized re- creation of Lancaster Sound, in the Canadian high Arctic. Training, research and feeding sessions with the whales occur throughout the day. Both exhibits have above- and underwater viewing and interpretive galleries with hands-on exhibits.

The aquarium is open 365 days a year, 9:30 a.m. to 7 p.m. in July and August and 10 a.m. to 5:30 p.m. the remainder of the year. Admission is $11.95 (Canadian) for adults, $10.55 for seniors and youths 13 to 18, $7.95 for children 4 to 12, and free to children 3 and younger. Group rates are available.

Whale Center

411 Campbell Street, P.O. Box 393, Tofino, British Columbia, V0R 2Z0 Canada
(250) 725-2132

The Maritime Museum displays artifacts from early native cultures, the first European explorers, traders, settlers, fishermen, and shipwrecks. The Whale Center, situated on the main floor, exhibits information, research developments, and artwork about living whales as well as whale bones, artifacts, and historical accounts from the early whaling era. The center offers guided tours, films, and lectures for groups; a marine charter reservation service; and a gift shop.

Hours are 9 a.m. to 8 p.m. daily from early March to October. Admission is free.

Wickaninnish Centre

Pacific Rim National Park, P.O. Box 280,
Ucluelet, British Columbia, V0R 3A0 Canada
(250) 726-7721

The Centre is situated at the surf line on the bay for which it was named. A window on the ocean side allows a view of whales, seals, and sea lions. Telescopes are available outside. Within the Centre are exhibits, displays, and films presented by heritage communicators.

Open daily 10:30 a.m. to 6 p.m. from mid-March to mid-October. Admission is free. During March and April, the communities along the west coast of Vancouver Island celebrate the spring migration of the gray whale with the Pacific Rim Whale Festival. Among the activities in the park are guided hikes, slide shows, movies, and lectures. For specific dates and more information, write Box 280, Ucluelet, British Columbia, V0R 3A0 Canada or phone (250) 726-7721.

MANITOBA

Manitoba Museum of Man & Nature

190 Rupert Avenue, Winnipeg, Manitoba, R3B 0N2 Canada
(204) 956-2830 or 943-3139 (recording)

This is an interpretive museum of the natural and human history of the province of Manitoba. Visitors walk through three-dimensional exhibits that depict the various areas of the province from the north to the south. The whale exhibit features the history of the beluga in Hudson Bay.

Victoria Day through Labor Day, open 10 a.m. to 6 p.m. The remainder of the year, closed Monday; open 10 a.m. to 4 p.m. Tuesday through Friday, 10 a.m. to 5 p.m. Saturday, Sunday, and holidays. Admission is $4.99 (Canadian) for adults, $3.99 for senior citizens 65 and older and youths 3 to 17. Free to children under 2. Group rates are available.

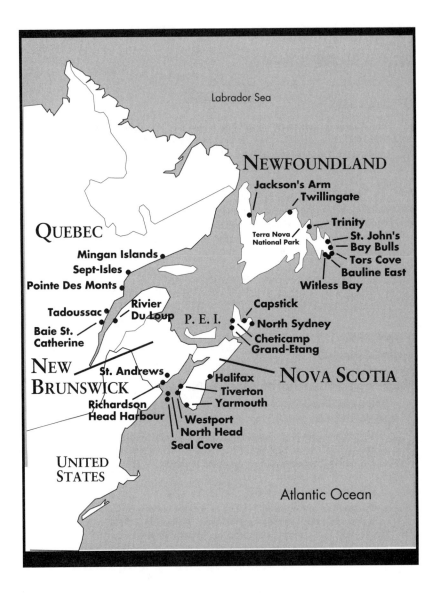

Labrador Sea

NEWFOUNDLAND

Jackson's Arm
Twillingate

QUEBEC

Terra Nova
National Park

Trinity
St. John's
Bay Bulls
Tors Cove
Bauline East
Witless Bay

Mingan Islands
Sept-Isles
Pointe Des Monts

Capstick

Tadoussac
Rivier
Du Loup
P. E. I.
North Sydney
Cheticamp
Grand-Etang

Baie St.
Catherine

NEW
BRUNSWICK
St. Andrews
Halifax
Tiverton
Yarmouth
NOVA SCOTIA

Richardson
Head Harbour
Westport
North Head
Seal Cove

UNITED
STATES

Atlantic Ocean

EASTERN CANADA

Visitors to Western Canada expect to see orcas and gray whales, but whale watchers who travel to the coastal areas of Eastern Canada may see blue whales, rare right whales, humpbacks, and belugas.

In Newfoundland, tour operators take people to see humpbacks, finbacks, minkes, and pilot whales from May through September. Those same species, plus right whales and the occasional sperm whale, can be seen off Nova Scotia and New Brunswick from June through September. Blue whales, along with finback, minke, and belugas, are found near the junction of the St. Lawrence Seaway and the Saguenay River, just off Quebec, from June through September.

As in Western Canada, whales may often be sighted from shore or encountered in the wild well beyond the reaches of the whale-watch tour operators.

TOURISM INFORMATION

MARITIME PROVINCES
Canada's Atlantic Coast Tourism Information
2695 Dutch Village Road, Suite 501, Halifax, B3L 4V2 Canada
(800) 565-2627

NEW BRUNSWICK
Tourism New Brunswick
P.O. Box 6000, Fredericton, New Brunswick, E3B 5H1 Canada
(800) 561-0123

NEWFOUNDLAND
Tourism Newfoundland
P.O. Box 8730, St. John's, Newfoundland, A1B 4K2 Canada
(800) 563-6353

NOVA SCOTIA
Nova Scotia Tourism
P.O. Box 130, Halifax, Nova Scotia B3J 2N7 Canada
(800) 341-6096

QUEBEC
Tourisme Quebec
C.P. 979, Montreal, Quebec H3C 2W3 Canada
(800) 363-7777

WHALE-WATCHING TRIPS

NEW BRUNSWICK

DEER ISLAND

Cline Marine

Box 18, Leonardville, Deer Island, New Brunswick, E0G 2G0 Canada
(800) 567-5880 for reservations or (506) 747-0114 for information;
Fax (506) 747-2287; E-mail clinemar@deerinet.nb.ca;
Web site www.deerinet.nb.ca/clinemarine

Whales:	Fin, minke, humpback, occasionally right
Season:	May through October
Boats:	One boat, the *M/V Cathy & Trevor*, which carries 60 passengers
Trips:	Two 3-1/2-hour trips daily at 9:30 a.m. and 1:30 p.m. mid-June through June 31 and in September. Four 2-1/2-hour trips daily at 9:30 a.m., 12:15 p.m., 3:15 p.m. and 6:15 p.m. July through August. Call for availability of trips in May, early June and October.
Fare:	Day trips cost $40 (Canadian) for adults; $20 for children 6 to 12; and free for children under 6 when accompanied by an adult. The sunset cruise costs $32 for adults and $16 for children. Reservations advised.
Departure:	Trips leave from Richardson Wharf on Deer Island.
Naturalist:	Captain R. Conrad Cline, a lifelong resident of Deer Island, narrates.

"Although we do not guarantee whales, Cline Marine is very proud of our 95-percent success rate," says Captain Cline. "Passengers can expect to see many varieties of seabirds, harbor porpoise and harbor seals in addition to three major species of whales. Come for an adventure on the sea with Cline Marine!"

GRAND MANAN ISLAND

Island Coast Boat Tours

P.O. Box 59, Castalia, Grand Manan Island, New Brunswick EOG 1L0 Canada
(506) 662-8181; Fax (506) 662-9904; E-mail icbt@nbnet.nb.ca;
We site www.angelfire.com/biz/icbt/

Whales:	Fin, humpback, minke, right and dolphins
Season:	July 1 through mid-September
Boats:	One 40-foot boat that carries 25 passengers
Trips:	Two 4-to-5-hour trips daily at 7:30 a.m. and noon
Fare:	Adults, $40 (Canadian); senior citizens, $35; children 12 and younger, $22. Reservations advised.
Departure:	Boat leaves from North Head Fisherman's Pier on Grand Manan Island, close to the ferry terminal.
Naturalist:	Captain with 24 years experience in the Bay of Fundy narrates trips.

Whale sightings are guaranteed or your money is refunded. The company has a 99 percent success rate, says Patricia Russell. A portion of each fare is donated to a whale conservation fund, which will be used for conservation efforts in the Bay of Fundy.

Sea-Land Adventures

P.O. Box 86, Castalia, Grand Manan Island, New Brunswick, E0G 1L0 Canada
(506) 662-8997

Whales:	North Atlantic right, fin, humpback
Season:	July to mid-September
Boats:	One schooner, *D'Sonoqua*; 20 passengers
Trips:	One 6-1/2-hour trip daily at 9:30 a.m.
Fare:	Adults, $75; children under 12 accompanied by a parent, $37. Lunch cooked aboard is included. Reservations advised.
Departure:	Boat leaves from North Head Wharf on Grand Manan Island, close to the ferry terminal.

Naturalist: Naturalist on board is marine biologist.

"Sea-Land Adventures' tours offer more than a search," owner James Bates says. "They offer an exciting sailing adventure aboard a traditionally rigged ocean-going schooner, expertly manned and equipped for your safety and comfort.

"Grand Manan is a special place—an island set aside in time and beauty. The magic of an island, the romance of sailing, and the thrill of marine life are all part of your holiday."

Sea Watch Tours

Seal Cove, Grand Manan Island, New Brunswick, E0G 3B0 Canada
(506) 662-8552

Whales:	Minke, fin, humpback, right
Season:	Mid-July to September 30
Boats:	One boat, *Sea Watcher*; 25 passengers
Trips:	Two 5-hour trips Monday through Saturday at 7:30 a.m. and 1:30 p.m. in peak season. Bring your own lunch.
Fare:	$44 (Canadian) per person. Reservations required.
Departure:	Boat leaves from Fishermens Wharf in Seal Cove on Grand Manan Island. Upon arriving in Seal Cove, turn down the road across from the two churches. Follow this road as it takes a sharp right, over to the last pier.
Naturalist:	Naturalist on board.

Peter Wilcox, owner of Sea Watch Tours, says, "There are very few North Atlantic right whales left, perhaps as few as 250. The Grand Manan Basin has become one of the most concentrated areas of right whales during the months of August and September, perhaps with 100 or more different animals.

"Their location is so predictable that it is almost certain that we will see them. In 15 years of whale watching, we have had only one day that we have not seen a whale."

ST. ANDREWS

Fundy Tide Runners

16 King Street, St. Andrews, New Brunswick, E0G 2X0 Canada
(506) 529-4481; E-mail welchdb@nbnet.nb.ca; Web site
www.townsearch.com/ftr.htm

Whales:	Fin, humpback, minke
Season:	May to October
Boats:	One boat, *Tide Runner I*, a 24-foot rigid-hulled Zodiac that carries 12 passengers. Flotation suit provided.
Trips:	Four 2-hour trips daily at 10 a.m., 1 p.m., 4 p.m., and 7 p.m. in season. Two trips daily in May and October. Call for details.
Fare:	Adults, $42.99 (Canadian); youths 5 to 13, $21.49. Trips may be too rigorous for expectant mothers, children under 5 or anyone in frail health. Reservations advised.
Departure:	Boat leaves from the wharf in St. Andrews.
Naturalist:	Trips are narrated.

In addition to the whale sightings, participants can expect to see eagles, porpoise, seals and marine birds. Also, narration provides unique insights into the region's history and culture, say owners Sandra and David Welch.

NEWFOUNDLAND

BAULINE EAST

Ocean Adventure Tours

Box 11, St. Michael's, A0A 4A0
(709) 334-3998

Whales:	Humpback, minke, fin
Season:	June, July, and August
Boats:	Two boats; the *Atlantic Iceberg* and the *Seabird*; 12 passengers each
Trips:	Nine 1- to 2-hour trips daily at 8 a.m., 9:30 a.m., 11 a.m., 12:30 p.m., 2 p.m., 3:30 p.m., 5 p.m., 6:30 p.m., and 8 p.m.
Fare:	Adults, $25 (Canadian); children under 12, $10. Reservations advised.
Departure:	Boats leave from East Bauline, just south of St. John's.
Naturalist:	Captain serves as naturalist.

Owner Jerry Colbert notes you will see majestic humpback, minke and fin whales, towering icebergs and many seabirds.

BAY BULLS

Gatherall's Puffin & Whale Watch

Northside Road, Bay Bulls, Newfoundland, A0A 1C0 Canada
(800) 419-4253 or (709) 334-2887; Fax (709) 334-2176

Whales:	Humpback, minke, fin
Season:	May to October
Boats:	Two boats; 30 and 40 passengers respectively
Trips:	Six 2-1/2-hour trips daily at 10 a.m., 11:30 a.m., 1 p.m., 2:30 p.m., 4 p.m. and 6:30 p.m.
Fare:	Adults, $28 (Canadian); children 6 to 12, $14.50; children 5 and younger, $7. Reservations advised.
Departure:	Departure from North Side Road in Bay Bulls on Route 10, about 30 minutes south of St. John's and 10 minutes from Route 1.
Naturalist:	Guide serves as naturalist.

"This is a guided boat tour—the guide is a well-qualified 'amateur' naturalist," says owner Rosemary Gatherall. "Our interpretative program will enrich and enhance the traveller's appreciation of nature, conservation, and the Newfoundland cultural heritage."

Gatherall's has been singled out for its whale watching and sensitivity to the marine environment and its wildlife, she notes. The Canadian government has named the Gatherall family "Canadian Tourism Ambassadors" for "outstanding hospitality to international visitors."

Mullowney's Puffin & Whale Tours

P.O. Box 1474, Station C, St. John's, Newfoundland, A1C 5N8 Canada
(709) 745-5061 or 334-3666; Fax (709) 334-3667

Whales:	Humpback, minke, fin
Season:	June, July, and August
Boats:	Two boats; 75 passengers each
Trips:	At least four 2-1/2-hour trips daily at 9 a.m., 11:30 a.m., 2:30 p.m. and 6 p.m.

Fare:	Adults, $25 (Canadian) plus tax; children under 12, $12. Reservations required.
Departure:	Boats leave from Bay Bulls, south of St. John's. A daily shuttle runs from major hotels in St. John's; reservations required.
Naturalist:	Tour guides narrate in English, French and German

Owner Greg Mullowney promises "an unforgettable experience" in the Witless Bay Ecological Reserve.

O'Brien's Bird and Whale Tours

150 Old Topsail Road, St. John's, Newfoundland, A1E 2B1 Canada
(709) 753-4850 or 334-2355; Fax (707) 753-3140

Whales:	Humpback, minke, fin
Season:	June, July, and August
Boats:	Two boats; 91 passengers each
Trips:	At least four 2-1/2-hour trips daily at 9:30 a.m., 11 a.m., 2 p.m. and 5 p.m.
Fare:	Adults, $28 (Canadian) plus tax; children 6 to 16, $15; 1 to 5, $10. Reservations required.
Departure:	Boats leave from Bay Bulls, Lower Road, south of St. John's. A daily shuttle runs from major hotels in St. John's; reservations required.
Naturalist:	Captain serves as naturalist.

"We are working on photographing whales that come to our area," says Captain Loyola O'Brien, president. Researchers identify the flukes of individual whales "so that we can put names on those that travel along the coast."

On board, the captain will sing for you and dance with you as part of the entire cultural experience.

JACKSON'S ARM

Pelley Inn

P.O. Box 428, Springdale, Newfoundland, A0J 1T0 Canada
(709) 673-3931; Fax (709) 673-3934;
Web site www.home.thezone.net/`godeep/whales

Whales:	Humpback, pilot
Season:	May 1 to September 30
Boats:	One; 6 to 10 passengers
Trips:	Whale watching included in week-long visit that starts at Pelley Inn in Springdale and moves to Little Harbour Deep Wilderness Lodge on White Bay. On shorter visits, whales may be seen during the 2-hour cruise to the lodge.
Fare:	$140 (Canadian) a day for single accommodations, $220 a day for double. $810 for single for 7 days, 6 nights; $1,620 for double. Reservations required.
Departure:	Boat leaves from Jackson's Arm, a 1-hour drive from Springdale.
Naturalist:	Naturalist available upon request.

Cyril R. Pelley says, "We own and operate the Pelley Inn, a twenty-two-room inn at Springdale, on the northeast coast of our island province. Our customers usually drive or fly via Deer Lake or Gander airport, where they are picked up by our limousine service and returned to the inn.

"However, our emphasis is on our new wilderness lodge in the great White Bay, just north of Springdale. A one-hour drive and a two-hour cruise get visitors to the lodge, where they may hike, fish, relax, or go on whale-watching or bird-watching excursions," Pelley says.

ST. JOHN'S

Adventure Tours of Newfoundland

P.O. Box 5395, St. John's, Newfoundland, A1C 5W2 Canada
(709) 726-5000; Fax (709) 722-3999

Whales:	Humpback, fin, minke
Season:	May 1 to October 1
Boats:	Several boats in prime whale-watching areas
Trips:	Four 2-hour trips daily at 10 a.m., 1 p.m., 4 p.m., and 7 p.m. The busiest day is Saturday.
Fare:	Adults, $30 (Canadian); $15 for children ages 4 to 14; free for children under 4. Reservations advised.
Departure:	Departure from Pier No. 7 in St. John's downtown harbor.
Naturalist:	Educational commentary provided.

Owner Charles Anonsen has provided whale-watching tours since 1976. He says that in addition to whale watching, his tours offer "listening to Newfoundland traditional music; meeting Bosun, our Newfoundland dog; sailing around North America's most easterly point; and enjoying the hospitality of the people from one of the oldest cities in North America, St. John's."

Wildland Tours

124 Water Street, P.O. Box 383, Station C, St. John's,
Newfoundland, A1C 5J9 Canada
(709) 722-3123; Fax (709) 722-3335; E-mail wildtour@nfld.com;
Web site www.wildlands.com

Whales:	Humpback, minke, fin
Season:	Early May to mid-August
Boats:	The best boats available to go where the whales are
Trips:	Tours of 7 days or longer to watch whales and view other wildlife in Newfoundland. June and July are the best months.
Fare:	Prices depend on package but start at $1,750 (Canadian). Packages include accommodations, boats, ground transportation and some meals. Reservations required.

Departure: All tours start in St. John's.

Naturalist: Biologist accompanies each trip.

David Snow, president, says, "Whales are a very special part of our product, but we do not ignore North America's largest puffin colony, the world's largest murre colonies, the world's largest storm petrel colonies, and huge collections of seabirds numbering in the millions visiting from the Arctic and Antarctic."

His company offers "probably the best marine wildlife-watching opportunities in the world, combined with small group travel. We are Canada's best-kept secret," Snow says. The Snows run a nature-oriented gallery in St. John's called Wild Things, where they sell their tapes of whale songs.

TERRA NOVA NATIONAL PARK

Ocean Watch Tours

Doryman Marine, Squid Tickle, Burnside, Newfoundland, A0G 1K0 Canada
(709) 533-6024

Whales: Humpback, minke

Season: Late June to Labor Day

Boats: One boat, the *Northern Fulmar*; 30 passengers

Trips: Four 3-hour trips daily at 9 a.m., 12:30 p.m., 3:30 p.m., and 7:30 p.m.

Fare: Adults, $28 (Canadian) plus tax for daytime trips, $22 for the evening trip. Children under 12, half price. Reservations advised.

Departure: Boat leaves from Salton's Marine Interpretation Center in Terra Nova National Park.

Naturalist: Internationally experienced naturalists.

Terra Nova, Canada's most easterly National Park, is famous for whales, icebergs, and bald eagles. You'll travel the ice-scoured fjords, through a maze of sheltered coves, looming cliffs, and narrow tickles, says a spokesman, who notes that "every trip is different in this world ruled by wind and tide."

TORS COVE

Molly Bawn's Great Island Whale & Puffin Tours

Site 1, Box 2, Tors Cove, Newfoundland, A0A 4A0 Canada
(709) 334-2621 or (709) 364-6440 or (709) 334-3395

Whales:	Humpback, minke, fin
Season:	June, July, and August
Boats:	One boat, the *Molly Bawn*; 12 passengers
Trips:	Nine 1-hour trips daily at 8:30 a.m., 10 a.m., 11:30 a.m., 1 p.m., 2:30 p.m., 4 p.m., 5:30 p.m., 7 p.m. and 8:30 p.m.
Fare:	Adults, $20 (Canadian) plus tax; children 6 to 16, $15; 1 to 5, $10. Reservations required.
Departure:	Boats leave from Tors Cove, south of St. John's. Reservations required.
Naturalist:	Captain serves as naturalist.

Tommy Reddick, the tour operator, and his family have been leading tours of the area since 1968. "Our memorable tours are highlighted by the antics of playful whales, and the colorful array of puffins, kittiwakes, murres and storm petrels."

TRINITY

Ocean Contact Ltd.

P.O. Box 10, Trinity, Newfoundland, A0C 2S0 Canada
(709) 464-3269; Fax (709) 464-3700; E-mail beamish@nf.sympatico.ca;
Web site www.nf.sympatico.ca/beamish

Whales:	Humpback, fin, minke, pilot
Season:	May to October
Boats:	One 26-foot rigid-hull inflatable; 6 to 12 passengers. Other power boats chartered as needed. Full-length flotation suits provided in inflatable.
Trips:	Half-day or whole-day excursions and multi-day expeditions offered.

Fare:	For excursions, rates start at $44 (Canadian) for adults, $32 for youths 13 to 15, $22.50 for children 4 to 12. Multi-day expedition rates start (for 3 days) at $423, $235, and $177 plus tax, respectively by age. Reservations advised. Hotel pack ages are available at the Village Inn. Write for details.
Departure:	Boats leave from Trinity, on Trinity Bay on the east coast.
Naturalist:	Naturalist on board.

Dr. Peter Beamish of Ocean Contact says, "Whale watching is free in Newfoundland! You can sit on a cliff near Trinity all day and watch whales. We, on the other hand, guide people into our spectacular marine environment so that the whales can watch us!"

Beamish, who has decades of experience, offers passengers the opportunity to make contact with whales by means of computer-driven acoustic signals. "The ensuing communications," he says, "may involve full breaches, tail or flipper slaps, exhalations, etc., and these are then easily predictable in time, allowing for spectacular photographs."

TWILLINGATE

Twillingate Island Boat Tours Ltd.

P.O. Box 127, Twillingate, Newfoundland, A0G 4M0 Canada
(800) 611-BERG or (709) 884-2242

Whales:	Humpback, fin, pilot, minke
Season:	Late May to late September
Boats:	One boat; up to 10 passengers
Trips:	Two 2-hour trips a day at 9:30 a.m. and 2 p.m. into Notre Dame Bay, on the "iceberg alley" route.
Fare:	Adults, $25 (Canadian); children, $12.50. Reservations advised.
Departure:	Boat leaves from Twillingate dock.
Naturalist:	No naturalist on board.

Owner Cecil G. Stockley says, "Whales swim around this island all year 'round on their migratory routes. Any place on this 15-mile-diameter island, whales can be seen a stone's throw away from the island's shore."

He adds that icebergs in all sizes and shapes "from peaked to pancake flat" usually appear in May, having taken two to three years to travel from Greenland, where the great ice packs break up and unleash their frozen landscape piece by piece into the southbound Labrador Current.

"As they pass by, the icebergs growl, rumble, and crackle like thunder. Sometimes they split in half or roll over. But mostly they just sail off into the sun to meet their fate—a final meltdown in the warmer waters off the Grand Banks."

WITLESS BAY

Murphy's Bird Island Boat Tours

P.O. Box 149, Puffin Cove, Witless Bay, Newfoundland, A0A 4K0 Canada
(709) 334-2002; Fax (709) 782-3232

Whales:	Humpback, fin, pilot, minke
Season:	Late May to late September
Boats:	One 53-foot boat; up to 50 passengers
Trips:	Four 2-1/2-hour trips a day at 10 a.m., 1 p.m., 4 p.m. and 7 p.m.
Fare:	Adults, $25 (Canadian); children, $15. Reservations advised.
Departure:	Boat leaves from Witless Bay, south of St. John's.
Naturalist:	Knowledgeable crew narrates trips.

Captain John W. Murphy notes that seabirds and whales often come into view just minutes after the boat leaves the dock.

NOVA SCOTIA

CAPSTICK

Captain Cox's Whale Watch

Bay St. Lawrence, Nova Scotia, B0E 1E0 Canada
(888) 346-5556 or (902) 383-2981;
Web site www.atlanticonline.ns.ca/captcox/indexhtml

Whales:	Finback, humpback, minke, pilot; rarely blue and beluga
Season:	June through October
Boats:	The *Northern Gannet*, a 35-foot Cape Island fishing boat; 34 passengers
Trips:	Three 2-1/2-hour trips daily in July and August at 10:30 a.m., 1:30 p.m. and 4:30 p.m.; fewer trips off season, according to demand.
Fare:	Adults, $25 (Canadian); senior citizens over 65, $22; children 13 to 16, $20, children under 12, $12; children under 6, free. Reservations advised.
Departure:	Trips leave from the Bay St. Lawrence Wharf, 2 kilometers past the Co-op Store on the left.
Naturalist:	Naturalist aboard.

Captain Dennis Cox and his wife, Lori Cox, operate out of Bay St. Lawrence on the northernmost tip of Cape Breton Island. Captain Cox is the most experienced whale-watch captain in Cape Breton Island, with an overall success rate of 96 percent. A lobster fisherman as well, Captain Cox also assists with a university research project on pilot whales.

"Our boat travels along the most isolated coast, and often there are sightings of nesting birds, fox, moose, bear and deer, as well as whales out on the water," he says.

CHETICAMP

Whale Cruisers (Cheticamp) Ltd.

P.O. Box 183, Cheticamp, Nova Scotia, B0E 1H0 Canada
(800) 813-3376 or (902) 224-3376; Fax (902) 224-1166;
Web site www.whalecruises.com

Whales:	Fin, minke, pilot
Season:	Mid-May to mid-October
Boats:	Two boats; 30 passengers each
Trips:	Two trips daily at 9 a.m. and 6 p.m. daily in May and June; three trips daily from July to August 14, at 9 a.m., 1 p.m. and 6 p.m.; three trips daily from August 15 through September 15, at 9 a.m., 1 p.m. and 5 p.m. From September 15 to October 15, two trips daily, at 10 a.m. and 4 p.m. All trips last about 3 hours.
Fare:	$25 (Canadian) per person. Reservations advised.
Departure:	Boats leave from Government Wharf at Cheticamp Harbour, opposite the large stone church.
Naturalist:	Experienced narrators aboard.

"We were the first whale-watch tour operation in Nova Scotia," says owner Poirier Calixte. "We never guarantee whales, but our success rate is over 90 percent. Also, the coastline is breathtakingly beautiful. From the water, we see Cabot Trail and the coastline of Cape Breton Highlands National Park."

TIVERTON

Ocean Explorations

Box 719, Tiverton, Long Island, Nova Scotia, B0V 1G0 Canada
(902) 839-2417; Fax (902) 839-2182; E-mail oceanexp@atcon.com;
Web site www.valleyweb.com/oceanexplorations

Whales:	Humpback, minke, right, finback
Season:	Mid-June through October

Boats:	Two Zodiac rigid-hull inflatable rafts; 6 to 12 passengers each
Trips:	Usually two half-day trips, at 8:30 a.m. and 1:30 p.m.; sometimes a third trip at 4:30 p.m.
Fare:	Adults, $45; teens, $25; children under 13, $20. Family and group rates available. Reservations advised.
Departure:	Trips leave from Gallery-by-the-Sea, an art and gift shop owned by the tour operator, at the main wharf in Tiverton, just 100 yards from the ferry wharf.
Naturalist:	Narration by owner Tom Goodwin, a marine biologist.

"We're the only whale tour in Nova Scotia owned and operated by a fully qualified marine biologist," says Tom Goodwin. "We emphasize education, and our passengers are invited to participate in various research efforts." Goodwin also operates a bed and breakfast, and he has a whale-watch video for sale. Write for information.

Pirate's Cove Whale Cruises

Tiverton, Long Island, Nova Scotia, B0V 1G0 Canada
(888) 480-0004 or (902) 839-2242; Fax (902) 829-2271;
E-mail pcove@clan.tartannet.ns.ca; Web site www.tartannet.ns.ca/pcove/htm/

Whales:	Humpback, fin, minke, right, dolphins
Season:	June through September
Boats:	Two boats, the 34-foot *M/V Todd and Cherida* that carries 20 passengers, and the 42-foot *M/V Fundy Cruiser*, 40 passengers
Trips:	Two 4-hour cruises daily, at 8 a.m. and 1 p.m. Occasional sunset cruise at 4:15 p.m.
Fare:	Adults, $35 (Canadian); teens, $27; children 6 through 12, $17.50; 5 and under, free. Ten percent discount for senior citizens and groups. Reservations required.
Departure:	Trips leave from Tiverton, on the tip of Long Island.
Naturalist:	Crew narrates trips.

The Sollows family owns and operates Pirate's Cove Whale Cruises. "Sighting success on our cruises is very high. In addition to whales, you will see seals and various seabirds—and we'll give you a raincheck if for some reason no whales are found."

226

WESTPORT

Brier Island Whale and Seabird Cruises, Ltd.

Westport, Brier Island, Nova Scotia, B0V 1H0 Canada
(902) 839-2995

Whales:	Humpback, fin, minke, pilot, right
Season:	June to October
Boats:	Two boats; the 45-foot *Cetacean Venture* and the 52-foot *Cetacean Quest*; up to 50 passengers each
Trips:	Four 4-hour trips a day at 8:30 a.m., 10:30 a.m., 1:30 p.m. and 3:30 p.m., with sunset trips sometimes available. Weekends are busiest.
Fare:	$37 (Canadian) per person. Charter, group, and family rates available. Reservations recommended.
Departure:	Departure from Westport, on Brier Island, at the southwestern end of Nova Scotia.
Naturalist:	Field researcher or naturalists from the Brier Island Research Division accompanies each trip.

Harold Graham, owner and operator, says the whale-watching trips are unusual in that the whales are normally close to the island and the four-hour trips are especially convenient.

"Brier Island is located at the southwestern tip of Nova Scotia. Highly saline marine water flows into the Bay of Fundy along the Nova Scotia coast, bringing large numbers of zooplankton. Plankton and fish productivity is enhanced by the nutrients brought to the surface by the strong tidal currents, which average 25 feet or more. Local tide rips and eddies concentrate plankton; these, in turn, attract large schools of herring and mackerel which the whales, dolphins, and seabirds feed on."

QUEBEC

MINGAN ISLANDS

Mingan Island Cetacean Study

760 B De L'epee, Outremont, Quebec, H2V3T9 Canada
(514) 948-3669; Fax (514) 948-1131; E-mail micshipolari@videotron.ca;
Web site www.rorqual.com

Whales:	Blue, humpback, fin, minke, orca
Season:	June to October
Boats:	Several 24-foot rigid-hull inflatables that carry 8 passengers each
Trips:	Several 3- to 10-day sessions with the Mingan Island Cetacean Study, a nonprofit research group in the Gulf of St. Lawrence. Participants live in motels and B&Bs, assisting research scientists out on the water with their work. Limited number of day trips on the St. Lawrence River for 35 to 40 passengers from late June to late October.
Fare:	Extended trips from $640 to $1,979 (Canadian) per person. Day trip: adults, $65; students, $55; groups of four or more, $55 a person. Reservations required.
Departure:	Most trips depart from Longue Pointe, the gateway to the Mingan Islands, east of Sept-Iles. MICS representatives will meet participants who arrive by air at Sept-Iles.
Naturalist:	Naturalists are scientists with the research group.

MICS is the first organization in the world to have carried out long-term studies of the blue whale. Through photo-identification techniques developed by MICS, a catalog of more than 325 blue whales now exists for the northwest Atlantic.

Director Richard Sears says, "Our research sessions offer the public the opportunity to get away to the solitude of the sea and immerse themselves in an educational adventure."

POINTE DES MONTS

Le Gite du Phare de Pointe-des-Monts

1684 Joliet Boulevard, Baie Comeau, Quebec, G5C 1P8 Canada
(418) 939-2332 in summer or (418) 589-8408 in winter

Whales: Blue, humpback, fin, minke

Season: June 1 to September 10

Boats: A wooden fishing boat refitted for whale watching that carries 10 people

Trips: One 2-hour trip on the St. Lawrence River on weekdays, two 2-hour trips each Saturday and Sunday. Departure times depend on the tides.

Fare: Adults, $20 (Canadian); children under 12, $10. Reservations required. Lodge and chalets available; write for information.

Departure: Boats leave from Pointe-des-Monts in Trinity Bay.

Naturalist: Guide serves as naturalist.

Owner Jean Louis Frenette teaches wildlife management at the Baie-Comeau College. He says that Pointe-des-Monts is a perfect place for Americans to practice their French, though we try to communicate in English as best we can as Pointe-des-Monts is a place Americans will certainly love. Frenette notes, "You will see and hear the whales from your bedroom, as the sea is very deep right next to our shoreline."

Frenette's lodge is a restored 1830 lighthouse that he rents from the government.

RIVIERE DU LOUP

Croisieres AML

124, rue Saint-Pierre, Quebec City, Quebec, G1K 4A7 Canada
(800) 563-4643 or (418) 692-2634; Fax (418) 692-0845

Whales: Blue, humpback, beluga, minke, fin

Season: End of May to October 15

Boats:	The *Cavalier Grand des Mers*, which carries 165 passengers
Trips:	Three 3-1/2-hour trips daily at 9 a.m., 1 p.m., and 5 p.m.
Fare:	Adults, $35 (Canadian) plus tax; senior citizens, $31.95; children 6 to 12, $15; 5 and under, free. Reservations advised.
Departure:	Trips leave from the marina in Riviere du Loup.
Naturalist:	Experienced narrators on board.

"Our guides will help you discover the St. Lawrence River, this unique whale refuge," says a spokeswoman.

TADOUSSAC

Compagnie de la Baie de Tadoussac

9145 Bord-de-l'eau, Tadoussac, Quebec, G0T 2A0 Canada
(800) 757-4548 or (418) 235-4548; Fax (418) 235-4491

Whales:	Fin, minke, beluga, some blue
Season:	May 1 to November 15 (August and September are the best months)
Boats:	Eight rigid-hull inflatable rafts; 10 to 24 passengers each. Cruise suits provided.
Trips:	Three 3-hour trips a day on the St. Lawrence River at 8:30 a.m., 12:30 p.m. and 4 p.m. Special trips at 5 a.m.
Fare:	$34 (Canadian) per person. Ten percent discount for groups and students. Reservations advised.
Departure:	Boats leave from Tadoussac.
Naturalist:	Bilingual naturalist on board.

"We use inflatable boats, a smaller boat, closer to the marine environment and with smaller groups aboard. We offer a more intimate experience," says a staff member.

Famille DuFour Hotel Tadoussac

Summer: 165 Bord-de-l'Eau, Tadoussac, Quebec, G0T 2A0 Canada
(800) 463-5250 or (418) 235-4421; Fax (418) 235-4607

Winter: C.P. 490, Beaupre, Quebec, G0A 1E0 Canada

Whales:	Beluga, blue, humpback
Season:	May 13 to October 16
Boats:	Two boats, the historic 130-foot schooner *Marie-Clarisse* in Quebec City and the *Famille DuFour*; 100 and 450 passengers respectively
Trips:	Three 3-hour trips on the St. Lawrence River daily at 9:30 a.m., 1:30 p.m., and 4:45 p.m.; plus one trip on the Saguenay River at noon. Trips also available on a rigid-hull Zodiac at 8:30 a.m., noon, and 3 p.m. daily.
Fare:	Adults, $30 (Canadian); children, $15. Group rates available. Reservations required. Packages available at Hotel Tadoussac and other Famille DuFour properties. Write for information.
Departure:	Departure from Hotel Tadoussac.
Naturalist:	Naturalist on board.

Tadoussac is situated at the confluence of the freshwater Saguenay River and the saltwater St. Lawrence River. For this "whale sightseeing safari," owner Alain DuFour says, "Bring along your cameras and experience the thrill of a fascinating encounter with these giant nomads.

"Every summer, the whales return to the very rich and fertile waters of the St. Lawrence. After having given birth to their young in the waters of warmer climes during the winter, they find here the great quantities of food they must have."

TADOUSSAC AND BAIE ST. CATHERINE

Croisieres AML

124, rue Saint-Pierre, Quebec City, Quebec, G1K 4A7 Canada
(800) 563-4643 or (418) 692-2634; Fax (418) 692-0845

Whales:	Blue, humpback, beluga, minke, fin
Season:	End of May to October 15
Boats:	The *Cavalier Grand Fleuve*, which carries 500 passengers and several rigid-hull Zodiacs
Trips:	The *Cavalier Grand Fleuve* makes four 3-hour trips on the St. Lawrence River daily at 10 a.m., 1 p.m., 2:30 p.m., and 4:15 p.m. Trips include a visit on the Saguenay River. Zodiacs make four 3-hour trips daily at 6:30 a.m., 10 a.m., 1:15 p.m. and 4:30 p.m.
Fare:	On the big boat: Adults, $32 (Canadian) plus tax; senior citizens, $28.95; children 6 to 12, $15; 5 and under, free. On the Zodiacs: $35 plus tax for adults and $20 for children 6 to 12. Reservations advised.
Departure:	Trips leave from the village wharves in Tadoussac and Baie St. Catherine.
Naturalist:	Experienced narrators on board.

"Our guides will help you discover the St. Lawrence River, this unique whale refuge," says a spokeswoman.

MUSEUMS, AQUARIUMS, AND SCIENCE CENTERS

Marine Interpretation Centre

Terra Nova National Park, Glovertown, Newfoundland, A0G 2L0 Canada
(709) 533-2801; Fax (709) 533-2706

Overlooking picturesque Newman Sound, a large saltwater inlet, the Marine Interpretation Centre features aquariums, interactive computer displays, murals, videos, a jellyfish tank and a touch tank.

The Centre is open from 9 a.m. to 9 p.m. daily from May to October. Reduced hours are in effect before late June and after Labor Day. Admission is included in the park entry fee, which ranges from $6.50 to $22.50 per day per family depending on the time of year. Individual rates range from $3.25 per day to $12.25 per day.

Ocean Sciences Centre

Memorial University of Newfoundland
St. John's, Newfoundland, A1C 5S7 Canada
(709) 737-3706; Fax (709) 737-3220

Situated in a building designed to resemble the internal anatomy of a sea anemone, the center is a research unit of the Science Faculty of Memorial University. The focus of study is cold oceans. Guides offer hour-long tours of the research facility.

Visitors meet a wide variety of fish, crabs, lobsters, sea stars, anemones and other sea creatures in the aquaria and touch tank in the Discovery Room. You will also meet the Centre's family of harbour seals. Other sights include special videos and exhibits, a display of diving gear and an energy recompression chamber.

Tours are available every half hour from 10 a.m. to 5 p.m., seven days a week from mid-June to early September. Admission is $4.50 (Canadian) for adults, $3.50 for senior citizens and students, and free to children under 6. Group rates available if booked in advance.

NOVA SCOTIA

Nova Scotia Museum of Natural History

1747 Summer Street, Halifax, Nova Scotia, B3H 3A6 Canada
(902) 424-7353 or 424-6099 (recording); Fax (902) 424-0560

An Aquatic Environments gallery features freshwater and saltwater exhibits with specimens or models of Nova Scotia seaweeds, invertebrates, amphibians, reptiles, fish, and mammals. Among these are the skeleton of a pilot whale and life-sized models of sharks and a 48-foot sei whale.

From June 1 to October 15, the museum is open 9:30 a.m. to 5:30 p.m. daily except Wednesday, when it is open 9:30 a.m. to 8 p.m., and Sunday, when the hours are 1 p.m. to 5:30 p.m. From October 16 to May 31, the museum is closed on Monday and closes at 5 p.m. Sunday, Tuesday, Thursday, Friday, and Saturday.

Admission is $3.50 for adults, $3 for senior citizens, $1 for children 6 to 17 and free for children 5 and younger.

QUEBEC

The Interpretative Center of Marine Mammals

108 rue de la Cale-seche, Tadoussac, Quebec, G0T 2A0 Canada
(418) 235-4701

Using exhibits, an aquarium, marine mammal skeletons, a model of a 32-foot fin whale, posters, videos, and slide shows, the center teaches about whales and their marine environment. A movie features the endangered beluga whales of the St. Lawrence River.

The center is associated with the Group of Research and Education on the Marine Environment, a nonprofit organization dedicated to preserving the marine environment and educating the public.

The center is situated near the marina in Tadoussac. Hours are 9 a.m. to 8 p.m. from June through mid-October. Admission is $5.50 (Canadian) for adults and $3 per child, with family rates.

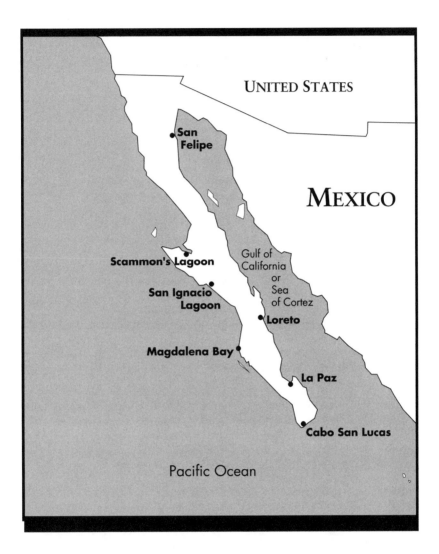

UNITED STATES

San
Felipe

MEXICO

Scammon's Lagoon

Gulf of
California
or
Sea
of Cortez

San Ignacio
Lagoon

Loreto

Magdalena Bay

La Paz

Cabo San Lucas

Pacific Ocean

MEXICO

Those photographs that you've seen of exhilarated whale watchers leaning out of tiny boats to pet gray whales were taken in the lagoons off Baja California, in Mexico. Every year the grays migrate south from the Bering and Chukchi seas, supporting a flourishing whale-watch industry along the entire Pacific Coast of the United States. Once in the calm, warm waters of Mexico, the whales mate and give birth, and people watch.

Aluminum skiffs, Zodiac rafts, and sea kayaks now dot Scammon's Lagoon, San Ignacio Lagoon, and Magdalena Bay in February, March, and part of April. On the other side of the peninsula, in the Sea of Cortez, boats go forth in March and April to see blue, humpback, fin, and pilot whales.

As it's unlikely that anyone would go to Baja California by chance—it's difficult to reach, though well worth the trouble—most whale-watch trips to the area are a week long. Among the groups sponsoring the trips are commercial tour operators; research organizations and scientific institutions, most of which travel by boat; and adventure outfitters, who offer kayaking and camping.

The sponsoring organizations are primarily based in the United States and Canada. Therefore, the listings in this chapter are organized by destination rather than by departure point. Separate index listings are given for destinations and departure points. Should you find yourself in Baja under other circumstances, you will be able to find a fisherman who will happily take you out in a boat for the afternoon to see the whales. By all means, go.

WHALE-WATCHING TRIPS

MEXICO

BAJA PENINSULA, EAST AND WEST COASTS

Baja Expeditions

2625 Garnet Avenue, San Diego, CA 92109
(800) 843-6967 or (619) 581-3311, Fax (619) 581-6542;
E-mail travel@bajaex.com; Web site www.bajaex.com

Whales: Gray, blue, humpback, finback

Season: Mid-January through mid-March

Boats: The 80-foot *Don Jose*, which holds 14 passengers in 7 state rooms. Participants live aboard. Whale watching from boats and skiffs.

Trips: Eight 8-day trips that combine a visit to Magdalena Bay with a trip around Cabo San Lucas to the Sea of Cortez, with a stop at Cabo Pulmo and Espiritu Santo Island. Trips conclude in either La Paz or Magdalena Bay.

Fare: $1,695 per person. Price includes land arrangements, accommodations, meals, beverages, and most related trip equipment. Airfare, tips, and airport taxes are not included.

Departure: Trips leave from La Paz and Magdalena Bay, with bus transportation to the boat.

Naturalist: Naturalist accompanies all trips.

This itinerary combines two days in Magdalena Bay with a trip around the tip of Baja to view humpback whales and others migrating south or to the Sea of Cortez.

Baja Expeditions made its first trip in 1974, inspired by John Steinbeck's "Log from the Sea of Cortez." Founder Tim Means notes that the company is the largest and oldest outfitter of natural history and adventure travel in Mexico.

Linblad Special Expeditions

720 Fifth Avenue, New York, NY 10019
(212) 765-7740, Fax (212) 265-3770; E-mail explore@specialexpeditions.com;
Web site www.expeditions.com

Whales:	Gray, humpback, fin
Season:	December through April
Boats:	The *M/V Sea Lion* and the *M/V Sea Bird*. Each carries 70 passengers. Participants live aboard. Whale watching from the ship and Zodiacs.
Trips:	Three- and 9-day trips to Magdalena Bay and among the islands in the Sea of Cortez, including Islas Los Islotes, Espiritu Santo, and Isla Santa Catalina. Trips conclude in Phoenix, Arizona.
Fare:	From $2,100 to $4,190, depending on accommodations. Fares do not include air transportation or tips.
Departure:	Trips leave from La Paz.
Naturalist:	Naturalists accompany all trips.

Linblad Special Expeditions' voyages travel with top naturalists who know the region intimately and are experts on flora and fauna. Each itinerary offers several whale-watching opportunities in Magdalena Bay, and the use of the Zodiac landing craft permits close-up views. Hiking on islands in the Sea of Cortez and snorkeling at coral reefs complete the experience.

Natural Habitat Adventures

2945 Center Green Court, Suite H, Boulder, CO 80301
(800) 543-8917 or (303) 449-3711; Fax (303) 449-3712

Whales:	Gray, blue, common and bottlenose dolphin
Season:	January through March
Boats:	The 80-foot *Don Jose*, which sleeps 14, and the 152-foot *Sea Bird* and the *Sea Lion*, which each carry 70 passengers. Participants live aboard. Whale watching from Zodiacs.
Trips:	Eight- and 9-day trips to Magdalena Bay and the Sea of Cortez, with visits at Espiritu Santo Island and other stops.
Fare:	From $1,695 to $5,390, depending on the boat and class of cabin. Round-trip airfare from Phoenix is included in the 9-day trip; airfare to and from La Paz for the 8-day trip is not. Meals and guide fees are included for both trips.

Departure: The 8-day trips begin and end in La Paz, Mexico. The 9-day trips begin and end in Phoenix.

Naturalist: Naturalists aboard.

Ben Bressler, director of Natural Habitat Adventures, says, "We take adventurers, photographers, and animal enthusiasts of all ages to visit some of the most incredible animals on the face of the Earth. We are committed to the idea that it is far better to see the animals as they live, wild and free, in their own natural environment."

Oceanic Society Expeditions

Fort Mason Center, Building E, San Francisco, CA 94123
(800) 326-7491 or (415) 441-1106, Fax (415) 474-3395;
Web site www.oceanic-society.org

Whales: Blue, fin, gray, humpback, sperm, minke, orca, several species of dolphin

Season: Mid-February through early April

Boats: The 88-foot *Spirit of Adventure*, with 14 cabins for 28 passengers and staff. Participants live on board. Whale watching from small skiffs.

Trips: A 12-day trip with stops at San Benito Islands, San Ignacio Lagoon, Magdalena Bay, Cabo San Lucas, Los Islotes Island, Santa Catalina Island, and San Jose Island. Trip concludes in Cabo San Lucas.

Fare: $2,295 per person. Price does not include airfare or transfers.

Departure: Trips leave from San Diego.

Naturalist: Experienced naturalists affiliated with Oceanic Society Expeditions accompany all trips.

"Our movement from temperate to tropical waters makes this one of the richest and most varied expeditions possible," notes Oceanic Society Expeditions. Slide shows and informal lectures are held each evening on board, and assorted optional activities are available each day. Oceanic Society Expeditions has conducted nature study tours since 1972.

Smithsonian Study Tours Travel Program

The Smithsonian Associates, 1100 Jefferson Drive S.W.,
Washington, D.C. 20560
(202) 357-4700

Whales:	Finback, blue
Season:	February
Boats:	The *M/V Sea Lion*; private baths, outside cabins with lower berths and air conditioning, with accommodations for up to 65 people. Participants live aboard.
Trips:	One 7-day trip in the Sea of Cortez, with a stop at Magdalena Bay, a breeding and calving area for gray whales.
Fare:	$2,790 to $3,880, depending on cabin location. Price includes meals, accommodations, transfers, and services of study leader and naturalists.
Departure:	Trips leave from and return to Phoenix, Arizona.
Naturalist:	Smithsonian study leader accompanies the trip.

The Smithsonian Institution sponsors numerous study tours. The Baja Whale Watch trip features whale watching, bird watching, walks on the beaches, and lectures on the islands, the flora and fauna.

MAGDALENA BAY

Baja Expeditions

2625 Garnet Avenue, San Diego, CA 92109
(800) 843-6967 or (619) 581-3311, Fax (619) 581-6542;
E-mail travel@bajaex.com; Web site www.bajaex.com

Whales:	Gray
Season:	January, February, and March
Boats:	The 80-foot *Don Jose* accommodates 14 passengers in 7 state-rooms. Participants live aboard on all trips. Whale watching from boat and from small skiffs.
Trips:	Several 4- and 7-day trips to Magdalena Bay. Trips conclude in La Paz.

Fare: From $995 to $1,895 per person. Price includes land arrangements, accommodations, meals, beverages, and most related trip equipment. Airfare, tips, and airport taxes are not included.

Departure: Trips leave from La Paz, with bus transportation to the boat.

Naturalist: Naturalist accompanies all trips.

"Magdalena Bay is formed by a long, low barrier island barely half a mile wide but 40 miles long," notes a spokesman for Baja Expeditions. "The Pacific shore is wild and windswept, the remains of boats and whales, large and small, can be found buried in the beach or half covered by a dune. On the eastern shore, mangrove-lined estuaries are the winter home of thousands of migratory birds."

Baja Expeditions made its first trip in 1974, in a rented fishing boat with a well-thumbed copy of John Steinbeck's "Log from the Sea of Cortez" aboard. Tim Means, founder, notes that today the company is the largest and oldest outfitter of natural history and adventure travel in Mexico.

Baja Expeditions

2625 Garnet Avenue, San Diego, CA 92109
(800) 843-6967 or (619) 581-3311, Fax (619) 581-6542;
E-mail travel@bajaex.com; Web site www.bajaex.com

Whales: Gray

Season: January through March

Boats: Sea kayaks. Participants camp, except for the first and last nights, which are spent in a hotel. Skiffs carry the camping supplies throughout the trip.

Trips: Weekly departures for 7-day trips to Magdalena Bay. Novice paddlers welcome. Trips conclude in La Paz.

Fare: $1,050 per person. Price includes land arrangements, accommodations, meals, beverages, hotels scheduled in itinerary, and all specialized equipment, including tents, kayaking gear, cookware, and utensils. Sleeping bags may be rented. Airfare, gratuities, and airport taxes are not included.

Departure: Trips leave from La Paz, with bus transportation to Magdalena Bay.

Naturalist: Naturalist accompanies all trips.

"Kayaks allow us to observe at close quarters the fascinating behaviors of the gray whale as we explore the lagoon and mangrove estuaries," says a spokesman at Baja Expeditions. Skiffs are used to carry camping equipment and to view whales.

SAN IGNACIO LAGOON

Baja Discovery

P.O. Box 152527, San Diego, CA 92115
(800) 829-BAJA or (619) 262-0700

Whales:	Gray
Season:	January through March
Boats:	Whale watching from 22-foot fiberglass skiffs
Trips:	Several 5, 6, and 8-day trips to Baja Discovery's "safari style" camp on an island in San Ignacio Lagoon. Participants go out in skiffs twice a day. Full meal service provided in the dining tent. Trips restricted to 20 participants.
Fare:	$995 to $1,700 per person, which includes round-trip charter flight to San Ignacio, meals, accommodations, equipment, guides, and one night in a hotel. Custom itineraries available.
Departure:	Trips begin and end in San Diego.
Naturalist:	Naturalist aboard.

"The Baja Discovery adventure focuses on one of the most spectacular wildlife phenomena in the world—the annual gathering of thousands of gray whales in the shallow, warm waters of the Baja lagoons," says owner Karen Ivey. "Our land-based shore camp on an inner lagoon lies adjacent to the largest concentration of whales in Laguna San Ignacio."

Baja Discovery has operated the environmentally conscious camp since 1966.

Baja Expeditions

2625 Garnet Avenue, San Diego, CA 92109
(800) 843-6967 or (619) 581-3311, Fax (619) 581 6542;
E-mail travel@bajaex.com; Web site www.bajaex.com

Whales:	Gray
Season:	January through March
Boats:	Whale watching from skiffs
Trips:	Several 5-day trips to Baja Expeditions' "safari style" camp on an island in San Ignacio Lagoon. Participants go out in skiffs twice a day. Full meal service provided in the kitchen tent.
Fare:	$1,625 per person, which includes charter flight to San Ignacio, meals, accommodations, equipment, and guides.
Departure:	Trips begin and end in San Diego.
Naturalist:	Naturalist accompanies all trips.

Kristin Kirk, public relations coordinator, says it is not unusual for San Ignacio's "friendly" whales to approach the boats and allow themselves to be touched.

Baja Expeditions made its first trip in 1974. Founder Tim Means notes that the company is the largest and oldest outfitter of natural history and adventure in Mexico.

Ecosummer Expeditions

5640 Hollybridge Way, #130, Richmond, British Columbia V7C 4N3 Canada
(800) 465-8884 or (604) 214-7484; Fax (604) 214-7485;
Web site www.ecosummer.com

Whales:	Gray
Season:	January through March
Boats:	Sea kayaks
Trips:	Many 7-day trips to the Pacific lagoons with gray whales. The trips are specifically geared to whale watching. Participants camp except for the first and last nights spent in a hotel in La Paz.
Fare:	$1,145 for the 7-day trip, which includes guides, group equipment, ground transportation, meals and hotel accommodations.
Departure:	Trips begin and conclude in La Paz.

Naturalist: Guides familiar with Baja's flora and fauna accompany each trip.

"Sharing the waters with the magnificent gray whales will provide you with an understanding of the absolute necessity of preserving their breeding habitat, intact, for the success of their future generations," says Steve Booth, Ecosummer's expedition director.

Founded in 1976, Ecosummer Expeditions began as an adventure company that promoted environmental education, working primarily with high school students. Founder Jim Allan was soon deluged with requests from adults who wanted activity-oriented natural history wilderness trips—and so Ecosummer Expeditions evolved.

Natural Habitat Adventures

2945 Center Green Court, Suite H, Boulder, CO 80301
(800) 543-8917 or (303) 449-3711; Fax (303) 449-3712

Whales: Gray, bottlenose dolphin

Season: January through March

Boats: Whale watching from skiffs. Participants sleep and eat at a base camp right on the beach at the lagoon.

Trips: Several 5-day trips

Fare: $1,625 per person, double occupancy. Fare includes round-trip airfare from San Diego, accommodations meals, guide services, taxes.

Departure: Trips begin and end in San Diego, Calif.

Naturalist: Naturalists on site.

"Over 300 whales enter this particular lagoon and our small boat gives us unbelievably close-up encounters," says Ben Bressler, director of Natural Habitat Adventures.

Oceanic Society Expeditions

Fort Mason Center, Building E, San Francisco, CA 94123
(800) 326-7491 or (415) 441-1106, Fax (415) 474-3395;
Web site www.oceanic-society.org

Whales:	Gray
Season:	Mid-February to late March
Boats:	The 88-foot *Spirit of Adventure*, with 14 cabins and accommodates 28 passengers and staff. Participants live aboard. Whale watching from small skiffs.
Trips:	Nine-day trips to San Ignacio Lagoon, with stops at San Benito Islands, Cedros Island, and Todos Santos Island. Trips conclude in San Diego.
Fare:	$1,730 per person. Price does not include airfare or airport transfers.
Departure:	Trips leave from San Diego, California.
Naturalist:	Two naturalists from Oceanic Society Expeditions accompany each trip.

Oceanic Society Expeditions is a national nonprofit environmental organization and has conducted nature study trips since 1972. "On this expedition, we will enjoy close encounters with some of the hundreds of whales that frequent this lagoon," a spokeswoman said. Trips include slide shows and informal lectures each evening and a choice of optional activities each day.

Pacific Sea Fari Tours

2803 Emerson Street, San Diego, CA 92106
(619) 226-8224; Web site www.hmlanding.com

Whales:	Gray
Season:	Late January to late March
Boats:	One boat, the 88-foot *Big Game*, which holds 30 passengers in 14 cabins. Participants live aboard. Whale watching from skiffs.
Trips:	Eight- and 9-day trips to San Ignacio Lagoon, with stops at San Martin Island, San Benito Islands, Cedros Island, Todos Santos Island, and Ensenada. Trip concludes in San Diego.

Fare:	$1,800 to $2,250 per person. Price includes meals and snacks, accommodations, related equipment, and services of a naturalist staff. Tips aboard, airfare, and transfers not included.
Departure:	Trips leave from San Diego, California.
Naturalist:	All trips accompanied by naturalists.

Pacific Sea Fari Tours' natural history program has been developed under the leadership of Dr. Theodore J. Walker, a noted author, lecturer, and researcher. Considered one of the world's foremost experts on gray whales, Dr. Walker wrote "Whale Primer," the first authoritative work of its kind, and founded the whale observatory at the Cabrillo National Monument. No two trips are exactly alike.

Sea Quest Expeditions/Zoetic Research

P.O. Box 2424R, Friday Harbor, WA 98250
(360) 378-5767; E-mail sequest@pacificrim.net;
Web site www.sea-quest-kayak.com

Whales:	Gray, dolphins
Season:	February and early March
Boats:	Sea kayaks and motorized skiffs
Trips:	Several trips with varied 5- to 8-day itineraries that include camping on remote beaches and stays in hotels en route to the whale sanctuary.
Fare:	$999 to $1,199 per person depending on length of trip. Price includes everything except airfare to Mexico.
Departure:	Trips originate in Loreto, Mexico.
Naturalist:	A professional educator serves as naturalist.

"If you would like the unforgettable experience of looking a giant whale in the eye and sharing physical contact with a leviathan, this is the trip for you," says Mark Lewis, executive director. "Laguna San Ignacio is home to the unusual 'friendlies,' gray whales that enjoy human contact and often approach boats for petting and rubbing sessions."

Thompson Voyages and Research

P.O. Box 217, Laguna Beach, CA 92652
714) 497-1055, Fax (714) 494-7764

Whales:	Gray
Season:	February and March
Boats:	Outboard-powered skiffs for whale watching. Participants live in a shore-based camp in tents equipped with cots.
Trips:	Two 5-day trips
Fare:	$1,595 per person, which includes airfare from San Diego, meals, accommodations, guides and whale watching.
Departure:	Trips begin and end in San Diego, California.
Naturalist:	Naturalists accompany trips.

"This adventure will transport you into the wildness of San Ignacio Lagoon, the ancestral breeding grounds of the gray whale," says owner Doug Thompson. "In the lagoon, we'll observe the spectacular activities of the gray whales ... breaching, fluking, spyhopping, courting and nursing."

Thompson has been making trips to Baja California since 1972, and says, "I'm still just as excited as I was the first time."

SAN IGNACIO LAGOON AND SEA OF CORTEZ

American Cetacean Society Expeditions

P.O. Box 1391, San Pedro, CA 90733
(310) 548-6279; Fax (310) 548-6950; E-mail acs@pobox.com;
Web site www.acsonline.org

Whales:	Gray
Season:	February and March
Boats:	The 95-foot sportfishing vessel *Searcher*; 16 cabins accommodate up to 31 passengers. Participants live aboard. Whale watching from small skiffs.

Trips: Three trips, one 8-day trip in mid-February, a 9-day trip in late February, and an 11-day trip late in March. Trips focus on San Ignacio Lagoon with stops at Scammon's Lagoon, San Martin Island, San Benito Islands, Cedros Island, and Todos Santos Island. Trips conclude in San Diego, Cabo San Lucas or La Paz.

Fare: For ACS members: the 8-day trip is $ 1,725; the 9-day trip is $2,050 plus $250 back to San Diego; the 11-day trip is $2,350 plus $215 back to San Diego. Add 10 percent for nonmembers. Fares do not include tips, personal items, or alcohol.

Departure: Trips leave from San Diego, California.

Naturalist: Naturalists from American Cetacean Society accompany all trips.

The American Cetacean Society has conducted specialized trips for small groups to see whales since 1973. "Our trips take place in some of the great wilderness areas and are led by experienced naturalists. All our trips are really spectacular!" says a spokeswoman.

"San Ignacio Lagoon is the home of the friendly gray whales; you will enjoy close-encounter whale watching from small skiffs."

SEA OF CORTEZ

Baja Expeditions

2625 Garnet Avenue, San Diego, CA 92109
(800) 843-6967 or (619) 581-3311, Fax (619) 581-6542;
E-mail travel@bajaex.com; Web site www.bajaex.com

Whales: Blue, finback

Season: April, May, and June

Boats: The 80-foot *Don Jose* has 7 cabins that accommodate 2 people each. Participants live aboard.

Trips: Ten-day trips in the Sea of Cortez, with stops at Espiritu Santo Island, San Jose Island, Santa Catalina Island, Ildefonso Island, and Raza Island.

Fare: $1,895 per per on. Price includes land arrangements, accommodations. meals, beverages, and most related trip equipment. Airfare, gratuities, and airport taxes are not included.

Departure: Trips begin and end in Loreto.

Naturalist: Naturalist accompanies all trips.

Baja Expeditions made its first trip in 1974, in a rented fishing boat with a well-thumbed copy of John Steinbeck's "Log from the Sea of Cortez" aboard. The company's offerings to the Sea of Cortez recapture the sights, sounds, and experiences of Steinbeck's trip.

Tim Means, founder, notes that today the company is the largest and oldest outfitter of natural history and adventure travel in Mexico.

Dolphin Charters

1007 Leneve Place, El Cerrito, CA 94530
(800) 472-9942 or (510) 527-9622; Fax (510) 525-0720;
E-mail dolphin3@earthlink.net; Web site www.dolphincharters.com

Whales: Blue, maybe humpback, gray and fin

Season: March

Boats: The 95-foot *Searcher*, with accommodations for 24 passengers. Participants live aboard.

Trips: Several 11-day trips into the Sea of Cortez, with stops at Espiritu Santo Island, Santa Catalina Island, Los Islotes, and La Paz.

Fare: $2,270 per person, depending on length of trip. Price includes accommodations, meals and transportation while aboard the vessel. Rates do not include transportation to Mexico, airport departure taxes, meals or lodging en route, or tips.

Departure: Most trips leave from San Diego and conclude in Cabo San Lucas.

Naturalist: Naturalist accompanies all trips.

"We proudly feature a cruise that combines the color and charm of Baja with all the might and majesty of the world's largest animals. You will be awed by their size and astonished by their gentle behavior."

Ronn Patterson, an authority on whales, has sponsored natural history trips to Baja California since 1970.

Ecosummer Expeditions

5640 Hollybridge Way, #130, Richmond,
British Columbia V7C 4N3 Canada
(800) 465-8884 or (604) 214-7484; Fax (604) 214-7485;
Web site www.ecosummer.com

Whales:	Humpback, blue, gray
Season:	January through March
Boats:	Sea kayaks
Trips:	Five 14-day trips among the islands of the Sea of Cortez. Participants camp except for the first and last nights spent in a hotel in La Paz.
Fare:	$1,845 per person. Price includes guides, group equipment, ground transportation, meals and hotel accommodations.
Departure:	Trips begin and conclude in La Paz.
Naturalist:	Guides familiar with Baja's flora and fauna accompany each trip.

"This exciting itinerary follows the most breathtaking coastline Baja has to offer between the historic mission town of Loreto and the pleasant capital of Baja del Sur, La Paz," says Steve Booth, expedition director.

Founded in 1976, Ecosummer Expeditions began as an adventure company that promoted environmental education, working primarily with high school students. Founder Jim Allan was soon deluged with requests from adults who wanted activity-oriented natural history wilderness trips—and so Ecosummer Expeditions evolved.

Mingan Island Cetacean Study

760 B De L'epee, Outremont, Quebec, H2V 3T9 Canada
(514) 948-3669; Fax (514) 948-1131; E-mail micshipolari@videotron.ca;
Web site www.rorqual.com

Whales:	Blue, finback, orca, humpback, gray, several species of dolphin
Season:	March
Boats:	Two 22-foot fiberglass boats that carry 3 or 4 passengers and a 24-foot rigid-hull inflatable that carries 8 passengers.
Trips:	Several 8-day trips in March, with a Loreto hotel as the base of operations.
Fare:	$1,285 for double occupancy

Departure: All trips begin and end in Loreto, Mexico.

Naturalist: Naturalist accompanies all trips.

The Mingan Island Cetacean Study operates a research station in the Mingan Island region of the Quebec North Shore from May to November, studying local populations of blue, humpback, finback, and minke whales. Since 1983, founder Richard Sears has also offered educational research programs in the Sea of Cortez.

"Guests are invited to the coastal community of Loreto on the Sea of Cortez, Mexico, to participate in our winter/spring research season," Sears says. "The striking blue waters of this area offer a rich environment in which to observe a great variety of marine mammals, birds, and fishes."

National Audubon Society Nature Odysseys

700 Broadway, New York, NY 10003
(212) 979-3067, Fax (212) 353-0190; E-mail travel@audubon.org;
Web site www.audubon.org/market/no

Whales: Gray, humpback, blue

Season: February

Boats: The 152-foot *Sea Lion*; 70 passengers in 36 outside cabins. Participants live aboard. Whale watching from motorized inflatable rafts.

Trips: One 9-day trip to the Sea of Cortez, with stops in Magdalena Bay, Cabo San Lucas, Espiritu Santo, Gorda Banks and Isla Partida La Paz. Trips conclude in Phoenix, Arizona.

Fare: For Audubon Society members, $2,790 to $4,190, depending on the location of the stateroom. Fare includes all meals, accommodations on board and transfers. Airfare, tips not included.

Departure: Trips leave from La Paz.

Naturalist: Natural history staff from the Audubon Society and guest lecturers accompany trips.

"The *M/V Sea Lion* is ideal for exploring the region. Built to glide effortlessly, it will get you as close as possible to the whales and other sea life," says an Audubon spokeswoman. "Where the *Sea Lion* can't go, the ship's fleet of rubber landing craft will be launched, ready to land you almost anywhere at will."

Natural Habitat Adventures

2945 Center Green Court, Suite H, Boulder, CO 80301
(800) 543-8917 or (303) 449-3711; Fax (303) 449-3712

Whales:	Blue
Season:	March and April
Boats:	The 80-foot-long *Don Jose*, which carries 14 passengers
Trips:	Several 8-day trips
Fare:	$1,625 per person, double occupancy. Fare includes accommodations and meals on the Don Jose, one night at a hotel in Loreto, and guide services.
Departure:	Trips begin in La Paz, Mexico, and end in Loreto, Mexico.
Naturalist:	Naturalists accompany trips.

"We will search for blue whales on our trip, and each day we will stop at various islands for snorkeling, hiking, beachcombing, and bird watching," says Ben Bressler, director of Natural Habitat Adventures.

Pacific Sea Fari Tours

2803 Emerson Street, San Diego, CA 92106
(619) 226-8224; Web site www.hmlanding.com

Whales:	Gray
Season:	Late February to mid-Aprill
Boats:	Two boats, the 88-foot *Spirit of Adventure*, which holds 28 passengers in 14 cabins, and the 78-foot *Horizon*, which holds 20 passengers in 9 cabins. Participants live aboard the boat. Whale watching from skiffs.
Trips:	Eight- and 11-day trips to the Sea of Cortez, with stops at San Benito Islands, San Ignacio Lagoon, Magdalena Bay, Cabo San Lucas, Espiritu Santo Island, San Jose Island, Santa Catalina Island, Ildefonso Island, and La Paz. Trip concludes in La Paz.
Fare:	$1,800 to $2,850 per person includes meals and snacks, accommodations, related equipment, and services of a naturalist staff. Tips aboard, airfare, and transfers not included.

Departure: Trips leave from San Diego, California.

Naturalist: All trips accompanied by naturalists.

Pacific Sea Fari Tours' natural history program has been developed under the leadership of Dr. Theodore J. Walker, a noted author, lecturer, and researcher. Considered one of the world's foremost experts on gray whales, Dr. Walker wrote "Whale Primer," the first authoritative work of its kind, and founded the whale observatory at the Cabrillo National Monument. No two trips are alike.

Sea Quest Expeditions/Zoetic Research

Zoetic Research, P.O. Box 2424R, Friday Harbor, WA 98250
(360) 378-5767; E-mail sequest@pacificrim.net;
Web site www.sea-quest-kayak.com

Whales: Fin, blue, occasionally humpback, gray, orca

Season: November through April

Boats: Sea kayak

Trips: Several trips with varied 5- to 10-day itineraries in the Sea of Cortez. Participants camp overnight on uninhabited nature preserve islands.

Fare: $699 to $1,199 per person. Price includes everything except airfare to Mexico.

Departure: Trips originate in Loreto, Mexico.

Naturalist: Biologist with field research and teaching experience accompanies trips.

Executive director Mark Lewis notes that whale and dolphin watching is excellent from February through April in what he calls the "Blue Triangle." So far, nearly 300 individual blue whales have been identified in the area, including cows with calves. The desert sea-scapes and snorkeling with tropical fish are added attractions.

Sea Quest also offers research trips that qualify for college credit, and they will design custom trips.

WHERE WHALES ARE WHEN

This chapter is a calendar that tells where whales are when. The time span shown encompasses the early weeks, when a few whales are present; the height of the season; and the end of season, when just a few laggers may still be around. Dolphins' migratory patterns are not as well known as those of the great whales, so the listings here emphasize the whereabouts of the larger animals.

This calendar has not been reviewed or approved by whales and may not correspond exactly with their comings and goings. Also, keep in mind that whales do not observe our territorial boundaries and may spill over into neighboring states and even countries other than those listed here.

JANUARY

Gray whales: Off the coasts of California and Oregon

Humpback whales: In Hawaiian waters

FEBRUARY

Gray whales: Off the coasts of California and Oregon and in the lagoons off the west coast of Baja California, Mexico

Humpback whales: In Hawaiian waters

MARCH

Blue whales, fin whales, and pilot whales: In the Sea of Cortez, off the east coast of Baja California, Mexico

Gray whales: Off the coasts of California, Oregon, and Washington; in Alaskan waters; in the lagoons off the west coast of Baja California, Mexico; and off British Columbia

Humpback whales: In Hawaiian waters and in the Sea of Cortez, off the east coast of Baja California, Mexico

APRIL

Blue whales: In the Sea of Cortez, off the east coast of Baja California, Mexico

Fin whales: Off the northeast U.S. coast

Gray whales: Off the coasts of northern California, Oregon and Washington; in the lagoons off the west coast of Baja California, Mexico; and off British Columbia

Humpback whales: In Hawaiian waters; in the Sea of Cortez, off the east coast of Baja California, Mexico; and off the northeast U.S. coast

Minke whales: Off the northeast U.S. coast

Right whales: Off the northeast U.S. coast

MAY

Beluga whales: Off the Northwest Territories in Canada

Bowhead whales: Off the Northwest Territories in Canada

Fin whales: Off the northeast U.S. coast

Gray whales: Off the coasts of Oregon and Washington

Humpback whales: In Alaskan waters and off the northeast U.S. coast

Minke whales: In Alaskan waters and off the northeast U.S. coast

Narwhals: Off the Northwest Territories in Canada

Orcas: In Alaskan waters

Right whales: Off the northeast U.S. coast

JUNE

Beluga whales: Off the Northwest Territories and in the St. Lawrence River in Quebec, Canada

Blue whales: In the St. Lawrence River in Quebec, Canada

Bowhead whales: Off the Northwest Territories in Canada

Fin whales: Off the northeast U.S. coast, in Alaskan waters, off Nova Scotia and Newfoundland, and in the St. Lawrence River in Quebec, Canada

Humpback whales: In Alaskan waters, off the northeast U.S. coast, off Newfoundland and Nova Scotia in Canada, and off the Oregon coast

Minke whales: In Alaskan waters, off the northeast U.S. coast, off Nova Scotia and Newfoundland, and in the St. Lawrence River in Quebec, Canada

Narwhals: Off the Northwest Territories in Canada

Orcas: In Alaskan waters, off British Columbia, in the San Juan Islands, and off the Oregon coast

Right whales: Off the northeast U.S. coast and Nova Scotia

JULY

Orcas: In Alaskan waters, off British Columbia, in the San Juan Islands, and off the Oregon coast

Right whales: Off the northeast U.S. coast and Nova Scotia, Canada

Sperm whales: Off the coast of California

AUGUST

Beluga whales: Off the Northwest Territories, in the St. Lawrence River in Quebec, and in Manitoba, Canada

Blue whales: In the St. Lawrence River in Quebec, Canada, and off the coast of California

Fin whales: Off the northeast U.S. coast; off Nova Scotia, Newfoundland, and New Brunswick; and in the St. Lawrence River in Quebec, Canada

Humpback whales: In Alaskan waters, off the northeast U.S. coast; off Newfoundland, New Brunswick, and Nova Scotia in Canada; and off the California and Oregon coasts

Minke whales: In Alaskan waters, off the northeast U.S. coast, off Nova Scotia and Newfoundland, and in the St. Lawrence River

Orcas: In Alaskan waters, off British Columbia, in the San Juan Islands, and off the Oregon coast

Right whales: Off the northeast U.S. coast and Nova Scotia, Canada

Sperm whales: Off the coast of California

SEPTEMBER

Beluga whales: In the St. Lawrence River in Quebec, Canada

Blue whales: In the St. Lawrence River in Quebec, Canada, and off the coast of California

Fin whales: Off the northeast U.S. coast, off Nova Scotia and Newfoundland, and in the St. Lawrence River in Quebec, Canada

Humpback whales: In Alaskan waters, off the northeast U.S. coast, off Newfoundland and Nova Scotia in Canada, and off the California and Oregon coasts

Minke whales: In Alaskan waters, off the northeast U.S. coast, off Nova Scotia and Newfoundland, and in the St. Lawrence River in Quebec, Canada

Orcas: In Alaskan waters and off British Columbia

Right whales: Off the northeast U.S. coast and Nova Scotia, Canada

OCTOBER

Beluga whales: In the St. Lawrence River in Quebec, Canada

Blue whales: In the St. Lawrence River in Quebec, Canada

Fin whales: Off the northeast U.S. coast and in the St. Lawrence River in Quebec, Canada

Humpback whales: Off the northeast U.S. coast

Minke whales: Off the northeast U.S. coast and in the St. Lawrence River in Quebec, Canada

Right whales: Off the Northeast U.S. Coast

NOVEMBER

This is a great month to plan whale-watch trips!

DECEMBER

Gray whales: Off the coast of Oregon

Humpback whales: In Hawaiian waters

ADDITIONAL TRIPS

Some tour operators sponsor whale-watch (and other nature study) trips to destinations other than those included in this book. Here is a list of those tour operators. Write for more information.

Bluewater Adventures

#3-252 East First Street, North Vancouver, British Columbia, V7L 1BC Canada

(604) 980-3800; Fax (604) 908-1800;

Web site www.home.istar.ca/`blueh2o

Canadian Nature Tours

Federation of Ontario Naturalists

355 Lesmill Road, Don Mills, Ontario, M3B 2W8 Canada

(416) 444 8419

Dolphin Charters

1007 Leneve Place, El Cerrito, CA 94530

(800) 472-9942 or (510) 527-9622; Fax (510) 525-0720;

Web site www.dolphincharters.com

Earthwatch

680 Mt. Auburn Street, Box 9104, Watertown, MA 02471

(617) 926-8200

Ecosummer Expeditions

5640 Hollybridge Way, #130, Richmond,
British Columbia, V7C 4N3 Canada

(800) 465-8884 or (604) 214-7484; Fax (604) 214-7485;

Web site www.ecosummer.com

Island Institute

4004 58th Place S.W., Seattle, WA 98116

(206) 938-0345

National Audubon Society Nature Odysseys

700 Broadway, New York, NY 10003

(212) 979-3067; Fax (212) 353-0190;

Web site www.audubon.org/market/no

Natural Habitat Adventures

2945 Center Green Court, Suite H, Boulder, CO 80301

(800) 543-8917 or (303) 449-3711; Fax (303) 449-3712

Oceanic Society Expeditions

Fort Mason Center, Building E, San Francisco, CA 94123

(800) 326-7491 or (415) 441-1106, Fax (415) 474-3395;

Web site www.oceanic-society.org

Sea Quest Expeditions/Zoetic Research

P.O. Box 2424R, Friday Harbor, WA 98250

(360) 378-5767;

Web site www.sea-quest-kayak.com

Smithsonian Study Tours Program

The Smithsonian Associates, 1100 Jefferson Drive S.W., Washington, D.C. 20560

(202) 357-4700

WHALE CONSERVATION AND RESEARCH ORGANIZATIONS

L ike-minded people have come together all over the United States and Canada to work for the conservation of whales and other endangered species. Some of the organizations listed here concentrate on research, some on direct aid to the animals, some on political activism, and some on education; some ably combine all four missions. A few of the organizations sponsor occasional whale-watch trips for members, and some even recruit people to assist in research projects. For details, write to those organizations that interest you.

Alaska Geographic Society
P.O. Box 93370, Anchorage, AK 99509
(907) 562-0164

Allied Whale
College of the Atlantic, 105 Eden Street, Bar Harbor, ME 04609
(207) 288-5644; Web site www.coa.edu.alliedwhale

American Zoo and Aquarium Association
Oglebay Park, Wheeling, WV 26003
(304) 242-2160; Web site www.aza.org

American Cetacean Society
P.O. Box 1391, San Pedro, CA 90733
(310) 548-6279; Web site www.acsonline.org

American Oceans Campaign
725 Arizona Avenue, Suite 102, Santa Monica, CA 90401
(800) 862-3260 or (310) 576-6162;
Web site www.americanoceans.org

Animal Protection Institute of America

P.O. Box 22505, 2831 Fruitridge Road, Sacramento, CA 95820

(916) 731-5521; E-mail api4animals@aol.com

Animal Welfare Institute

P.O. Box 3650, Washington, D.C. 20007

(202) 337-2333; Web site www.animalwelfare.com

Brier Island Ocean Study

Westport, Digby County, Nova Scotia, B0V 1H0 Canada

(902) 839-2960; Web site magi.com/`kk/bios/

British Columbia Wildlife Federation

Suite 103, 19292 60th Avenue, Surrey,

British Columbia, V3G 8E5 Canada

(604) 533-2293

Canadian Nature Federation

1 Nicholas Street, Suite 606, Ottawa, Ontario K1N 7B7 Canada

(613) 562-3447; Web site www.magma.ca\`cnfgeu

Canadian Wildlife Federation

2740 Queensview Drive, Ottawa, Ontario, K2B I8Z Canada

(613) 721-2286; Web site cwf-fcf.org

Center for Coastal Studies

59 Commercial Street, Box 1036, Provincetown, MA 02657

(508) 487-3622 Web site www.provincetown.com/coastalstudies

Center for Marine Conservation

1725 DeSales Street NW, Suite 500, Washington, D.C. 20036

(360) 378-5835; Web site www.rockisland.com/`orcasurv

Center for Whale Research

1359 Smuggler's Cove, Friday Harbor, WA 98250

(206) 378-5835

Cetacean Research Unit
P.O. Box 159, Gloucester, MA 01930
(978) 281-6351; Web site www.cetacean.org

Cetacean Society International
P.O. Box 953, Georgetown, CT 06829
(203) 544-8617

Cousteau Society
870 Greenbrier Circle, Suite 402, Chesapeake, VA 23320
(757) 523-9335; Web site www.cousteau.org

Defenders of Wildlife
1101 14th Street NW, Suite 1400, Washington, D.C. 20005
(202) 682-9400; Web site www.defenders.org

Delta Society
289 Perimeter Road East, Renton, WA 98055
(425) 226-7357; Web site deltasociety.org

Dolphin Research Center
P.O. Box 2875, Marathon Shores, FL 33052
(305) 289-0002

Earth Island Institute
300 Broadway, Suite 28, San Francisco, CA 94133
(415) 788-3666; Web site www.earthisland.org

Earthtrust Wildlife Society
P.O. Box 5361, Lahaina, Maui, HI 96761
(808) 667-0437; Web site www.aloha.net/`WILD

Earthwatch
680 Mt. Auburn Street, Box 9104, Watertown, MA 02471
(617) 926-8200; Web site www.earthwatch.org

Environmental Defense Fund
257 Park Avenue South, New York, NY 10010
(212) 505-2100; Web site www.edf.org

Friends of the Animals
1841 Broadway, Room 812, New York, NY 10023
(212) 247-8120

Friends of the Earth
1025 Vermont Avenue NW, Third Floor, Washington, D.C. 20005
(202) 783-7400; Web site www.foe.org

Fund for Animals
200 W. 57th Street, New York, NY 10019
(212) 246-2096; E-mail camory@fund.org

Greenpeace USA
1436 U Street NW, Washington, D.C. 20009
(202) 462-1177; Web site www.greenpeace.org

Humane Society of the United States
2100 L Street NW, Washington, D.C. 20037
(202) 452-1100; Web site www.hsus.org

International Fund for Animal Welfare
P.O. Box 193, Yarmouthport, MA 02675
(508) 362-4944; Web site www.ifaw.org

International Wildlife Coalition
70 East Falmouth Highway, East Falmouth, MA 02536
(508) 548-8328; Web site www.iwc.org

Manitoba Wildlife Federation
70 Stevenson Road, Winnipeg, Manitoba, R3H 0W7 Canada
(204) 633-5967

Marine Mammal Stranding Center
P.O. Box 773, 3625 Brigantine Boulevard, Brigantine, NJ 08203
(609) 266-0538; Web site www.mmsc.org

Mingan Island Cetacean Study
Summer:
124 Bord de la Mer, Longue-Pointe-de-Mingan,
Quebec, G0G 1V0 Canada
(418) 949-2845
Winter:
285, rue Green, St. Lambert, Quebec, J4P 1T3 Canada
(514) 465-9176

National Audubon Society
700 Broadway, New York, NY 10003
(212) 979-3000; Web site www.audubon.org

National Wildlife Federation
1400 16th Street NW, Washington, D.C. 20036
(202) 797-6800; Web site www.nwf.org

Nature Conservancy
1815 North Lynn Street, Arlington, VA 22209
(703) 841-5300; Web site www.tnc.org

New Brunswick Wildlife Federation
190 Cameron Street, Moncton, New Brunswick, E1C 5Z2 Canada
(506) 857-2056

Newfoundland/Labrador Wildlife Federation
14 Fairhaven Place, St. John's, Newfoundland, A1E 4S1 Canada
(709) 364-8415

Nova Scotia Wildlife Federation
P.O. Box 654, Halifax, Nova Scotia, B3J 2T3 Canada
(902) 423-6793

Oregon Natural Resources Council

5825 North Greeley, Portland, OR 97217

(503) 283-6343; Web site www.onrc.org

Pacific Whale Foundation

101 North Kihei Road, Kihei, Maui, HI 96753

(800) 942-5311 or (808) 879-8811

St. Lawrence National Institute of Ecotoxicology

460, du Champ-de-Mars, Suite 504, Montreal, Quebec, H2Y 1B4 Canada

(514) 499-283-6252; Fax (514) 283-6252

Save the Whales

P.O. Box 3650, Washington, D.C. 20007

(202) 337-2332; Web site www.animalwelfare.com

Sea Shepherd Conservation Society

P.O. Box 628, Venice, CA 90294

(310) 394-3198; Web site seashepard.org

Sierra Club

85 Second Street, Second Floor, San Francisco, CA 94105

(415) 977-5750; Web site www.sierraclub.org

Society for Animal Protective Legislation

P.O. Box 3719, Georgetown Station, Washington, D.C. 20007

(202) 337-2334

Whale Conservation Institute

191 Weston Road, Lincoln, MA 01773

(781) 259-0423; Web site www.whale.org

Whale Center

411 Campbell Street, Tofino, British Columbia, VOR 2Z0 Canada

(250) 725-2132; E-mail jforde@mail.tofino/bc.com

The Wilderness Society

900 17th Street NW, Washington, D.C. 20006
(202) 833-2300; Web site www.wilderness.org

Wildlife Conservation Society

2300 Southern Boulevard, Bronx, NY 10460
(718) 220-5155; Web site www.wcs.org

Wildlife Preservation Trust

1520 Locust Street, Suite 704, Philadelphia, PA 19102
(215) 731-9770; Web site www.homeoffice@wpti.org

Wildlife Society

5410 Grosvenor Lane, Bethesda, MD 20814
(301) 897-9770; Web site www.wildlife.org

Worldwatch Institute

1776 Massachusetts Avenue NW, Washington, D.C. 20036
(202) 452-1999; Web site www.worldwatch.org

World Wildlife Fund

1250 24th Street NW, Washington, D.C. 20037
(202) 293-4800; Web site www.worldwildlife.org

ADOPT-A-WHALE PROGRAMS

If whales have captured your heart or your imagination, you may want to "adopt" a whale for yourself or as a gift for a friend or family member. The sponsoring organizations (most of them research or conservation programs) typically provide adoptive parents with a photo of the adoptee, an official certificate, news about sightings of your whale, a one-year membership in the organization, a newsletter subscription, and other materials related to whale research and conservation.

When you adopt a whale, you aren't signing up to help save a nameless, faceless whale. Research scientists who study annual whale migrations recognize individual animals year after year, based on cross-referenced photo-identification files. Whales can be distinguished from one another by specific markings, coloring, scars from boat propellers, and for humpbacks the unique patterns on the underside of the tails. If you go whale watching at the right time in the right place, you may very well meet your adopted whale.

Write or call the organizations listed here for more information.

BELUGA WHALES

Adopt A Beluga

St. Lawrence National Institute of Ecotoxicology
460, du Champ-de-Mars, Suite 504, Montreal,
Quebec, H2Y 1B4 Canada

(514) 499-283-6252; Fax (514) 283-6252

Nearly 80 individuals of the 400 to 500 belugas in the St. Lawrence River have been identified. The minimum donation to adopt a beluga is $5,000.

BLUE WHALES

Adopt a Blue Whale

Oceanic Society
Fort Mason Center, Building E, San Francisco, CA 94123

(800) 326-7491; Fax (415) 3395

Web site www.oceanic-society.org

Blue whales feed in California waters outside San Francisco Bay. Adopt a blue whale for $35 or name and adopt a blue whale for one year for $250.

Adopt A Giant

Mingan Island Cetacean Study
760 B De L'epee, Outrement, Quebec, H2V 3T9 Canada

(514) 948-3669; Fax (514) 948-1131

Web site www.rorqual.com

The Adopt A Giant program offers 210 blue whales that live in the Gulf of St. Lawrence and 160 in the Sea of Cortez. Each whale costs $100 per person, $1,000 for a corporate adoption, and a minimum of $50 for school children.

FINBACK WHALES

Adopt-A-Finback-Whale Program

Allied Whale, College of the Atlantic,
105 Eden Street, Bar Harbor, ME 04609

(207) 288-5644; Fax (207) 288-4126

Web site www.coa.edu/ASSOCIATED
PROGRAMS/AlliedWhale/HOMEPAGE

About thirty-five individual finback whales are available for $30; a mother and calf cost $50.

HUMPBACK WHALES

Adopt-A-Whale Project

Pacific Whale Foundation, Kealia Beach Plaza, Suite 21,
101 North Kihei Road, Kihei, Maui, HI 96753

(800) 942-5311; Fax (808) 879-2615

Humpback whales from Hawaii and Australian waters are available.
There is a $35 fee for a non-exclusive adoption plus an annual support
fee. An exclusive adoption costs $75—you get to name the whale—
plus an annual support fee of $50.

Adopt a Humpback Whale

Oceanic Society, Fort Mason Center, Building E,
San Francisco, CA 94123

(800) 326-7491; Fax (415) 474-3395

Web site www.oceanic-society.org

This program is a joint project with OCS and Cascadia Research
Collective. Humpbacks feeding in California waters outside San
Francisco Bay may be adopted for $35 or you may name and adopt a
humpback whale for $100 for one year.

Adopt A Whale

Cetacean Research Unit
P.O. Box 159, Gloucester, MA 01930

(508) 281-6351; Fax (508) 281-5666;

Web site www.cetacean.org

Several North Atlantic humpback whales are available for adoption at
$30 per year. CRU was founded in 1978.

Humpback Whale Adoption/Project Megafam

The Whale Conservation Institute,
191 Weston Road, Lincoln, MA 01773
(781) 259-0423

Individual whales are available for adoption for $25 each.

Save the Whales International

Earthtrust, P.O. Box 1358, Lahaina, Maui, HI 96767
(808) 661-8755
Web site www.earthtrust.org

Save the Whales International, a project under the auspices of
Earthtrust, calls its adoption program a "hanai" program, wherein interested people welcome a Hawaiian humpback whale into their family.
Adoption costs $15 per whale. Earthtrust is a non-profit organization
and adoption profits go towards our anti-whaling campaigns.

Whale Adoption Project

International Wildlife Coalition
70 East Falmouth Highway, East Falmouth, MA 02536
(508) 564-8328; Fax (508) 548-8542
Web site www.iwc.org

More than sixty individual humpback whales that linger in the Gulf of
Maine from April to November are available for $17 each.

Wild Whale Research Foundation

P.O. Box 139, Holualoa, Hawaii 96725
(888) WHALES6 or (808) 322-0028
Web site ilovewhales.com

Three humpbacks from Hawaiian waters are available for adoption for
$40 each, or, for $150, you may choose either a humpback whale or
a pilot whale and give it a name.

ORCAS

Orca Adoption Program

The Whale Museum, 62 First Street North,
P.O. Box 945, Friday Harbor, WA 98250

(360) 378-4710; Fax (360) 378-5790

Web site www.whale-museum.org

More than 80 orcas (killer whales) that spend summers in the San Juan Islands are available for adoption. For $40, you receive a museum membership as well as an adoption; $25 covers just an adoption. A special classroom package for $60 gives each student a certificate inscribed with his or her name and the teacher receives the museum membership.

Whale Adoption Program

Vancouver Aquarium, P.O. Box 3232,
Vancouver, British Columbia, V6B 3X8 Canada

(604) 659-3430

Web site www.killerwhale.org

Northern residents and transient killer whales off British Columbia are available for adoption to help support the aquarium's field research on wild whales. The annual fee is $49 (Canadian) for individual or family adoption. Entire pods are available for $39 per whale. Annual renewal is $25.

RIGHT WHALES

Know Your Rights

The Whale Conservation Institute, 191 Weston Road,
Lincoln, MA 01773

(781) 259-0423

Eight right whales regularly observed off Peninsula Valdes in Patagonia, Argentina, are available for adoption for $25 each. These endangered whales have been studied since 1970, and adoption fees support that research.

Right Whale Adoption Program

New England Aquarium, Central Wharf, Boston, MA 02110;

(617) 973-6582 or 973-5253

Web site www.neaq.org

A sponsorship package is available for $45 each; for $100, you get the complete package plus a "Right Whale Research Project" tee-shirt. The northern right whale is the rarest whale on Earth, very close to extinction. Proceeds go to defray costs of field research and analysis.

DOLPHINS

Oceanic Project Dolphin

Oceanic Society Expeditions, Fort Mason Center, Building E, San Francisco, CA 94123

(800) 326-7491 or (415) 441-1106; Fax (415) 474-3395

Web site www.oceanic-society.org

This program was created to photo-document individual spotted dolphins off the Bahamas so scientists may learn how dolphins feed, socialize, rest, and communicate, and to analyze the importance of their habitat. An adoption costs $35 a year. For a $250 tax-deductible donation, supporters may adopt and name a spotted dolphin.

SUGGESTED READING

NONFICTION

Audubon Society. *A Field Guide to North American Fishes, Whales and Dolphins.* Alfred A. Knopf, 1983.

Baker, Mary L. *Whales, Dolphins, and Porpoises of the World.* Doubleday, 1987.

Balcomb, Kenneth C. III. *The Whales of Hawaii.* Marine Mammal Fund, 1987.

Beamish, Peter. *Dancing With Whales.* Creative Publishers, 1993.

Beland, Pierre. *Beluga: A Farewell to Whales.* Lyons & Burford, 1996.

Bennett, Ben. *Oceanic Society Field Guide to the Gray Whale.* Legacy, 1983.

Bonner, Nigel. *Whales.* Blanford Press, 1980.

Bonner, Nigel. *Whales of the World.* Facts on File, 1989.

Brower, Kenneth. *Wake of the Whale.* Friends of the Earth/Dutton, 1979.

Burton, Robert. *The Life and Death of Whales.* 2d ed. Universe Books, 1980.

Caldwell, D.K. and M.C. *The World of the Bottlenosed Dolphin.* Lippincott, 1972.

Clapham, Phil. *Humpback Whales.* Voyageur Press, 1996.

Connor, Richard and Micklethwaite Peterson, Dawn. *The Lives of Whales and Dolphins.* Henry Holt and Company, 1996.

Cousteau, Jacques. *The Whale—Mighty Monarch of the Sea.* Doubleday, 1972.

Cousteau, Jacques, and Yves Paccalet. *Whales.* Harry N. Abrams, 1988.

Daugherty, A.E. *Marine Mammals of California.* Rev. ed. California Department of Fish and Game, 1972.

Day, David. *The Whale War.* Sierra Club Books, 1987.

Dietz, Tim. *Tales of the Sea.* Guy Gannett, 1983.

Dietz, Tim. *Whales and Man.* Yankee Books, 1987.

Doak, Wade. *Encounters with Whales and Dolphins.* Sheridan House, 1989.

D'Vincent, Cynthia. *Voyaging with the Whales.* Oakwell Boulton, 1989.

Ellis, Richard. *Men and Whales.* Alfred A. Knopf, 1992.

Ellis, Richard. *Dolphins and Porpoises.* Alfred A. Knopf, 1982.

Ellis, Richard. *The Book of Whales.* Alfred A. Knopf, 1980.

Flaherty, Chuck. *Whales of the Northwest.* Cherry Lane Press, 1990.

Gatenby, Greg. *Whales: A Celebration.* Little, Brown and Company, 1983.

Gilders, Michelle A. *Reflections of a Whale Watcher.* Indiana University Press, 1995.

Gilmore, R.M. *The Story of the Gray Whale.* Gilmore, 1961, rev. 1972.

Gordon, David G. and Chuck Flaherty. *Field Guide to the Orca.* American Cetacean Society, 1990.

Gormley, Gerald. *Orcas of the Gulf: A Natural History.* Sierra Club Books, 1990.

Hand, Douglas. *Gone Whaling: A Search for Orcas in Northwest Waters.* Simon and Schuster, 1994.

Harrison, Richard, and Michael Bryden. *Whales, Dolphins, and Porpoises.* Intercontinental Publishing, 1988.

Heyning, John. *Masters of the Ocean Realm.* University of Washington Press, 1995.

Hodge, Judith. *Whales.* Barron, 1997.

Hoyt, Erich. *Meeting the Whales.* Camden House, 1991.

Hoyt, Erich. *Seasons of the Whale.* Chelsea Green, 1990.

Hoyt, Erich. *Orca: The Whale Called Killer.* Rev. Ed. E. P. Dutton, 1990.

Hoyt, Erich. *The Whale Watcher's Handbook.* Doubleday, 1984.

Jones, Mary Lou, Steven L. Swartz, and Stephen Leatherwood. *The Gray Whale.* Academic Press, 1984.

Katona, Steven K., Valerie Rough, and David T. Richardson. *A Field Guide to the Whales, Porpoises, and Seals of the Gulf of Maine and Eastern Canada.* 4th ed. Scribner's, 1983.

Kelly, John E., Scott Mercer, and Steve Wolf. *The Great Whale Book.* Center for Environmental Education, 1981.

Knudtson, Peter. *Orca: Vision of the Killer Whale.* Sierra Club Books, 1996.

Leatherwood, Stephen, and Randall R. Reeves. *The Bottlenose Dolphin.* Academic Press, 1989.

Leatherwood, Stephen, and Randall R. Reeves. *The Sierra Club Handbook of Whales and Dolphins.* Sierra Club Books, 1983.

Leatherwood, Stephen, Randall R. Reeves, William F. Perrin, and William E. Evans. *Whales, Dolphins, and Porpoises of the Eastern North Pacific and Adjacent Arctic Waters.* 2d ed. Dover, 1988.

Lien, Jon and Steven Katona. *A Guide to the Photographic Identification of Individual Whales*. American Cetacean Society, 1990.

Lilly, John. *Man and Dolphin*. Doubleday and Company, 1961.

Martin, Anthony. *Beluga Whales*. Voyageur, 1996.

Matthews, L. H. *The Natural History of the Whale*. Columbia University Press, 1978.

Matthews, L. H. *The Whale*. Simon and Schuster, 1968.

May, John. *The Greenpeace Book of Dolphins*. Sterling Publications, 1990.

McIntyre, Joan. *Mind in the Waters*. Scribner's/Sierra Club, 1974.

McIntyre, Joan. *The Delicate Art of Whale Watching*. Sierra Club Books, 1982.

McNally, Robert. *So Remorseless a Havoc*. Little, Brown and Company, 1981.

Miller, Tom. *The World of the California Gray Whale*. Baja Trail Publications, 1975.

Minasian, Stanley M., Kenneth C. Balcomb III, and Larry Foster. *The World's Whales*. Smithsonian, 1984.

Mowat, Farley. *A Whale for the Killing*. Bantam Books, 1972.

Nakamura, Tsuneo. *Gentle Giant: At Sea With the Humpback Whale*. Chronicle Books, 1984.

National Geographic Staff. *Whales, Dolphins & Porpoises*. National Geographic, 1995.

National Geographic Staff. *Blue Whales*. Random House, 1995.

Nickerson, Roy. *Brother Whale*. Chronicle Books, 1977.

Nickerson, Roy. *The Friendly Whales: A Whale Watcher's Guide to the Gray Whales of Baja California*. Chronicle Books, 1987.

Nicklin, Flip. *With The Whales*. NorthWord Press, 1990.

Nollman, Jim. *Whales and Humans*. Henry Holt, 1998.

Nollman, Jim. *Whales and Dolphins*. Henry Holt, 1997.

Norris, K. *Whales, Dolphins and Porpoises*. University of California Press, 1966.

Paine, Stefani. *The World of Arctic Whales*. Sierra Club Books, 1997.

Payne, Roger. *Among Whales*. Scribner, 1995.

Reeves, Randall R., and Stephen Leatherwood. *The Sea World Book of Dolphins*. Harcourt, Brace, Jovanovich, 1987.

Scammon, Charles M. *The Marine Mammals of the Northwest Coast of North America*. Reprinted by Dover, 1968; originally published in 1874.

Scheffer, Victor. *A Natural History of Marine Mammals*. Scribner's Sons, 1976.

Sears, Richard, Frederick Wenzel and J. Michael Williamson. *The Blue Whale*. Mingan Island Cetacean Study, 1987.

Small, G.L. *The Blue Whale*. Columbia University Press, 1971.

Stewart, Frank. *The Presence of Whales: Contemporary Writings on the Whale*. Alaska Books, 1995.

Walker, Theodore J. *Whale Primer*. Cabrillo Historical Association, 1962 (since revised several times).

Watson, Lyall. *A Sea Guide to Whales of the World*. E. P. Dutton, 1982.

Watson, Paul. *Sea Shepherd: My Fight for Whales and Seals*. Norton, 1982.

Weyler, Rex. *Song of the Whale*. Anchor Press, 1986.

Whitehead, Hal. *Voyage to The Whales*. Stoddart Publishing, 1989.

Williams, Heathcote. *Falling for a Dolphin*. Harmony Books, 1989.

Williams, Heathcote. *Whale Nation*. Harmony Books, 1988.

Winn, Lois King, and Howard E. Winn. *Wings in the Sea: The Humpback Whale*. University Press of New England, 1985.

Yates, Steve. *Marine Life of Puget Sound, the San Juans, and the Strait of Georgia*. Globe Pequot Press, 1988.

FICTION

Abbey, Lloyd. *The Last Whales*. Grove Weidenfeld, 1989.

Carrighar, Sally. *The Twilight Seas*. Dutton, 1989.

Lucas, Jeremy. *Whale*. Summit Books, 1981.

Melville, Herman. *Moby Dick; or The Whale*. Numerous editions and publishers, 1851.

Scheffer, Victor. *The Year of the Whale*. Scribner's, 1969.

Searls, Hank. *Sounding*. Ballantine, 1982.

Siegel, Robert. *Whalesong*. Berkeley, 1981.

Spain, Stanley. *Rajac: A Story*. MacMillan, 1982.

END NOTE

Ten percent of the author's income from this book will go to whale conservation and research organizations working to ensure that the world's whales do not become extinct.

In an effort to include every whale-watch tour operator serving customers in the geographical areas in this book, the author has checked, rechecked, and cross-checked with known tour operators, local chambers of commerce, state and local tourist bureaus, museums, aquariums, and conservation organizations and foundations. If you were inadvertently left out, or if you know someone who was, please make sure the omission will be remedied in revised editions by writing immediately to Patricia Corrigan in care of NorthWord Press, Creative Publishing International, 5900 Green Oak Drive, Minnetonka, MN 55343.

INDEX

TOUR OPERATORS

NORTHEAST U.S. COAST

Maine

Acadian Whale Watcher
(Bar Harbor): 55

Bar Harbor Whale Watch
Company (Bar Harbor): 56

Cape Arundel Cruises
(Kennebunkport): 57

Indian Whale Watch
(Kennebunkport): 58

Olde Port Mariner Fleet
(Portland): 59

Ugly Anne (Ogunquit): 58

Whale Watcher Inc.
(Bar Harbor): 56

Massachusetts

A. C. Cruise Line (Boston): 61

Boston Harbor Cruises
(Boston): 61

Boston Harbor Whale Watch
(Boston): 62

Cape Ann Whale Watch
(Gloucester): 64

Cape Cod Cruises
(Provincetown): 68

Captain Bill & Sons Whale
Watch Cruises (Gloucester): 67

Captain John Boats
(Plymouth): 67

Captain Tim Brady & Sons, Inc.
(Plymouth): 67

Dolphin Fleet of Provincetown
(Provincetown): 69

Hyannis Whale Watcher
Cruises (Barnstable): 60

Nantucket Whale Watch
(Nantucket): 66

New England Aquarium
(Boston): 63

Portuguese Princess Whale
Watch (Provincetown): 69

Provincetown Whale Watch
Inc. (Provincetown): 70

Salem Whale Watch
(Salem): 71

Seven Seas Whale Watch
(Gloucester): 64

Yankee Whalewatch
(Gloucester): 65

New Hampshire

Al Gauron Deep Sea Fishing
(Hampton Beach): 72

Atlantic Fleet (Rye): 73

New Hampshire Seacoast
Cruises (Rye): 74

Oceanic Whale Watch
Expeditions (Portsmouth): 72

New Jersey

Cape May Whale Watch
and Research Center (Cape
May): 75

THE PACIFIC NORTHWEST

Oregon

Bayfront Charters
(Newport): 91

Betty Kay Charters
(Charleston): 87

HAWAII

Hawaii

Kauai

Maui

MUSEUMS, AQUARIUMS, AND SCIENCE CENTERS

NATIONAL PARKS AND MARINE SANCTUARIES

NOTES

_____

_____

_____

_____

_____

_____

_____

_____

_____

_____

NOTES

ABOUT THE AUTHOR

PATRICIA CORRIGAN, secretly a mermaid, lives in land-locked St. Louis, Missouri, with one orange cat and one tortoise cat. As a mermaid who likes her dessert, she is the author of a heavenly cookbook, "Angels in the Kitchen" (Pocket Books). She also is the author of "Dolphins For Kids," "Sharks For Kids," "Manatees For Kids," and "Beavers For Kids," all published by NorthWord Press. She is the proud mother of a grown son. Right now she is fulfilling a childhood dream working as a reporter and columnist for the St. Louis Post-Dispatch. Eventually, she hopes to fulfill a more recent dream and move to the southern coast of Oregon. There she plans to watch whales from her living room window, when she isn't out on a boat in some equally whale-rich area of the world.

ABOUT THE ILLUSTRATOR

DAVID PETERS is a commercial artist and author and illustrator of "Giants of Land, Sea and Air—Past and Present" (Sierra Club/Alfred A. Knopf, 1986); "A Gallery of Dinosaurs and Other Prehistoric Reptiles" (Alfred A. Knopf, 1988); "From the Beginning: The Story of Human Evolution" (Morrow Junior Books, 1990); and "The Strangest Animals of All Times" (Morrow Junior Books, 1991). He lives in St. Louis, Missouri, with his wife and two daughters.